T0339374

THE BATTLE for NORTH AFRICA

THE BATTLE
for
NORTH AFRICA

El Alamein and the Turning Point for World War II

GLYN HARPER

INDIANA UNIVERSITY PRESS

This book is a publication of

Indiana University Press
Office of Scholarly Publishing
Herman B Wells Library 350
1320 East 10th Street
Bloomington, Indiana 47405 USA

iupress.indiana.edu

Library of Congress Cataloging-in-
Publication Data

Names: Harper, Glyn, author.
Title: The battle for North Africa :
    El Alamein and the turning point for
    World War II / Glyn Harper.
Description: Bloomington : Indiana
    University Press, 2017. | Series:
    Twentieth-century battles | Includes
    bibliographical references and index.
Identifiers: LCCN 2017020636 (print) |
    LCCN 2017019231 (ebook) |
    ISBN 9780253031433 (e-book) |
    ISBN 9780253031426 (cloth)

Subjects: LCSH: El Alamein, Battle of,
    Egypt, 1942.
Classification: LCC D766.9 (print) |
    LCC D766.9 .H335 2017 (ebook) |
    DDC 940.542321—dc23
LC record available at https://lccn.loc
    .gov/2017020636

1 2 3 4 5   22 21 20 19 18 17

CONTENTS

LIST OF MAPS

ACKNOWLEDGMENTS

All publications are a team effort. For me, one of the most enjoyable parts of the publishing process is being able to acknowledge the assistance I have received in writing a book and to thank people for their contributions.

I must begin by offering my thanks to Spencer C. Tucker, the initial editor of this series of books. In 2010, Spencer took a great deal of interest in a visiting Fulbright Scholar to the Virginia Military Institute. A friendship developed and it was at Spencer's invitation that I commenced work on this book. I remain immensely grateful for the faith he placed in me and for his ongoing support. Indiana University Press has been delightful to work with and has easily overcome the tyranny of distance in dealing with an author who lives a long way from the USA. Also overcome, but perhaps not so easily in my case, has been the different spellings used in both countries. I also wish to acknowledge the work of Janice Frisch, Peggy Solic, and Ashley Runyon and thank them for their support, efficiency, and sound advice.

The primary source material for this book has been obtained from research institutions in four separate countries. Without fail, the staffs at all these institutions have been friendly, courteous, and helpful. I am deeply indebted to them for their professionalism, assistance, and dedication. I must especially acknowledge Neil Frances and the staff of the Wairarapa Archive in Masterton, New Zealand. Neil and his colleagues searched their photograph collections of the Second World War and provided all the images used in this book. They did not charge for this service and I am grateful for their generosity.

Paul Lumsden produced the excellent maps from his farm near Ward in New Zealand's South Island. As I live in New Zealand's other large island, this process also meant there were problems of distance involved. Thanks to the internet, the rural phone service, and Skype, any problems were easily overcome.

Massey University, New Zealand's defining university, was fully supportive of this project. The University gave me the time to undertake the research and to write this book. Massey University's School of Humanities also provided some financial assistance toward its publication.

Finally, I wish to acknowledge and thank my wife, Susan Lemish, for her support and all the work she has put into this book. Susan read all the first drafts twice, assisted with the research, checked all the footnotes and bibliography, and undertook a myriad of other tasks necessary to bring this book to publication. It is not surprising, then, that Susan does not want to hear about the battles of El Alamein for some time now.

Glyn Harper
Palmerston North, New Zealand
January 2017

THE BATTLE
for
NORTH
AFRICA

INTRODUCTION: THE EYES
OF THE WHOLE WORLD,
WATCHING ANXIOUSLY

On the evening of October 23, 1942, Lieutenant General Bernard Montgomery settled in for a good night's sleep. Montgomery later claimed that he retired to his caravan early as was his habit, read a few pages from a novel "and some time after nine o'clock he went to sleep."[1] If this was true, it was a remarkable display of calm, steely resolve and composure given what was at stake. Earlier Montgomery had written a Personal Message to be read to the men of his Eighth Army that morning. Part of his Message read:

> When I assumed command of the Eighth Army I said that the mandate was to destroy ROMMEL and his Army, and that it would be done as soon as we were ready.
>
> We are ready NOW.
>
> The battle which is now about to begin will be one of the decisive battles of history. It will be the turning point of the war. The eyes of the whole world will be on us, watching anxiously which way the battle will swing.[2]

Montgomery was in no doubt that the battle would swing his way. It was part of the reason he claimed to sleep so soundly that night. Earlier he had dined with Lieutenant General Sir Oliver Leese, his 30 Corps commander. On learning that Leese intended to watch the opening barrage timed for 9:40 p.m. that evening, Montgomery counseled against it. Leese recalled what Montgomery said to him:

> My job, he said, was to go to bed early so as to appear fresh in the morning and be able by my appearance to give confidence to the troops. I had then to be on top of my form so as to accept the inevitable shocks of battle; and be able to plan quickly and soundly the next night's attacks. He could not have been more right.[3]

Montgomery may have been right, but Leese ignored his advice and later moved to a slight ridgeline from which he could observe the opening barrage. It was the largest fired by the British Army in the war up to that time. But Montgomery, despite his claims, was also awake watching the barrage. His Chief of Staff, Brigadier Francis (Freddie) de Guingand, was at a vantage point on the coast road that night and his notes on the battle make it clear that Montgomery was with him.[4] And Montgomery recorded the event in his diary. The opening barrage was:

> a wonderful sight, similar to a Great War 1914/18 attack. It was a still night and very quiet. Suddenly the whole front burst into fire, it was beautifully timed and the effect was terrific; many large fires broke out in enemy gun areas.[5]

This was clearly not the dream of a slumbering army commander. It shows that Montgomery, despite what he wrote later, knew how important this battle was to the Allied war effort and to his own career.

At 9:40 p.m., the artillery barrage opened right on time. The noise from nearly 900 guns was a crescendo of sound that made the air vibrate; the muzzle flashes lit up a cloudless black light. Twenty minutes after this opening barrage, the infantry from five divisions and a Free French brigade crossed their start lines. Montgomery had been correct in his assessment. A turning-point battle of the war had commenced and the eyes of the world were turned to this life-and-death struggle in North Africa.

Twenty minutes after the sound of the guns shredded the night air, the first enemy artillery rounds passed over Lieutenant General Bernard Freyberg's forward headquarters. The GOC of the 2nd New Zealand Division had just received news that the "Infantry are off – both bdes [brigades] are away to a good start." General Freyberg turned to his G1, the principal staff officer, and remarked:

> If there was ever justice in a cause this is it. I don't think the Itys will stick it and I don't think the Boche will either—they didn't in the last war. . . Auchinleck could have won the war by putting in Blamey instead of Ritchie. Mind you this is going to be a stiff fight.[6]

Freyberg was right, but this had also been anticipated by Montgomery. That day, Montgomery, no stranger to the cost of large-scale set piece battles, had written in his diary a grave reality:

The battle will be expensive as it will really become a killing match. I consider that the dog fight of the "crumbling" operations may last for a week, during which time we shall never let go our stranglehold. I have estimated for 10,000 casualties in this week's fighting.

All we need now is average luck and good weather.[7]

Both Freyberg and Montgomery were correct. The Eighth Army had a stiff fight ahead in what would become a real "killing match." But this October battle of El Alamein would be the turning-point military action of the North African campaign. Montgomery's opponent was the famed Field Marshal Erwin Rommel, who commanded Panzerarmee Afrika, the name of his Italian-German desert army from mid-1942. Up until this October battle, Rommel and the Panzerarmee had held the initiative and had dominated this theater of war. The multinational Eighth Army, comprising soldiers from the British Empire and some of Britain's allies, decisively defeated the Axis opponents during this battle. Freyberg was right in that the Italians and Germans on the Alamein position could not "stick it" against the weight of manpower and materiel wielded against them by an Army commander who demonstrated considerable skill in their use.

While this second battle of Alamein has been praised by some commentators as a great and important victory, it was a battle that never ran to the detailed and careful script Montgomery had prepared. The intense infantry fighting that required soldiers to close with and defeat an entrenched enemy was primarily carried out by just four of the eleven divisions of Eighth Army. The three armored divisions of Eighth Army had mixed performances, and some units demonstrated considerable reluctance to follow Montgomery's repeated orders to engage with the enemy. While Rommel was defeated on this battlefield, he was able to extricate the remnants of his shattered Panzerarmee Afrika and reconstitute it to fight yet more battles in North Africa. Three times wide encircling movements, described as "left hooks," almost managed to "bag" the Afrika Korps, Panzerarmee's main German component. That they failed to do so was the product of excessive caution by the Eighth Army, combined with their faulty tactics and several poor command decisions. The pursuit of the defeated Axis forces after the battle has attracted less attention and considerable criticism than the battle itself.

* * *

It is hard to exaggerate the importance of this battle to the British Empire and its people. To date there had been little to celebrate in this war, as by mid-1942 there had been few victories and a string of defeats and disasters. A future Prime Minister of the United Kingdom wrote that the disasters of the first six months of 1942 "marked the lowest point of our fortunes and put the greatest strain upon our morale."[8] The United Kingdom had endured much since the start of the war in September 1939, but the "continued misfortunes" of the spring and summer of 1942 "were harder to bear."[9] General Harold Alexander recalled that when he arrived in the Middle East in August 1942 to assume command of an army that was baffled and suffering a crisis of morale, "the situation did not look good." Alexander wrote that on his appointment, "For me the war so far had been nothing but defeats, rearguard actions and efforts to stave off disaster." But he believed that things would soon change.[10] Alexander was right and both he and Montgomery, the man who by accident had been appointed Eighth Army commander, were primarily responsible for the change in the United Kingdom's fortunes. The change was sudden, too, and occurred within weeks of both men assuming their respective commands. It was a remarkable transformation. The October Alamein battle was at the heart of this change. It was never a forgone conclusion that the Eighth Army would win this battle, nor did the battle go according to plan. Few battles ever do and this one, so profound in its impact on the Axis and the Allies, never did stick to the script that had been written for it.

Victory at El Alamein in October 1942 saved reputations and established others. According to Stephen Bungay, this battle saved the reputations of both Churchill and the British Army. Churchill was not exaggerating when he wrote that "all our fortunes turn upon the speedy and decisive defeat of Rommel."[11] The British Army at last showed it could beat the German Army in battle, even though that army had been made up largely of Italians. It also affected Churchill's reputation, enabling him to become "not just the rallier of a nation in defeat but the standard bearer of a nation in victory."[12] It also firmly established the reputation of the Eighth Army and made its commander famous almost overnight. He was later awarded the impressive title Field Marshal the

Viscount Montgomery of Alamein. After so many disasters and defeats, many of them in the last year in this very theater of war, the October battle of El Alamein "seemed to be a true watershed in Britain's fortunes during the war."[13] Bungay wrote that although "not a very big battle by the standards of the war," the October Alamein battle was one that Montgomery, Eighth Army, and the British Empire "had to win."[14]

While the October battle of Alamein was an undoubted victory and a turning-point battle, it was not without its controversies. This book examines what happened at El Alamein in October 1942 and its place in the history of the North African campaign and the Second World War. It also looks at the two earlier battles on the El Alamein position. At first, it had been intended to include both these battles in a background chapter. However, as they were both pivotal to what occurred in the final battle at Alamein, more detailed explanations of them was necessary. They have therefore been allocated a separate chapter each.

There were three battles fought on the Alamein position. These earlier battles have often been ignored by military historians, especially the one that occurred in July. This July battle, known now as the First Battle of El Alamein, was a confused and seemingly unconnected series of engagements, but it was this battle that halted Rommel's triumphant advance into Egypt. The August battle, the battle of Alam Halfa, was significant in that Rommel's last attempt to get to Cairo was halted by a combination of factors, including exemplary air-land cooperation and the skillful use of signals intelligence intercepts. At last British military commanders were learning how to use their vast military assets correctly. It is not possible to understand what occurred during the October or Second Battle of El Alamein without some knowledge of what had occurred in the recent months leading up to it. Finally, this book also considers whether the reputations won and lost at El Alamein were deserved and analyzes the significance of the battle to the Allies and to Germany.

So why write another book on the battles of El Alamein? Without doubt, the Second World War was one of the most catastrophic and harrowing events in human history. It is deservedly one of the most written-about subjects in history. A search of the British Library catalogue on the topic of the Second World War in July 2016 showed them holding almost 10,000 titles on the subject.[15] Amongst these holdings, the campaigns in

North Africa were well served with 1,807 titles devoted to Montgomery and 140 to his opponent Rommel.[16] In 2011, the library held 308 titles on the North African campaign, which amounted to more than four books a year on the subject or a book every three months of the sixty-nine years since the November battle.[17] The United States Library of Congress has similarly impressive holdings. In July 2016, it held 10,000 titles on World War II. In relation to the North African campaign, the US Library of Congress held 359 titles on the topic Alamein and 270 titles on North Africa–World War II. The titles it held on Bernard Montgomery numbered 189; those on his opponent Rommel were more than triple at 611.[18]

With such impressive coverage, it would seem that another book on the El Alamein battles of 1942 is not necessary. There are, however, several reasons for doing so. First, interest in the North African campaign remains high. A reason for this is that so many countries were involved in what was a unique theater of war. From December 1940 and lasting for more than two years, "over a million men from ten faraway countries fought here, and more than 50,000 of them died."[19] As John North has written, the October Alamein battle is the story of "a great battle . . . fought in the desert" and of "two armies . . . locked in deadly combat for months on end."[20] With the 75th anniversary of the battles approaching, interest in what happened at Alamein and why it was important is unlikely to wane. Second, a large number of the books on the North African campaign have taken a partisan approach to the various commanders involved or have told the story of the Alamein battles from a particular national perspective. This book attempts to avoid these limitations. Third, there is no doubt that the October Alamein battle was an important turning point in the war. It marked, albeit on a smaller scale than other turning-point battles of the war, the first decisive defeat on land of an army commanded by a German general and containing panzer and infantry formations of the Wehrmacht. While Rommel's defeated Panzerarmee contained many Italian formations, it is a myth that these units did not fight well in North Africa in the Alamein battles. Such an important event in the history of the Second World War is always worthy of further study. It is hoped that this book will provide a fresh and unbiased perspective of a critical battle of the Second World War. Finally, the battles of Alamein, even after so many years, remain contested ground. Part of this was fueled after the war in a "third battle of El Alamein," when so many of the participants published their accounts of what happened. The state of Eighth Army in early August 1942, who was responsible for success at Alam Halfa and the October battle, and how important all three battles were all still remain controversial and debated topics. As Jonathan Fennell wrote in 2011, "After close to seventy years of scholarship, the causes of Eighth Army's success at El Alamein are still contested."[21] It is not expected that this book will resolve these debates, although it is hoped that it adds substantially to them.

NOTES

1. Nigel Hamilton, *Monty: The Making of a General 1887–1942*. (London: Hamish Hamilton, 1981), 774.

2. Ibid., 770.

3. Ibid., 768–769.

4. Niall Barr, *Pendulum of War: The Three Battles of El Alamein*. (London: Pimlico, 2005), 309.

5. Ibid., 309.

6. Freyberg's War Diary 23 October 1944, WA II 8/44, Archives New Zealand. Te Rua Mahara o te Kāwanatanga (ANZ).

7. Hamilton, *Monty*, 771.

8. Harold Macmillan, *The Blast of War 1939–1945*. (London. Macmillan & Co. Ltd., 1967), 81.

9. Ibid., 166.

10. John North, ed., *The Alexander Memoirs: 1940–1945*. (London: Cassell & Company Ltd., 1962), 12.

11. I.S.O. Playfair, and C.J.C. Molony, with F.C. Flynn, T.P. Gleave, *The Mediterranean and the Middle East, Volume IV. The Destruction of the Axis Forces in Africa*. (London: HMSO, 1966), 1.

12. Stephen Bungay, *Alamein*. (London: Arum Press, 2003), 215.

13. Barr, *Pendulum of War*, xxxvii.

14. Bungay, *Alamein*, 3.

15. The British Library, accessed July 13, 2016, www.bl.uk. The exact figure was 9,794.

16. Ibid.

17. Jonathan Fennell, "'Steel my soldiers' hearts': El Alamein Reappraised," in *Journal of Military and Strategic Studies* (Vol.14, Issue 1, Fall 2011): 1.

18. Library of Congress, accessed July 13, 2016, https://www.loc.gov.

19. Bungay, *Alamein*, 2.

20. North, *The Alexander Memoirs*, 5.

21. Fennell, "Steel my soldiers' hearts," 2.

ONE

THE MILITARY BACKGROUND

Since late 1940, after Italy joined the war on the side of the Axis on June 10 that year, both sides had waged military offensives in the Western Desert with varying degrees of success. Egypt was a vital cog in Britain's war effort, described by John Connell as "the fulcrum of the British Empire."[1] Egypt protected the sources of oil in the Middle East and its route to the United Kingdom. It was a center of communications for the far-flung parts of the Empire "east of Suez" and a critical base for naval operations in the Mediterranean. For these reasons, Egypt became the largest British military base outside of the United Kingdom. It was a vital, strategic asset. But, after June 1940, one of Britain's Axis enemies was just across the border in Libya with a huge military force. Italian forces in Libya, under Marshal Rodolfo Graziani, numbered 250,000 organized into two armies and fourteen divisions. British forces in Egypt under General Sir Archibald Wavell had just 36,000 men and consisted primarily of an understrength armored and two infantry divisions. The Western Desert Force, as these were called—there were not yet enough assets to form a corps or an army—was short of much essential equipment including artillery, tanks, transport, and logistical support.

Given their overwhelming force, it was natural that the Italians should strike first. They took some time doing so, though. It was not until September 13 that the Italians crossed the border and began a slow, ponderous advance into Egypt. After four days, all the time harassed by artillery fire, minefields, and bombed by the Royal Air Force (RAF), the Italians reached Sidi Barrani, just sixty-five miles into Egypt. There they halted, dug in, and planned their next moves.

They were still contemplating them when, on December 9, the Western Desert Force launched Operation *Compass*. It achieved complete surprise and was a stunning success. Within two days, the Sidi Barrani position was captured, four Italian divisions destroyed, and the remainder of the Italian force sent reeling back in utter defeat. Amongst the 38,000 Italian prisoners taken were four generals. Also captured were 237 guns, seventy-three tanks, and more than 1,000 vehicles. Losses in the Western Desert Force were 624 killed, missing, or wounded.[2] As an exultant Anthony Eden informed British Prime Minister Winston Churchill, "debasing a golden phrase" in the process, "Never before has so much been surrendered by so many to so few."[3]

In the pursuit phase that followed the Italians' rout, British forces advanced deep into Libya. On January 3, 1941, they captured Bardia just over the border and pushed on. On January 22, Tobruk was captured, Derna eight days later, and Benghazi fell on February 7. Two days later, the Western Desert Force, now renamed 13 Corps, reached El Agheila, where they halted. This was the first British offensive of the Second World War and their first land victory. It was a significant one, too. In just two months, a British force, never numbering more than 30,000 men, had advanced some 500 miles, destroyed ten Italian divisions, captured 130,000 prisoners, 850 guns, 400 tanks, and given the British Commonwealth something to celebrate in the darkest of times. British casualties had been fewer than 2,000.[4] It was an impressive victory and the Allies would not have another like it for nearly two years.

The success of the British forces in Operation *Compass* had the effect of tarnishing the reputation of the Italian army there. But Operation *Compass* was an aberration where Italian troops had been inexperienced, lacked vital equipment, and were poorly led. The Italians fought in North Africa for almost three years, "its longest campaign of the Second World War." From 1941–43, in concert with its German allies, "most Italian soldiers fought well against the British forces."[5] Italian losses in various actions were similar to German losses, indicating that their formations had fought equally hard. The North African campaign would eventually result in twenty-six Italian divisions being destroyed, with 12,000 Italian soldiers being killed in action.[6]

Two developments occurred in capital cities thousands of miles from the fighting that were to have profound implications on this theater of war. First, on the same day that Bardia fell, Churchill took the decision that offensive operations in the Middle East were to be halted, the advance should not proceed beyond Benghazi and the position there made secure. Then all military assistance should be rendered to Greece in their fight against the Italian invaders there. This was to be the military priority now. From his already stretched resources, Wavell was directed to prepare a sizable expeditionary force to Greece. Then, just over a month later on February 2, 1941, Adolf Hitler wrote to Mussolini expressing his concerns about events in North Africa and offering a German armored division to assist in the defense of Tripoli. Mussolini reluctantly accepted the assistance and things moved quickly from here. On February 6, Adolf Hitler summoned one of his favourite generals to see him. After giving "a detailed account of the situation in Africa," Hitler informed Erwin Rommel that Rommel "had been recommended to him as the man who would most quickly adapt himself to the altogether different conditions of the African theatre."[7] Rommel was elated with his new appointment and wrote to his wife, Lucie-Maria, that evening apologizing for cutting short his leave. "Things are moving fast," he informed her. "The new job is very big and important."[8]

Things were certainly moving fast. On February 11, Lieutenant General Erwin Rommel arrived in Rome to discuss military arrangements. Only three days later, the first German units arrived in Tripoli and were immediately dispatched to the front. They would eventually become the famed Deutsches Afrika Korps (DAK). The timing was crucial. Just as the British were winding down their operations and diverting their forces to meet other commitments, "a new and formidable factor had entered the desert war."[9] It would soon be the British forces' turn to be surprised and it began the period for them that David Fraser called "the habit of defeat."[10] On February 16, just two days after their arrival, the Germans were in action against the depleted British forces and Rommel had taken command of the battle front. At the end of March, despite the reluctance of his Italian allies and in defiance of orders from the German Oberkommondo des Heeres (Army High Command), Rommel launched a raid in force against the British positions in Libya. It turned into much more than that. Rommel wrote to his wife on April 3 that their attack had met with "dazzling success" and that the British forces were "falling over each other to get away."[11] It was true. By April 10, the Axis forces had pushed the British back across the Egyptian border, leaving just the isolated Tobruk garrison holding out now eighty miles behind the frontline. By the end of April, the Axis were occupying all the old Italian positions along the frontier and had established a forward out-post at Halfaya Pass, ten miles inside Egypt. Axis casualties had been light and three British generals, including the Army commander Richard O'Connor, had been captured. Rommel and the Axis had clearly won this round of the "Benghazi Handicap" as the race across North Africa was now called. His success was as immensely satisfying to him as it was galling to his British opponents. He wrote to his wife that, "It's wonder-ful to have pulled this off against the British."[12] But there was a tactical thorn that threatened to prick his growing reputation. The town of To-bruk and its wide defended perimeter held out against the Axis. It was defended largely by the 9th Australian Division, which was determined not to lose it. As Barrie Pitt has written, Tobruk "was to prove a continual distraction to Rommel's further ambition and his attempts to storm its defences were to cause him serious losses in both men and material dur-ing the months which followed."[13] It would cause considerable losses for the British forces, too.

While Tobruk was besieged, with its harbor providing a tenuous lifeline, three attempts were made by the British to drive the Axis forces back from the Libyan-Egyptian border and lift the siege. The British Army in these early years of the war was hampered by two serious flaws, both of them a legacy of the First World War. While the British Army had pioneered tank development in the 1914–18 war, it had then seriously neglected its development in the decades that followed. Tanks, many felt, were a marginal asset and were certainly unreliable. They were expensive and definitely not as likeable as horses. So it was then that "the British Army entered the Second World War without a coherent doctrine of armoured operations, and with little general understanding of how those operations might change the whole pattern of warfare."[14] It was a seri-ous gap in the British Army's warfighting doctrine, one that would be responsible for several disasters ahead and that would affect how the last

Alamein battle would be fought. It was also the reason that the British failed to produce a quality tank during the war that could match those of the Germans. In response to the German challenge, "we produced tanks with too thin a skin or too feeble a weapon, or both."[15] It was not until mid-1942 during the Gazala battle that the M3 Grant provided the British with a tank that could match the best of the German tanks. Later in the year, the British received an even better US-designed M4 tank: the Sherman, which would eventually become the mainstay of British armored formations. The other flaw reflected the shadow of the barbed wire of the trenches of the Western Front. The defense, it was assumed, was the strongest and the wisest method of war. It also engendered, as the historian/soldier David Fraser admitted, "a spirit of caution and hesitancy [that] was never completely eradicated from all parts of the British Command." But as Fraser acknowledged, often bold offensive moves can lead to fewer casualties when a cautious approach can accumulate many casualties for small gains.[16]

The first attempt to relieve Tobruk was the appropriately named Operation *Brevity* launched on May 15. The offensive began well. The British forces achieved a tactical surprise and initially captured the key border locations of Halfaya Pass, Sollum, and Fort Capuzzo. But the offensive was brought to an abrupt halt when the Axis forces launched spirited counterattacks and the British tanks encountered for the first time in this theater the powerfully effective 88 millimeter (mm) anti-aircraft gun being used in an anti-tank role. The range and hitting power of this weapon was devastating on the lightly armored British tanks. The 88 mm gun came to have an important effect on the morale of British armored formations from this time. It soon became "the most feared weapon in North Africa."[17] Curiously, the British had their equivalent of the 88 mm in the 3.7-inch (94 mm) anti-aircraft gun, but hide-bound British staff officers refused to allow it to be used in a dual role. One anti-aircraft gunner, Lieutenant David Parry, felt there was "no excuse for the sheer stupidity" of this decision.[18] An 88 mm gun had three times the effective range of a two-pounder gun. Unfortunately, the two-pounder gun was the standard armament of British tanks and their anti-tank weaponry at this stage of the war. An 88 mm gun "could completely destroy a Crusader tank with one shot from a distance of one-and-a-half miles."[19]

With its range and sheer velocity, the 88 mm gun "wrought havoc" on the North African battlefields and "remained queen of the desert."[20]

After ten days and with the loss of five tanks and around 200 men, the offensive was called off. It was a humiliating defeat for the British 13 Corps. Rommel, who recaptured the last position lost to the British on May 27, recorded a succinct summary of the fighting:

> The British were soon driven out and fled in panic to the east, leaving considerable booty and material of all kinds in our hands. Our losses were comparatively insignificant.[21]

It was an inauspicious start to lifting the siege of Tobruk.

The next attempt, Operation *Battleaxe*, launched on June 14, was even worse. Barrie Pitt summed it up as "a disastrous failure."[22] Reinforced by the arrival of more than 200 new tanks and pressured by Winston Churchill to use them as soon as possible, the attack revealed just how much the British had to learn in this type of warfare. The army commander Wavell was not confident and identified part of the problem in a report on May 28. Wavell wrote:

> Our infantry tanks are really too slow for a battle in the desert, and have been suffering considerable casualties from the fire of the powerful enemy anti-tank guns. Our cruisers have little advantage in power or speed over German medium tanks.

Wavell, however, hoped to "succeed in driving the enemy west of Tobruk."[23] Wavell's dashed hopes would lose him the command of the Middle East. As indicated above, the new tanks were not suited for desert conditions and their crews were unfamiliar with how they could be used. Worse still was the fact that an all-arms approach to the battle was not yet part of British doctrine. British armored units did not know how to work in tandem with the infantry, artillery, and engineer formations that made up their land force in this theater. Cooperation and coordination with the Royal Air Force was also nonexistent. These were fundamental flaws and doomed Operation *Battleaxe* to failure. And by the time *Battleaxe* was launched, Rommel's forces had been strengthened by the arrival of an additional formation—the 15th Panzer Division.

On the first day, the British armor skirted around the fortified positions on the border but came up against strong German defenses at

Fort Capuzzo. There they were attacked by the tanks of the 15th Panzer Division and routed. Within the space of a few short hours, the British armored formations had lost more than half their tanks. The next day, the third of the battle, Wavell called off the operation and his army retired ignominiously to their start lines. Inferior British equipment, poor planning, faulty doctrine, inadequate training, and British generalship that was "remote and inexpert" had caused this defeat.[24] In the United Kingdom, Winston Churchill described the failure of *Battleaxe* as "a most bitter blow." Victory in the Western Desert was of "supreme consequence" and "all our hearts at home had been set on beating Rommel."[25] Churchill was deeply disappointed by the British forces' dismal performance in *Battleaxe* and decided a new commander was needed to deliver him the victory he so desperately needed in the Middle East. "The fact remains," he wrote somewhat defensively in his history of the war, "that after 'Battleaxe,' I came to the conclusion that there should be a change."[26] Wavell was informed on June 21 that he was being relieved of command of the armies in the Middle East.

The Germans soon recovered their lost tanks and many of the British ones, too, and restored them to working order. So severe had been their defeat that the original intent of destroying Rommel's forces and lifting the Tobruk siege was kept hidden from the British public. It was described to them as "merely a reconnaissance in force."[27] The Germans were not deceived, though, and Rommel was elated with his success. He described it to his wife as a "complete victory." After the battle, Rommel went around the front line troops to thank them personally.[28] The morale of the Afrika Korps troops was "tremendous" and Rommel's confidence soared. "Now the enemy can come," he wrote, and "he'll get an even bigger beating."[29] The enemy would not be coming for several months now.

* * *

Appointed as the commander to deliver Churchill the elusive land victory against German ground forces he so desperately wanted was an impressive-looking general nicknamed "The Auk." This was General Sir Claude Auchinleck, who had limited experience for such a crucial appointment. Auchinleck was a major general at the start of the war in

1939, and the following year had commanded Allied land forces during the latter half of the ill-fated Narvik expedition in Norway. He then commanded a corps in England and was promoted as the GOC Southern Command. Auchinleck's star was definitely on the rise in 1940 and in November, he was promoted to general and appointed as the Commander-in-Chief India. It was in this role that Auchinleck's swift dispatch of soldiers to deal with an uprising in Iraq in 1941 caught Churchill's eye. He appeared to be the decisive, skilled commander he needed to replace Wavell. But Auchinleck was, like the Duke of Wellington, a "Sepoy General" from the Indian Army. In the British Army, "he was not widely known, nor did he widely know others." This would lead to a fatal flaw. While his own soldierly qualities were clearly evident, Auchinleck was a poor selector of subordinates. As David Fraser has written, Auchinleck "did not choose subordinates wisely, nor judge their performance as shrewdly as was needed."[30] In the battles ahead, this would become glaringly obvious and cost Eighth Army dearly.

Auchinleck arrived to take over the Middle East command in July 1941. His instructions were simple. He was to take offensive action against the Axis forces immediately and expel them from Egypt first and then from North Africa. But Auchinleck refused to be rushed. After a good look at his forces and the terrain over which they must fight, Auchinleck's first cable to Churchill made it clear that immediate offensive action was too risky. Instead, Auchinleck needed time to secure his main base and build up his forces, including having an adequate reserve of armor. An "adequate" armored reserve for Auchinleck meant 50 percent of the total with this being equally divided between those in workshops under repair and those available for immediate replacement of battle casualties. Churchill was furious, writing: "Generals only enjoy such comforts in heaven . . . And those that demand them do not always get there."[31] In the months that followed, additional reinforcements were sent to the Middle East from the United Kingdom as well as considerable materials, including vast supplies of fuel, munitions, armor, and vehicles. With each new shipment came pressure from Whitehall for military action. It was not until mid-November, though, that Auchinleck felt ready to move. On November 18, 1941, he launched the newly named Eighth Army against the Axis forces with the aim of driving them back and relieving Tobruk.

Operation *Crusader*, the codename of this new offensive, would be "the third lap of the Benghasi Handicap."[32]

The Eighth Army was an unusual creation. It was a multinational force comprising soldiers from across the British Empire. It also contained soldiers from Allied nations, including Poles, Free French, and Greek units or formations. Such a polyglot force caused serious problems. Until the arrival of Lieutenant General Bernard Montgomery in August 1942, Eighth Army lacked a sense of shared purpose. Niall Barr wrote that in July 1942, at a time of severe crisis in the North African campaign, Eighth Army was still "not a unified army with a strong sense of collective identity but a collection of units with sometimes competing identities."[33] This lack of cohesion, this understanding of a shared purpose in working together as part of a larger team, contributed significantly to the many disasters ahead for Eighth Army.

Operation *Crusader* was a critical if greatly confused battle in the North African campaign. The New Zealand official historian warned that it was "A play with a cast of 250,000, a setting the size of Italy, and a plot like a pot of eels, twisting and turning in all directions."[34] It was an apt description of what became a real soldier's battle. Generalship on both sides "was at second best level."[35] Twice Rommel led spectacular armored thrusts, which certainly unnerved his opponent but diverted crucial assets away from the battle's tipping point around Tobruk. But Eighth Army commander Lieutenant General Sir Alan Cunningham performed so poorly that Auchinleck was forced to relieve him of command midway through the fighting. He was replaced with a staff officer, Major General Neil Ritchie, whose last combat experience had been as a major in Palestine in 1918. Ritchie, "a large, affable Scot," had risen from major to Major General in the space of four years but always in staff roles. Bierman and Smith attribute this rapid promotion "more to his ability to get on with people than to a particularly sharp mind."[36] In this theater and at this stage of the war, being "clubbable" or a "good chap" was essential to receiving an army command.

Meanwhile, as much of the British armor had been destroyed in piecemeal clashes, British Commonwealth infantry bore the brunt of the fighting around key pieces of terrain such as Sidi Rezegh, Belhamed, and Ed Duda. Their losses soon mounted, especially for the South Africans and New Zealanders. In the end, victory went to the side with the biggest purse. After his two impetuous armored dashes into Egypt, Rommel was critically short of armor, fuel, ammunition, and other vital supplies. The often-forgotten efforts of the Royal Air Force and Royal Navy had sent most of the Axis supplies to the bottom of the Mediterranean and it made a telling difference. In mid-December, Rommel reluctantly made the decision to abandon the siege of Tobruk and withdrew his forces back to El Agheila. He wrote two telling letters to his wife. The first informed her that, "We're pulling out. There was simply nothing else for it." The next offered some explanation why the withdrawal was necessary:

> Retreat to Agedabia. You can't imagine what it's like. Hoping to get the bulk of my force through and to make a stand somewhere. Little ammunition and petrol, no air support. Quite the reverse with the enemy.[37]

If Churchill now had his victory, it was a pyrrhic one at best. British casualties, some 17,700, were heavy; unnecessarily so. Of those formations involved, one, the 2nd New Zealand Division, had suffered more than 30 percent of them, some 4,620 in total.[38] This "victory" had cost the New Zealanders far more in casualties than their two previous military disasters of Greece and Crete. There was also the strong feeling throughout Eighth Army that the victory had been won by default and was undeserved.

After *Crusader*, rather than being elated with their success, many Eighth Army soldiers had little confidence in their army's military leadership and believed their weapons systems to be thoroughly inferior to their opponents'. This especially applied to Eighth Army's main anti-tank weapon—the two-pounder gun. Introduced in 1936 and reasonably effective in 1939, the two-pounder anti-tank gun was "dangerously obsolete" in 1941.[39] It could penetrate the heavier armored German tanks only at close range. The 75 mm guns of the German tanks easily outranged them. In contrast, the Afrika Korps was equipped with two of the best anti-tank guns of the war. These were the 5 cm Pak gun, which had a low profile and a range of 1,000 yards—double that of the British two-pounder—and the much-vaunted 88 mm anti-aircraft gun. When used in the anti-tank role, the 88 mm "could destroy British tanks at 2,000 yards range."[40] Little wonder British tanks greatly feared the

88 mm anti-aircraft gun, although both guns were formidable weapons. Also important was the fact that the Afrika Korps used its anti-tank guns as part of a combined arms team working closely with infantry and the armored formations.

British tanks were also obsolete in 1941–42. In the *Crusader* battle, Eighth Army had used seven different types of tanks and not one had been able to match the German tanks in terms of firepower. Their mainstays, the Crusader, Matilda, and Valentine, armed with a two-pounder gun, were outmatched by the German tanks. The Crusader tank, designed as a light cruiser tank, had a top speed of thirty miles per hour, "far faster than any other tank in North Africa."[41] But speed was only one factor in armored warfare and not as crucial as armament and protection. All British tanks at this time mounted a two-pounder gun. This designation referred to the weight of the shell it fired, although it actually weighed 2.38 pounds. In terms of muzzle diameter, the two-pounder was equivalent to a 39 mm gun.[42] The two-pounder gun had a maximum range of 500 yards; German tanks had twice that range. The two-pounder guns had another problem. Their small bore permitted the firing of only armor-piercing rounds. They could not fire high explosive or other types of ammunition so that while they could take on tanks at close range, they were ineffective against infantry and anti-tank gun positions. Field Marshal John Harding recalled after the war being told in London that a Crusader tank mounted with a two-pounder anti-tank gun "was about the best weapon there was." It was a dangerous illusion as Harding found out the hard way; the sad reality was that "it wasn't, because it couldn't really destroy a German tank at all."[43] As Niall Barr has written, "the two-pounder had never really been suitable as a tank-mounted weapon."[44] Only the new US Grant tank, which did not enter service with Eighth Army until April 1942, could match German tanks in terms of armor and fire power. But the Grant tank lacked a revolving turret for its main weapon, a 75 mm gun, which was mounted in a sponson on the side of the hull. As well as the limited traverse of the main gun, Grant tanks had a high profile and the positioning of the 75 mm gun meant it could not fight in a hull down position. The new US Sherman M4 medium tank would not arrive in theater until September 1942. They would be a match for the Germans, even if a design fault with its ammunition storage made the Sherman "brew up" all too easily when hit in the turret.

After *Crusader*, many in Eighth Army developed a strong admiration for the abilities of both Rommel and the Afrika Korps. It was a dangerous situation not helped by the fact that British training and doctrine was clearly inadequate for this type of warfare. This did not bode well for the next leg of the Benghazi stakes.

The Eighth Army did not have long to wait. In the closing months of 1941, the Royal Navy had lost four capital ships and two cruisers to Axis torpedoes and two more cruisers had been badly damaged by mines. Until these losses could be replaced, the British had lost control of the mid-Mediterranean. The results were immediately apparent. A German convoy bringing much-needed panzers had reached North Africa prior to Christmas 1941, followed by an even larger convoy in the New Year. Arriving on January 5, this latter convoy brought the Afrika Korps fifty-five more panzers, twenty armored cars, and a large consignment of fuel. As Fritz Bayerlein, the Korps' Chief of Staff, remarked, this convoy's safe arrival was "as good as a victory in battle."[45]

Rommel did not wait long to use these assets. On January 21, 1942, without informing his own High Command and against the protests of the Italian senior officers in theater, Rommel advanced against Eighth Army positions in front of El Agheila. On the eve of the attack Rommel wrote in his diary:

> The Army launches its counter-attack in two hours' time. After carefully weighing the pros and cons, I've decided to take the risk. I have complete faith that God is keeping a protective hand over us and that He will grant us victory. [46]

The risk certainly paid off. Rommel wrote to his wife on January 22 that, "Our opponents are getting out as though they'd been stung."[47] Within ten days, Rommel's counterstroke recaptured most of Cyrenaica including Benghazi and taking him to within thirty-five miles of Tobruk. Much abandoned equipment including guns, tanks, armored cars, rations, fuel, and ammunition fell into German hands, which helped to sustain the advance. The Eighth Army lost another seventy-two tanks, forty guns, and "yet more confidence in its leaders . . . equipment, tactics, and command ability" during this withdrawal.[48] The habit of defeat was back.

The new frontline eventually stabilized in early February in Eastern Cyrenaica around Gazala-Bir Hacheim-Tobruk. On February 4, an elated Rommel wrote to Lucie-Maria, "we have Cyrenaica back. It went like greased lightning."[49] It was an accurate assessment. Once again, Rommel had done the unpredictable and it had paid dividends. Amongst his opponents, confidence in Eighth Army's leadership was further diminished by this success. The "Rommel legend" took a firm hold. On the Gazala line, both sides planned their next moves for the opening months of summer. Rommel struck first and inflicted an even heavier defeat on Eighth Army.

The Gazala Stakes

Despite a marked inferiority in numbers of guns, tanks, vehicles, and men, Rommel launched a major offensive against the Gazala line on May 26, 1942. It would mark "the climax of Rommel's performance as a daring battlefield commander."[50] Rommel's Panzerarmee Afrika (the new name for Panzergruppe Afrika from this battle on) started this offensive with 90,000 men, 561 tanks, and 542 aircraft. For this operation, Rommel would divide his army into two wings. In the north, the infantry under General Ludwig Crüwell would make the initial attack against the British line. In the south, the main effort of the battle would be Operation *Venezia*. In this Rommel would personally command the Afrika Korps and two Italian armored divisions. Standing on the defensive at Gazala, the British Eighth Army had more than 100,000 men, 849 tanks, and 604 aircraft.[51] Some 167 of these tanks were the new American M3 Grant tank, which had thick armor and a 75 mm gun mounted in a sponson on the side of the hull.[52] Despite the inferiority of some of its other equipment, Eighth Army had considerable advantages. Not only did they outnumber their opponents, but the army sheltered behind dense minefields designed to channel any attack by Axis forces. The army was well supplied; its fighting units were experienced in desert warfare, well rested, and at full strength. Eighth Army also possessed a critical advantage in intelligence. Ultra decrypts of German Enigma radio traffic provided by the code breakers at Bletchley Park confirmed that Rommel was planning an offensive against the Gazala position in late May 1942.[53] Auchinleck was confident of defeating Rommel's new attack. On May 15, he assured the CIGS, Sir Alan Brooke, that "our plans to meet such an attack are made, all preparations are in hand."[54] Despite this assurance, on May 20, Churchill advised Auchinleck to "assume direct command of Eighth Army" and to move the New Zealand Division immediately from Syria to Libya.[55] Auchinleck did not accept this advice.

* * *

Despite all of these advantages of Eighth Army, Rommel's attack against the Gazala position was a stunning success. Poor leadership and faulty tactical doctrines resulted in a decisive defeat for Eighth Army in Cyrenaica. While they may have had more tanks than the Panzerarmee, British commanders still did not know how to use this advantage. The Eighth Army "as usual did not concentrate their armour; the Germans were able to tackle and defeat the 7th and 1st Armoured Divisions separately."[56] The Gazala battle, wrote David Fraser, "constituted a serious and avoidable reverse for British arms."[57] As Niall Barr has written, at times the Eighth Army commander, Ritchie, "seemed to be making decisions in slow motion."[58] Another historian has accused Ritchie of letting "the days slip by in a blur of indecisiveness."[59] These criticisms may be justified, but they are harsh. In many ways Ritchie had been set up to fail, being promoted well above his ceiling and expected to command an army that was clearly dysfunctional. Barrie Pitt wrote:

> Sandwiched as he was between Auchinleck's determination to "hold his hand" at almost every stage of the operation, and indifference to his opinion by his corps commanders and almost contempt for them from lower levels, it is not surprising that Ritchie's grip on the battle as it developed was at first weak and in the end nonexistent.

Pitt was correct when he stated that "ultimate responsibility for the disasters of Gazala" lies with Auchinleck. It was Auchinleck who appointed Ritchie and then watched him flounder. Even when it was abundantly clear that Ritchie possessed neither the experience, command skills, or the intellect to command Eighth Army against the Panzerarmee, Auchinleck took no immediate action. When Auchinleck finally acted, it was too late to avert disaster.[60]

Rommel had no problems making quick decisions and commenced his new attack on the afternoon of May 26. The turning point of the battle had been an attack on the Knightsbridge position on June 5 and 6. What had been intended as a vital blow against the Panzerarmee resulted in "a decisive defeat . . . from which Eighth was not to recover."[61] In the Cauldron battle, as it is known, the fighting was "remarkably hard," with gallant actions on both sides. But as David Fraser has written of the battle, "To the Panzerarmee the enemy operations appeared uncoordinated and tactically inept, and were defeated without especial difficulty."[62] Most noticeable was the lack of coordination between the British armor, infantry, and artillery. By the end of June 6, Rommel had destroyed hundreds of British tanks, overrun several formation headquarters and had taken more than 3,000 prisoners. The British counterattack had been "decisively defeated."[63]

Only the Free French Brigade at the Bir Hacheim Box in the southern sector of the Gazala line offered Rommel any determined resistance. Rommel had attacked the position on May 26 believing that he could destroy the position within an hour. Instead, the Free French held out at Bir Hacheim, isolated and desperately short of essential equipment, for two weeks. Only on the night of June 10 did their commander, General Pierre Koenig, decide to break out from their encirclement. In doing so, 2,500 from a garrison of 3,700 managed to escape.[64]

On June 11–12, Eighth Army lost a staggering 260 tanks, "virtually writing off 8th Army's armoured forces."[65] After two weeks of intense fighting, by June 13, Eighth Army was reduced to just fifty cruiser and twenty infantry tanks. The remnants of this defeated army fled back to the Egyptian frontier, exposing the fortress of Tobruk to the victorious Panzerarmee Afrika. So many British tanks had been destroyed that "there was no longer an effective armoured force that could keep open communication with the garrison of Tobruk or launch a counter-attack against the enemy forces arrayed before the town." Hope that Tobruk would hold out in another siege "did not last long."[66]

Tobruk, the very "symbol of British resistance," was taken on June 21 and Rommel received his Field Marshal's baton for taking this prize that had eluded him in 1941.[67] The fortress of Tobruk had fallen within twenty-four hours. It was "the biggest British setback of the war in North Africa."[68] "It was a heavy blow, for no one had expected it quite so early," recalled de Guingand.[69] The 35,000 prisoners of war taken with the fortress made this the second-largest capitulation of the war, second only to the fall of Singapore. Equally significant was "the vast quantity of petrol and other stores that had laboriously been accumulated there for many months past."[70] It included three million rations, 7,000 tons of water, and 1.5 million gallons of fuel.[71] Rommel would be the beneficiary of this labor, and he put his captured booty to good use. Although he did not know it, the capture of Tobruk marked "the pinnacle of his military career."[72] On the day of its capture, a jubilant Rommel wrote to his wife, "Tobruk! It was a wonderful battle."[73]

For Eighth Army though, the Gazala battle had been anything but wonderful. With the fall of Tobruk, "the British humiliation was complete."[74] "We have been out-gunned, out-manoeuvred, out-generalled; in other words, led up the garden path," wrote one veteran of the retreat. Another captured the bitterness and bewilderment equally well. He wrote:

> Let me try to analyse the last few months. We had started out as a well-equipped regiment, well trained, good administration, very good officers and NCOs, plenty of experience in tank warfare in the desert. It boiled down to one thing, the enemy had out-gunned us with superior armament and fire power, plus a few very bad decisions by the high command. We must try again. It was just like seeing your favourite football team reaching the final and getting licked 6–0.[75]

Catching the bewilderment, bitterness, and loss of confidence, Albert Martin of the 2nd Rifle Brigade wrote a telling entry in his diary two days before Tobruk capitulated. It read, "Everything has been a jumble. Does anyone at the top know what they are doing?"[76]

Prime Minister Winston Churchill, then in the USA, must have been asking himself the same question. This was one of his worst moments in the war. Churchill, who learned of the news in President Franklin Roosevelt's study, at first could not believe such dire news. He was mortified and later wrote that Tobruk's loss:

> was one of the heaviest blows I can recall during the war. Not only were its military effects grievous, but it had affected the reputation of the British armies.... It was a bitter moment. Defeat is one thing; disgrace is another.[77]

But his US allies rose to the occasion. "What can we do to help?" asked President Roosevelt. "Give us as many Sherman tanks as you can spare and ship them to the Middle East as quickly as possible," replied Churchill without hesitating. Within days, 300 Sherman tanks and one hundred 105 mm self-propelled guns were loaded onto six of the fastest ships the US had and sent on their way to Cairo. Churchill was right to call it a sympathetic and chivalrous act.[78]

To add to Churchill's bitterness, upon returning to the United Kingdom he faced a no-confidence motion in the House of Commons. While this motion was massively defeated, it was pivotal to Churchill's decision to travel to the Middle East to finally sort out what bedeviled Britain's only active land army.

Churchill had good reason to feel dishonored. In mid-May 1942, Eighth Army had been well dug in on a strong defensive position with a considerable numerical superiority over its enemy in armor, artillery, and infantry. A month later, "it had been utterly defeated and flung back nearly three hundred miles."[79] Reading of the Gazala battle and the poor performance of British armored units during it, a senior New Zealand officer was reminded of an Edgar Allan Poe story. It was "a dreadful tale" that left his "hair standing on end and eyes staring wide with horror."[80] The American military attaché at the US Embassy made an astute assessment of the problems afflicting Eighth Army at this time. On June 20, 1942, part of Colonel Bonner F. Fellers' report to Washington stated:

> With numerically superior forces, with tanks, planes, artillery, means of transport, and reserves of every kind, the British army has twice failed to defeat the Axis forces in Libya. . . . The Eighth Army has failed to maintain the morale of its troops; its tactical conceptions were always wrong, it neglected completely cooperation between the various arms; its reactions to the lightning changes of the battlefield were always slow.[81]

This must have been music to Rommel's ears. The Italian Military Intelligence Service (SIM), in "a magnificent coup," had broken the American diplomatic cipher and Fellers' reports were being sent directly to Rommel.[82] Rommel greatly appreciated the information provided by the "Good Source" or "my little Fellers," as he called them. One of Rommel's intelligence staff officers, Hans-Otto Behrendt, stated after the war that the steady stream of intelligence originating from Colonel Fellers was "stupefying in its openness" and "contributed so decisively . . . to our victories in North Africa."[83]

Little wonder, then, that Rommel did not stop at Tobruk. The Axis forces pushed deep into Egypt, forcing Eighth Army back to a strong defensive position first at Mersa Matruh and then back further to positions around El Alamein. This was a calamity for the British in Egypt. Auchinleck relieved Ritchie of command of Eighth Army on June 25, but did not appoint a new commander. He would be both theater and army commander in the remaining few weeks ahead of him. It was a move that Churchill had urged a month earlier. Auchinleck's decision to take over the direct running of the army "represented a real upheaval of the British command chain, a sign in itself of the deep crisis facing Middle East Command."[84] As Christopher Pugsley wrote, at this time Eighth Army "is an army in name only and is really a fragmented patchwork quilt of formations and units that lacks cohesion and more importantly lacks faith in itself."[85] A senior officer in the 7th Armoured Division described Auchinleck as being "manifestly unlucky in his choice of subordinates." Lieutenant Colonel Ronald Belchem later recalled this time as "a moment of utter crisis" for the Eighth Army.[86] Senior staff officer Freddie de Guingand recalled the time when Eighth Army's fortunes were at their lowest. With Auchinleck, he watched the army in retreat from Tobruk:

> I had never seen such chaos; it looked like you'd never be able to save the situation. I've never seen the desert road crammed with every sort of vehicle, every unit muddled up higgledy-piggledy, no one knew what was going on. Luckily our Air Force was stronger than the enemy's, otherwise I think we would have been routed. We got back to El Alamein hoping that they had taken precautions beforehand to prepare defensive positions, that there was somewhere for us to go to, but it was touch and go for several days. One wondered whether we'd ever be able to hold the front and prevent Rommel from getting into Egypt and Cairo itself.[87]

Auchinleck's personal intervention may have been the only course he felt left open to him. But it marked a failure in his leadership skills and left him vulnerable. No one commander could cover both the operational and strategic command of the Middle East. In Cairo, government officials started burning official documents and an urgent call was sent to the 9th Australian Division and the 2nd New Zealand Division, both on garrison duty in Syria, to immediately return to Egypt.

The Australians were in the middle of a major field exercise when all battalion commanders were called to attend a conference at their brigade headquarters. The War Diary of 2/24 Infantry Battalion recorded its outcome: "The C.O. returned with warning advice that exercise was cancelled and that the Bn would move SOUTH."[88] The War Diary of 2/28 Infantry Battalion recorded that the 9th Australian Division "is to move as soon as possible to EGYPT" and that soon, "Hasty preparations for the move are under way." It noted that:

> All possible secrecy and deception is to be maintained relative to our move but already the tps have wind that something is doing so we are instructed to tell them that we are moving to ALLEPPO but unfortunately nobody is deceived. Rumours very close to the truth are soon current and it is impossible to say from where they originate.[89]

With all unit and formation symbols obscured, the 9th Australian Division was soon heading south by road and rail. The Australian soldiers, always inveterate gamblers, were soon taking bets as to whether they were returning to fight in the Western Desert or returning to Australia. "Hopes soared" that it was the latter. However, skirting around Cairo and still heading west, "the destination of the Bn ceased to be in doubt. It was the desert—and another crack at ROMMEL."[90]

The New Zealanders received the call to return to the Western Desert earlier than the Australians. Their commander, Lieutenant General Sir Bernard Freyberg, received an urgent summons to Cairo and flew there from Baghdad on June 13. Early the next morning, the New Zealand Division received a written order "to move forthwith to EGYPT, destination MATRUH."[91] The War Diary of one of its infantry brigades recorded on June 15 reads,

> Instruction from NZ Div that Bde be prepared to move immediately.
> Conference of Unit Commanders at 2000 hours. Advance party of 20 Aus Bde arrive at Aleppo.[92]

After handing over its garrison duties to 20th Australian Brigade on June 18, the next day the New Zealanders were heading south with utmost speed. En route to Egypt, on June 22 the leading New Zealand Brigade received the order from Freyberg "to proceed to MERSA MATRUH with all possible speed."[93]

When the Australians and New Zealanders arrived back in Egypt, after a 1,200-mile journey by road or rail, they were alarmed with what they found. A senior New Zealand officer recalled:

> Eighth Army poured through us, not looking at all demoralised except for the black South African drivers, but thoroughly mixed up and disorganised. I did not see a single formed fighting unit, infantry, armour, or artillery.[94]

The New Zealand commander, Lieutenant General Bernard Freyberg, cabled his government on June 24:

> There is no doubt our forces in Western Desert have suffered a major reverse and situation at the moment causes anxiety. General Auchinleck has a difficult task here with inadequate resources and inferior tank gun and anti-tank gun.[95]

What shocked Freyberg most was the confusion that gripped Eighth Army at the time, especially the lack of clear direction from its leadership. Freyberg later reported to the New Zealand government:

> This continued vacillation shook me, but not nearly as much as the tempo of the troops coming down the Sidi Barrani road.... What I was most anxious about was not to allow panic orders to put us in an impossible position. I was determined to appeal to the New Zealand Government if necessary and I went to see the Eighth Army Commander to protest against being shut up in Mersa Matruh. This could have ended in only one way. My next orders were to go into the Naghamish Wadi—almost an impossible position. Again I pointed out the inadvisability of committing a highly trained division to such a mission. Eventually I persuaded them to let us meet the full thrust of the German Army head on. We picked an area on high ground south of Mersa Matruh, where there was room to manoeuvre and to use our powerful guns to the full.[96]

The 2nd New Zealand Division took up position on an escarpment called Minqar Qaim in the belief that it was to take part in a major set-piece battle that would halt the Panzerarmee in its tracks. Its orders from 13 Corps were "to secure a box in the area MINQAR QAIM in order to deny the escarpment to the enemy, and to operate all round with mobile columns to attack and delay the enemy advance."[97] Unknown to the New Zealanders was the fact that Auchinleck had decided against fighting a set piece battle around Mersa Matruh. He and Eric Dorman-Smith, his Chief of Staff, were convinced that Eighth Army in its current state would be destroyed if it fought at Mersa Matruh. This was in spite of the fact that British forces outnumbered the Panzerarmee by a margin of two to one and that it was known that Rommel's troops were overextended and reaching the point of exhaustion. There was now no plan nor willingness to make a stand and fight it out around Mersa Matruh. Instead, Eighth Army would withdraw to the area around El Alamein some 150 miles further east. Auchinleck later explained: "El Alamein offered by far the strongest position in the Western Desert as both its flanks rested on impassable obstacles."[98]

Part of his decision was based on the state of the Army's armored formations. Both armored divisions of Eighth Army were determined not to engage with the advancing enemy and risk losing more tanks. According to Brigadier H.B. Latham, the armored units "had not recovered from the beating they had taken in June" and that "sheer bad tactical handling had knocked all the stuffing out of the tank crews."[99] Holding actions were to be the order of the day as the main elements of Eighth Army withdrew to the El Alamein position to make their stand there. This was a critical decision as all British planning since 1940 had been based on a last-ditch stand at Mersa Matruh as the "worst possible case."[100] It is surprising though, and a sad reflection on the state of the Army, that such a vital change in plan was not passed on to the New Zealanders and it almost caused the destruction of their Division.

Minqar Qaim

On the afternoon June 26, 1942, the 2nd New Zealand Division, minus one brigade, formed up a defensive position on the escarpment at Minqar Qaim. On its left flank was the 1st Armoured Division, with 159 tanks, of which sixty were the new Grant tank. An Indian Brigade covered the right flank. On the morning of June 27, the Afrika Korps, down to just thirty-nine serviceable tanks, approached the Minqar Qaim position. As they did so, the formations providing flank protection for the New Zealanders melted away. Harassed by the concentrated firepower of the New Zealand guns, including newly arrived six-pounder anti-tank guns, 21 Panzer Division advanced across the face of the Minqar Qaim position and then wheeled south and west to envelop the position. An "intense artillery duel" commenced at 1022 hours and was kept up for most of the day.[101]

With his division engaged with the enemy on three sides and German tanks astride his line of retreat, the New Zealand commander Lieutenant General Bernard Freyberg was extremely anxious about the safety of his command. Unable to contact the Corps Commander and "astonished and alarmed" when he was informed that the 1st Armoured Division were clearing off, Freyberg decided his division must attempt to break out of the encirclement by itself. At 1530 hours, the message was sent to the two infantry brigades:

> Received warning from NZ DIV HQ that NZ DIV was to delay enemy and inflict as much damage as possible, and, when posns became untenable to fall back on posns at EL ALAMEIN.

Later that afternoon came word that the New Zealanders were to be ready to move at 2300 hours.[102] But while searching for the best escape route in the afternoon, Freyberg was struck in the neck by a shell splinter. Things did not look good for the New Zealanders.

That evening the New Zealand Division attempted its breakout. It launched an attack with one of its infantry brigades on foot, with bayonets fixed. Explaining the action to a worried New Zealand government, the acting commander of the division described his withdrawal from Minqar Qaim as "crash tactics: that is a charge straight through." He assured his government that it had been "most effective."[103] Effective it may have been, but it was also disorganized and chaotic. The New Zealanders had been lucky too in that the weakened Afrika Korps was taken by surprise. The New Zealand Division's War Diary described a frantic and desperate event:

> Following Brig. INGLIS, our front vehicles gave the lead and direction by moving off at top speed to the left. For the moment it was no longer a question of convoy running. It was a case of getting clear as quickly and with as few casualties as possible—vehicle for vehicle in a Balaclava-like dash across country in the dark. Enemy fire pursued us in a steady stream. The noise of firing and fast-moving vehicles, the lightning streaks of tracer shells and bullets, with here and there a bursting sheet of flame lighting the night as a vehicle was hit, made it a hectic scene. Two miles on to the East, when we seemed to have broken through clear of the enemy, the group halted to rally. Vehicles had kept well together in spite of the speed and difficult going. Casualties in the group were about 11 vehicles, two of which were ambulances, and some personnel (number not finally known) killed or missing. The convoy proceeded East.[104]

* * *

The New Zealanders' break out from Minqar Qaim punched a hole through the German positions in front of them. An urgent signal was sent to Headquarters Afrika Korps informing them that: "The enemy attacks, which we thought to be feints, have developed into violent attacks on all parts of the front."[105] While not everything went according to plan, most of the New Zealand Division got through with some 10,000 men escaping captivity at Minqar Qaim. It seemed almost a miracle that "casualties and damage were . . . very slight."[106]

Rommel was disappointed with the outcome at Minqar Qaim. He wrote two days after the action:

> Unfortunately, the New Zealanders under Freyberg had escaped. This division, with which we had already become acquainted back in 1941–42, was among the elite of the British Army, and I would have been very much happier if it had been safely tucked away in our prison camps instead of facing us.[107]

This was almost the fate of two divisions of 10 Corps, which like the New Zealanders, had been left stranded, this time at Mersa Matruh. By the morning June 28, 10 Corps was cut off at Mersa Matruh with powerful units of the Panzerarmee well to the east of their position. At midday came an order from Auchinleck that 10 Corps was "to slip out to-night with whole force on a broad front, turn east on high ground and rally El Daba." Auchinleck offered 10 Corps the assurance that "13 Corps will cover you."[108] But 13 Corps was miles away and in disarray. That night the two divisions of 10 Corps attempted to "slip away" and found it was not as easy as it sounded. Both the 10th Indian and 50th Divisions had to fight their way clear and the 10th suffered particularly heavy losses in men and vehicles. While the majority of their soldiers escaped capture, "both divisions had been shattered."[109] The remnants of both divisions passed through the Alamein position and on to Alexandria where they began the painful process of piecing together their formations again.

Not only were the British formations being defeated in detail, but their abandoned supplies were providing Rommel with the means to keep his advance continuing. As the British formations retreated, there was little time to carry or destroy their logistical support bases. In July 1942, the Axis forces were using as many as 6,000 captured vehicles as well as numerous British field guns with ample ammunition stocks. It was somewhat ironic that the spearhead units of Panzerarmee were enjoying British bully beef and Imperial Tinned Peaches while driving Canadian Ford trucks filled with Iraqi fuel. In comparison, Eighth Army on the Alamein position "had been bled almost dry of the supplies and ammunition it would need to fight a further battle."[110]

The Mersa Matruh battle has been aptly described by Niall Barr as "another fiasco for the British."[111] It, together with Minqar Qaim, revealed much about the state of Eighth Army in June 1942. Its higher leadership was poor and defeatist, coordination between arms nonexistent. For Howard Kippenberger, it was a continuation of the Gazala horror story:

> Can anything be more deplorable than the conduct of what is called the Battle of Matruh? As you yourself have said, General Gott [13 Corps] should have fought the New Zealand Division and one armoured division as Corps and if he had 90 Light and 21 Panzer must have been destroyed.[112]

That an opportunity had been missed through faulty coordination and defeatism was the conclusion of the South African official historians. In a draft manuscript now in the British National Archives, they recorded:

> General Lumsden afterwards admitted that co-ordination with the New Zealand Division was faulty—one of the Yeomanry tanks was knocked out by the New Zealand artillery—and the opportunity of annihilating 21st Panzer was lost. "We should have obliterated the lot" was General Lumsden's considered opinion.[113]

The New Zealanders rejoined Eighth Army, then forming defensive positions along a line from El Alamein to the Qattara Depression. The Eighth Army was greatly weakened by its headlong retreat in the face of Rommel's advance. In early July, it was down to just one complete infantry division, a reduced division, a brigade group, and the remnants of other divisions now dispersed into ineffective battle groups. Eighth Army had lost more than 1,000 tanks in just seventeen days of fighting in June. It had now only 137 serviceable tanks but most of these were obsolete and unreliable. Only thirty-six were the latest Grant tank. Its morale was poor, too. As Major General John Harding, at the time a senior staff officer in Cairo recalled, "the morale of the army as a whole was shattered because they were in a state of confusion and had been defeated."[114]

The day after the New Zealanders' escape from Minqar Qaim, a confident Rommel wrote to his wife:

> We're still on the move and hope to keep it up until the final goal. It takes a lot out of one, of course, but it's the chance of a life-time. The enemy is fighting back desperately with his air force. P.S. Italy in July might still be possible. Get passports![115]

On July 1, Rommel reached the Alamein position but he was down to only fifty-five serviceable tanks and his troops were exhausted. Instead of waiting, though, Rommel was determined to seize his chance of a lifetime. He took the decision to push on in the hopes of breaking through and eventually reaching Cairo. The scene was set for the first battle of El Alamein and Rommel's holiday in Italy with his wife would have to wait.

NOTES

1. John Connell, "Wavell's 30,000," in *History of the Second World War*, ed. Sir Basil Liddell Hart. (London: Phoebus Publishing, 1980), 91.

2. Ibid., 98.

3. Quoted in John Bierman and Colin Smith, *Alamein: War without Hate*. (London: Viking, 2002), 50.

4. Connell, "Wavell's 30,000," 105.

5. Richard Carrier, "Some Reflections on the Fighting Power of the Italian Army in North Africa, 1940–1943," in *War in History* (Vol.22, Number 4, November 2015): 526, 527.

6. Ibid., 527, 526.

7. Erwin Rommel, "African Mission," in *The Rommel Papers*, ed. B.H. Liddell Hart. (London: Arrow Books, 1987), 99.

8. Rommel to Dearest Lu, 3 April 1941, in Liddell Hart, *The Rommel Papers*, 99.

9. Connell, "Wavell's 30,000," 105.

10. David Fraser, *And We Shall Shock Them: The British Army in the Second World War*. (London: Book Club Associates, 1983), 131.

11. Rommel to Dearest Lu, 3 April 1941, in Liddell Hart, *The Rommel Papers*, 111.

12. Rommel to Dearest Lu, 10 April 1941, in Liddell Hart, *The Rommel Papers*, 118.

13. Barrie Pitt, *The Crucible of War: Year of Alamein, 1942*. (London: Jonathan Cape Ltd., 1982), xx.

14. Fraser, *And We Shall Shock Them*, 8.

15. Ibid., 89.

16. Ibid., 9.

17. Biereman and Smith, *Alamein: War without Hate*, 68.

18. Bierman and Smith, Ibid., 104.

19. James Holland, *Together We Stand: Turning the Tide in the West: North Africa 1942–1943*. (London: HarperCollins Publishers, 2005), 49.

20. Stephen Bungay, *Alamein*. (London: Arum Press, 2003), 30.

21. Rommel, diary entry, in Liddell Hart, *The Rommel Papers*, 137.

22. Pitt, *The Crucible of War*, xx.

23. Quoted in Liddell Hart, *The Rommel Papers*, 141.

24. Fraser, *And We Shall Shock Them*, 157–158.

25. Winston Churchill, *The Second World War, Vol. III*. (London: Cassel, 1950), 307, 298.

26. Ibid., 309.

27. Liddell Hart, *The Rommel Papers*, 141.

28. Rommel to Dearest Lu, 18 June 1941, in Liddell Hart, *The Rommel Papers*, 146.

29. Rommel, diary entry, 23 June 1941, in *The Rommel Papers*, 146.

30. Fraser, *And We Shall Shock Them*, 160.

31. Churchill, *Vol. III.*, 356.

32. Pitt, *The Crucible of War*, xxi. Because this book was written for Indiana University Press, American spelling has been used in most instances. However, British spelling has been retained when it was the name of a military unit or formation, and when used in direct quotation.

33. Barr, *Pendulum of War*, 45.

34. W.E. Murphy, *Official History of New Zealand in the Second World War 1939–34. The Relief of Tobruk*. (Wellington: War History Branch, Department of Internal Affairs. 1961), v.

35. Pitt, *The Crucible of War*, xxi.

36. Bierman and Smith, *Alamein: War without Hate*, 154.

37. Rommel to Dearest Lu, 20 and 22 December 1941, in Liddell Hart, *The Rommel Papers*, 175.

38. Glyn Harper, *Kippenberger: An Inspired New Zealand Commander*. (Auckland: HarperCollins (NZ), 2005), 129.

39. Barr, *Pendulum of War*, 53.

40. Ibid., 60.

41. Holland, *Together We Stand*, 44.

42. Ibid., 46.

43. John Harding quoted in Richard Holmes, *The World at War: The Landmark Oral History from the Previously Unpublished Archives*. (London: Ebury Press, 2007), 266.

44. Barr, *Pendulum of War*, 59.

45. Quoted in Pitt, *The Crucible of War*, 8. Also in in Liddell Hart, *The Rommel Papers*, 180.

46. Rommel, diary entry, 21 January 1942, in Liddell Hart, *The Rommel Papers*, 180.

47. Rommel to Dearest Lu, 22 January 1942, in Liddell Hart, *The Rommel Papers*, 181.

48. Fraser, *And We Shall Shock Them*, 180.

49. Rommel to Dearest Lu, 4 February 1942, in Liddell Hart, *The Rommel Papers*, 183.

50. Martin Blumenson, "Rommel," in *Hitler's Generals*, ed. Correlli Barnett. (London: Phoenix Giants, 1995), 303.

51. These figures are from Barr, *Pendulum of War*, 13.

52. David Fraser, *Knight's Cross: A Life of Field Marshal Erwin Rommel*. (London: HarperCollins Publishers, 1994), 314.

53. F.H. Hinsley, *British Intelligence in the Second World War: Volume 2: Its Influence on Strategy and Operations*. (London: HMSO, 1981), 350, 363.

54. CAB 44/96, No. 140, in Hinsley, *British Intelligence in the Second World War: Volume 2*, 363.

55. CAB 105/17, No.125 of 20 May 1942, in Hinsley, *British Intelligence in the Second World War: Volume 2*, 364.

56. Alan J. Levine, *The War Against Rommel's Supply Lines, 1942–1943*. (Westport CT: Praeger Publishers, 1999), 22.

57. Fraser, *And We Shall Shock Them*, 213

58. Barr, *Pendulum of War*, 14.

59. Holland, *Together We Stand*, 102.

60. Pitt, *The Crucible of War*, 117.

61. Hinsley, *British Intelligence in the Second World War: Volume 2*, 370.

62. Fraser, *Knight's Cross*, 330.

63. Ibid., 331.

64. Holland, *Together We Stand*, 129–130.

65. Blumenson, "Rommel," in *Hitler's Generals*, 303.

66. G.L. Verney, *The Desert Rats: The History of the 7th Armoured Division 1938–1945*. (London: Greenhill Books, 1990), 116.

67. Rommel, writings on the campaign, in Liddell Hart, *The Rommel Papers*, 225.

68. Bierman and Smith, *Alamein: War without Hate*, 179.

69. Francis de Guingand, *Operation Victory*. (London: Hodder & Stoughton, 1947), 123.

70. Verney, *The Desert Rats*, 116.

71. Holland, *Together We Stand*, 155.

72. Ronald Lewin, *Rommel as Military Commander*. (New York: Ballantine Books, 1968), 160.

73. Rommel to Dearest Lu, 21 June 1942, in Liddell Hart, *The Rommel Papers*, 231.

74. Robin Neillands, *The Desert Rats: 7th Armoured Division 1940–1945*. (London: Weidenfeld and Nicolson, 1991), 111.

75. Quoted in Neillands, *The Desert Rats: 7th Armoured Division*, 123.

76. Albert Martin, diary entry, 19 June 1942, quoted in Holland, *Together We Stand*, 149.

77. Winston S. Churchill, *The Second World War Volume IV: The Hinge of Fate*. (London: Cassell & Co., 1951), 343–44.

78. Ibid., 344.

79. Holland, *Together We Stand*, 182.

80. Howard Kippenberger, letter to J.A.I. Agar-Hamilton, 14 February 1950, 181/3/6, Correspondence of Howard Kippenberger 1947–1955, WA II 11/2, Archives New Zealand. Te Rua Mahara o te Kāwanatanga (ANZ).

81. The Contribution of the Information Service to the May-June 1942 Offensive in North Africa, RG457/1035, USNA, quoted in Barr, *Pendulum of War*, 17.

82. Hans-Otto Behrendt, *Rommel's Intelligence in the Desert Campaign 1941–1943*. (London: William Kimber & Co., 1985), 146.

83. Ibid., 146, 167.

84. Barr, *Pendulum of War*, 23.

85. Christopher Pugsley, *A Bloody Road Home: World War Two and New Zealand's Heroic Second Division*. (Auckland: Penguin Books, 2014), 264.

86. Lieutenant Colonel Ronald Belchem, quoted in Holmes, *The World at War*, 165–166.

87. Major General Francis de Guingand, quoted in Holmes, *The World at War*, 262.

88. War Diary, 2/24 Australian Infantry Battalion, 25 June 1942, AWM 52, Unit and Formation War Diaries, Australian War Memorial (AWM).

89. War Diary, 2/28 Australian Infantry Battalion, 25–27 June 1942, 8/3/24, AWM 52, AWM.

90. War Diary, 2/48 Australian Infantry Battalion, Brief Summary of Events, AWM 52, AWM.

91. War Diary, Headquarters 2 New Zealand Division, General Staff, 13–14 June 1942, WA II, I 1631, DA 21.1/1/30, ANZ.

92. War Diary, 6 New Zealand Infantry Brigade, 15 June 1942, WA II, I 1660, DA 58/1/21, ANZ.

93. War Diary, 5 New Zealand Infantry Brigade, 22 June 1942, WA II, I 1652, DA 52/1/30, ANZ.

94. Howard Kippenberger, *Infantry Brigadier.* (London: Oxford University Press, 1949), 127.

95. Freyberg, message New Zealand Prime Minister Wellington, 24 June 1942, WAII 8/24, Minqa Q'aim and Ruweisat Ridge, ANZ.

96. Freyberg to NZ Prime Minister, 14 October 1942, in *Documents Relating to New Zealand's Participation in the Second World War 1939–45.* (Wellington: War History Branch, 1951), Document 163, 129.

97. War Diary, Headquarters 2 New Zealand Division, General Staff, 26 June 1942, WA II, I 1631, DA 21.1/1/30, ANZ.

98. Auchinleck's Despatch, WO 32/10160, The National Archives of the UK (TNA).

99. H.B. Latham to Howard Kippenberger, 8 October 1953, WA II 11/2, ANZ.

100. Barr, *Pendulum of War,* 25.

101. War Diary, Headquarters 2 New Zealand Division, General Staff, 27 June 1942, WA II, I 1631, DA 21.1/1/30, ANZ.

102. War Diary, 5 New Zealand Infantry Brigade, 27 June 1942, WA II, I 1652, DA 52/1/30, ANZ.

103. Fearnleaf (Inglis), message New Zealand Prime Minister Wellington, 29 June 1942, WAII 8/24, Minqa Q'aim and Ruweisat Ridge, ANZ.

104. War Diary, Headquarters 2 New Zealand Division, General Staff, Night of 27/28 June 1942, WA II, I 1631, DA 21.1/1/30, ANZ.

105. 21 Panzer, message to HQ AK 0307 hrs 28 June 1942, Afrika Korps Messages, GMDS Files 22966/8 and 9, WA II 11/22 Translation of German and Italian documents – Afrika Korps, ANZ.

106. War Diary, 5 New Zealand Infantry Brigade, 29 June 1942, WA II, I 1652, DA 52/1/30, ANZ.

107. Rommel, diary entry, 29 June 1942, in Liddell Hart, *The Rommel Papers,* 240.

108. I.S.O. Playfair, *The Mediterranean and the Middle East, Volume III: British Fortunes Reach their Lowest Ebb (September 1941 to September 1942).* (London: HSMO, 1960), 294.

109. Barr, *Pendulum of War,* 30.

110. Ibid., 38, 39.

111. Ibid., 30.

112. Howard Kippenberger to Freyberg, 11 August 1955, WA II/11/2, ANZ.

113. South Africans Crisis in the Desert, May–July 1942, p. 33, CAB 44/20, TNA.

114. Major General John Harding, quoted in Julian Thompson, *Forgotten Voices: Desert Victory.* (London: Ebury Press, 2011), 162.

115. Rommel to Dearest Lu, 27 June 1942, in Liddell Hart *The Rommel Papers,* 237.

TWO

THE FIRST BATTLE: JULY 1942

The Alamein position was a unique one in the Western Desert. It presented the defenders with a shortened line only forty miles long—from the coast in the north where the railway station of El Alamein gave its name to this location, to the impassable Qattara Depression in the south. The Qattara Depression, the largest salt marsh in the Western Desert, was almost 450 feet below sea level. The Germans were quick to recognize its significance: "This depression and its northern rim protected the flank of the El Alamein line . . . the soft sand was . . . difficult to cross vehicles."[1] With the sea to the north and the Qattara Depression anchoring the south, the position could not be turned by a wide encircling movement on the open flank. It could only be taken by a direct assault and, therefore, it was the best defensive position available in Egypt. Any features offering good observation for considerable distances, the ridges and lips of depressions, became the key tactical features. The three low and narrow ridges running parallel with the coast were especially important. These were Miteiriya Ridge in the north, Ruweisat Ridge in the center, and Alam el Halfa being the most southerly of these. They would be hotly contested in all three battles to be fought here.

The Alamein position was not a complete defensive "line," either, as it is often misleadingly called. Auchinleck had far too few troops to garrison a line forty miles long. This would have required a force of at least sixteen divisions, which Auchinleck did not have.[2] Rather, he created strong defensive positions that aimed to channel Rommel's forces down corridors in the center of the position. Auchinleck could then strike with his limited mobile forces at the enemy's exposed flanks. These

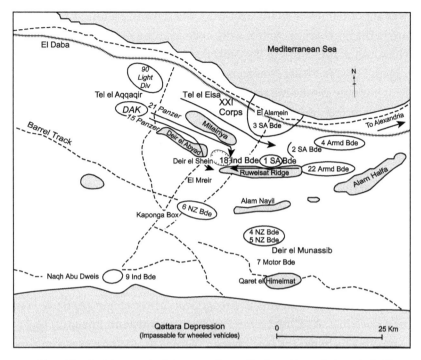

Map 1. The pivotal moment—July 1, 1942. Rommel's attempt to crash through the El Alamein position is thwarted mainly due to the resistance from 18 Indian Brigade at Deir el Shein. For Rommel, this was the first of many setbacks at El Alamein.

were the defensive positions known as "boxes." There were initially three of these. The first was in the north around the railway station. Halfway across the desert was another box in the center at Bab el Qattara with the southernmost box at Naqb Abu Dweiss. That was the plan, in any case, but it was not going to be easy. The defensive boxes were fifteen miles apart and therefore could not offer mutual support. The assumption had been that strong mobile forces would maneuver between the boxes and engage the enemy there. So wide was this gap between boxes and so weak was Eighth Army's armor, that Lieutenant General Norrie (Charles Willoughby Moke Norrie, 1st Baron Norrie) belatedly constructed another box at Deir el Shein, halfway between Alamein and Bab el Qattara.

There was a major flaw in Auchinleck's defensive plan. On the Alamein position were two vital stretches of high ground. These were two low ridges "imperceptible to the eye from a distance."[3] The Miteiriya Ridge was about ten miles south west from the railway station. It formed an arc in the northern sector for a distance of around six miles. Directly to the south of this ridge, in the central sector, was the largest ridge in the region. Ruweisat Ridge was some twenty miles south of the railway halt. This low rock mound ran west to east for almost ten miles. As mentioned above, any feature offering good observation would be hotly contested. Auchinleck later described Ruweisat Ridge as "vital" and "the key to our position."[4] Such recognition was belated, as Auchinleck did little to protect these key tactical features and they were soon in Axis hands. Much of the fighting in late July was fought to secure positions on both these ridges. Many Eighth Army soldiers died trying to wrest them back from the Axis forces.

After being thoroughly defeated in the Gazala battle, Eighth Army was now going to fight Rommel's Panzerarmee Afrika on the only possible defensive line before Alexandria. Auchinleck would need to meld his disparate army into an effective team while also changing its flawed tactical doctrines. As Christopher Pugsley has written, in July 1942, Eighth Army was "battered and bewildered ... a thing of bits and pieces, confused and humiliated."[5] Few people in Egypt at the time thought Auchinleck's depleted and demoralized Eighth Army had any chance of stopping Rommel's advance. At Alexandria, the population prepared to welcome the victorious Italians and Germans. One young girl recalled being thrilled at the prospect. Years later, Lucette de Saab recalled her reasoning:

> I loved the Italian chauffeurs. When we thought the Germans were going to enter Alexandria, everybody cried, but not me. I was thrilled. I wanted them to come and liberate our two Italian chauffeurs and carry off my English governess.[6]

Lucette was not the only Egyptian looking forward to the arrival of the Axis forces. Much of the Egyptian population, including military officers like Gamal Abdel Nasser and Anwar Sadat, "waited expectantly for their Axis 'liberators.'"[7]

Despite work commencing on defensive positions here since mid-1941, at the end of June 1942, as Rommel's forces approached, the Alamein positions "were still dangerously incomplete."[8] When the 1st South African Division occupied the Alamein Box in the north, they spent two frantic weeks improving the defenses. This included such basic defensive tasks as laying out thousands of yards of barbed wire, burying thousands of mines and constructing bomb-proof shelters. As the bulk of the New Zealand Division escaped from the escarpment of Minqar Qaim, its detached 6th New Zealand Infantry Brigade occupied the Kaponga Box (also known as Bab el Qattara, Qaret el Abd, and Fortress A) on the morning of June 28. Despite the Kaponga Box being designated as a key defensive position in the center of the El Alamein position, the New Zealanders were shocked by the lack of preparations that had been made. The War Diary of the 6th Brigade recorded of this:

> The Box was reasonably prepared including water storage and masonry HQ and A.D.S [Advanced Dressing Station]. At this stage, the Bde had no MT [mechanized transport], no guns and no mines; and the Box contained 10 tons of water, no food and no ammunition.[9]

Frantic preparations were made over the next three days to improve the Kaponga defenses. This included the laying of 2,000 mines and building up water and ammunition supplies. On June 30, 6th Brigade's War Diary recorded a more satisfactory state of affairs: "Box now fairly secure, and have 21 guns of 6 (NZ) Fd Regt and 20 6-prs of 33 A Tk Bty in position." The brigade was also allocated an additional battalion, the 28th (Maori) Battalion, to strengthen its defenses at Kaponga. However, the War Diary also noted that defenses nearby were inadequate:

> Both 18 Ind Bde to North and 9 Ind Bde to South in difficulties over supply. Helped former with 5000 mines and latter with water and ammunition.[10]

The 9 Indian Brigade was in the southernmost box at Naqb Abu Dweiss where it was critically short of water and fuel. Little wonder the brigade felt "considerable isolated."[11] While all of these defensive positions were occupied by June 30, no British armored units had reached the Alamein position. The defense here was still thin and all the infantry positions were remote and vulnerable.

To blunt Rommel's advance, Auchinleck focused on the two most obvious lines of advance: the coast road in the north and the "Barrel Track" in the south. The south was the least likely route to be used, so Auchinleck protected this with just two independent brigades and the few tanks of the 7th Armoured Division. In the north, the 1st South African Division garrisoned the El Alamein Box, a fifteen-mile crescent of platoon and company posts along the coast road and railway. Only one South Africa brigade was inside the perimeter, the other two occupied key locations nearby. One brigade was positioned on the northern slopes of Ruweisat Ridge; the other was sent some three miles southwest of the perimeter. To protect its flanks, 30 Corps commander Lieutenant General Norrie had sent 18 Indian Infantry Brigade to hold the Deir el Shein, some seven miles to the southwest of El Alamein. Two regiments of field artillery and an anti-tank platoon with the new six-pounder gun supported both positions. Auchinleck planned to hold Rommel's advance with these defensive boxes while the 22nd Armoured Brigade and the infantry of 2nd New Zealand Division struck a crushing blow against the Panzerarmee's flanks and rear as it launched its assault. This was the plan, in any case, but unfortunately for Auchinleck, Lieutenant General William H. E. "Strafer" Gott, the corps commander who would coordinate this strike, could not be located. Niall Barr wrote that on July 1, "Eighth Army had completely lost contact with 'Strafer' Gott."[12] That this happened at the moment Eighth Army was fighting for its existence was extraordinary.

Auchinleck's plan, though, was defense in considerable depth combined with a mobile strike force. As Auchinleck's Chief of Staff later wrote, "To the 'box-minded' 8th Army, these dispositions were revolutionary and untried tactical novelties."[13] As static defensive "boxes" alone had not halted Rommel in the past, it was high time that Eighth Army tried something different.

Auchinleck issued his first "Order of the Day" on June 30. It said in part:

> The enemy is stretching to his limit and thinks we are a broken army. . . . He hopes to take Egypt by bluff. Show him where he gets off.

According to his Chief of Staff, this message "did not impress the higher echelons of command."[14] It is likely, too, that few soldiers of Eighth Army ever read Auchinleck's message.[15]

The next day, July 1, would be a critical day. Rommel began his assault on the Alamein position with the 90th Light Division leading the way. He planned for 90th Light to move south of the El Alamein strong-point and cut the coast road well to the east of the position. Italian troops would pin the defenders by an attack on the strongpoint from the west while mobile Italian forces provided flank protection. The Axis forces had made no reconnaissance of the enemy positions at all. Rommel based his plan on past experience when British defenders had cut and run the moment it looked like their line of withdrawal was threatened. Rommel knew he was driving his exhausted troops hard, but he believed that the British forces around Alamein were incapable of mounting a determined defense. One more push could carry his Axis troops to Al-exandria and maybe even Cairo. Auchinleck's Order of the Day was to be put to the test.

Action in Early July

It was an exhausted and weak Afrika Korps that advanced in the early dawn of July 1 against the Alamein defenses. According to a senior German officer with the Afrika Korps, despite the enormous logisti-cal problems Rommel faced, "the sole reason why the German advance was halted was the lack of striking power."[16] Rommel's supply situation was precarious and would remain so for the rest of the campaign. Fore-warned by Ultra signals intercepts, the British ensured that very few supplies, especially of precious fuel, reached Rommel's Panzer Army. A senior German staff officer later recorded how successful the British had been in denying Rommel the vital sinews of war:

> They [British forces on Malta] succeeded in bringing German convoy traffic to an almost complete standstill. The Italian battleships were in port at Tarent and La Spezia, unable to operate because of lack of fuel. Losses in material and fuel were so heavy that it was barely possible to obtain adequate supplies from Germany. The sea routes to Tripoli and Benghasi were completely severed. Air transportation from Crete now played the major role but quite naturally the volume was far too small to meet even the most urgent demands of the front.[17]

Despite this, Rommel and the Panzerarmee were confident of suc-cess and expected to soon be pursuing retreating British forces towards Cairo. It was not to be. Auchinleck was well aware of Rommel's inten-tion as "Sigint now contributed intelligence of immediate operational value."[18] He was determined that Rommel would not breach the Alamein

position. Hard fighting continued all day around the El Alamein defenses, most of it occurring during a heavy sandstorm, but the British
positions around El Alamein held firm. Their artillery fire was particularly effective. Around Kaponga Box, the Afrika Korps' attack was easily
repulsed thanks to the guns now located there. The defending brigade
recorded in its War Diary:

> Bad dust and haze, visibility poor. Carriers and portees appeared moving SW
> and firing into haze. Believed to be escort with mine trucks, so opened fire on
> German tanks following them. As dust cleared 18-20 tanks and about 1000 MT
> could be seen at extreme range. Engaged them with fd arty vigorously until
> dark.[19]

The Deir el Shein was a depression with a series of conical ridges ris-
ing above it some four miles from the western edge of Ruweisat Ridge. It
was being defended by 18 Indian Brigade, and this new position surprised
Afrika Korps as it advanced to attack the Alamein Box. The fire coming
from Deir el Shein was intense and it blocked any Axis advance. General
Walther Nehring, commanding the Afrika Korps, knew this position had
to be eliminated and spent the rest of July 1 attempting to do this. The inexperienced 18 Indian Brigade had only arrived at the Alamein position
on June 27, being rushed "at full speed from Iraq."[20] Its three battalions
put up a fierce resistance having to fight most of the afternoon during
a heavy dust storm, which limited their visibility to only a few yards
ahead of them.[21] Only at 1930 hours, when most of their anti-tank guns
were destroyed, no anticipated armored support forthcoming, and their
support weapons out of ammunition, was the Deir el Shein captured. It
cost 21 Panzer Division eighteen of its precious fifty-five tanks to do so.
Most of 18 Indian Brigade managed to escape, but it had to leave behind
close on 1,000 casualties.[22] As Niall Barr has written, 18 Indian Brigade's
resistance was a considerable achievement and won a precious breath-
ing space for the rest of the Army. The stubborn resistance of 18 Indian
Brigade had gained one day for Eighth Army. It was a critical gain. Barr
writes:

> The fight against the Afrika Korps had indeed been one-sided. An ill-equipped
> and poorly supported brigade filled with inexperienced soldiers had drawn the
> entire weight of Rommel's two panzer divisions onto their position. . . . Not only
> had the offensive power of the Afrika Korps been blunted, but the main drive

through the British positions which Rommel wanted complete by the end of the day had been halted.[23]

Despite stemming the initial advance, this could hardly be regarded as a great start for Eighth Army. An important position had been lost and the fighting should not have been so one-sided. Needless to say, Auchinleck's strike against the advancing Panzerarmee failed to materialize.

While the Axis forces were steadily being eroded—at the end of July 1, 21st Panzer could muster just thirty-seven runners and 15th Panzer just seventeen—more British reinforcements arrived to strengthen their positions. By July 1, 1st Armoured Division was firmly established on Ruweisat Ridge with more than 100 tanks, thirty-eight of them Grant tanks, and liberally protected by the new six-pounder anti-tank guns.

Rommel now intended that the Afrika Korps was to finish mopping up the Deir el Shein then push onto Ruweisat Ridge some five miles away. At Ruweisat, the Korps was to advance east along the ridge then turn north to cut the coast road. Meanwhile, 90th Light would also advance to the coast on an inner arch. With all his German formations committed, Rommel was dependent on the Italian 20 Corps to protect his left flank. But nothing went according to plan. While the Afrika Korps' armored divisions managed to advance for around four miles, 90th Light made no headway at all. Its War Diary made for depressing reading:

> the enemy gave no sign of withdrawing. On the contrary, he gave the impression that he was trying with all his force to stop Panzerarmee from storming the Alamein position. It seemed that the German forces, exhausted by the heavy fighting and the hardships of the past days and weeks, would not be able by their own strength, to force this last British fortification.[24]

Adding to 90th Light's gloom was that it had been under constant air attack during the day. During this July battle, the RAF, now named the Desert Air Force (DAF) from February 1942, had achieved parity with the Luftwaffe. It made a critical difference and "was one of Auchinleck's best assets."[25] This was in spite of the DAF's shortage of aircraft and equipment. During the Gazala battle, the DAF had lost 202 fighter aircraft and during July 1942, most of the fighter squadrons were operating at half-strength.[26] On the two days of July 1–2, the Desert Air Force dropped 180 tons of bombs on the Axis forces.[27] Casualties caused were small, but the disruption to Rommel's timetable was significant. Rommel summarized the day's activities in his diary: "Under this tremendous weight of fire, our attack came to a standstill."[28] His advance beyond the Alamein position had been thwarted for the second time.

Despite this lack of progress, Rommel was still confident of success. He was particularly buoyed by news from the Luftwaffe that night that the British fleet had left Alexandria. He wrote on hearing this news:

> This determined me to go all out for a decision in the next few days. The British no longer seemed to trust their luck and were preparing for a retreat. I was convinced that a breakthrough over a wide front by my forces would result in complete panic.[29]

Far from showing "complete panic," Auchinleck struck first the next day. The 1st Armoured Division, in conjunction with other units from 13 Corps, launched a counterattack from Ruweisat Ridge against the Axis' southern flank in the early afternoon. There was also some sporadic fighting to the north but the Axis forces made little headway. This resistance surprised Rommel. He recorded in his diary:

> More and more British tanks and guns were arriving at the front. General Auchinleck, who had meanwhile taken over command himself at El Alamein, was handling his forces with very considerable skill and tactically better than Ritchie had done. He seemed to view the situation with decided coolness, for he was not allowing himself to be rushed into accepting a "second best" solution by any moves we made.[30]

The unexpected resistance also forced Rommel to change plans and make an unwelcome decision. He would call off the offensive after the next day's fighting if no breakthrough had been achieved. His tanks' strength in Afrika Korps had shrunk to just twenty-six runners.[31]

The next day's fighting on July 3 was a complete disaster for Rommel's forces. An exhausted 90th Light was to remain at its current location while the armored formations tried to push further east before wheeling north to cut the coast road. Rommel's advance made no progress at all, not least because the DAF flew 780 sorties against the Panzerarmee that day.[32] An officer on Rommel's headquarters staff described the outcome of two very disappointing days of action:

> The breakthrough was timed for July 2. When we were near Sidi Barrani Rommel said, "Look at the map. There's El Alamein, last fortified point before Cairo,

there's a fortified mountain position lower down. El Alamein below on the coast has been strongly fortified. The enemy wonders will Rommel go forward to the right or to the left. I'm doing it differently --- I'm going through the middle."

It was well prepared but it failed because someone or some unit arrived half a day late, being held up by ground, mts [mountains] and sand dunes.

The next day, to force the issue, he pushed the 90th Lt past El Alamein in S.E. direction towards Cairo. This made the force; Marcks, Menny and Menton.

They made good progress in a sandstorm but this cleared and they were taken under heavy arty fire from El Alamein. They came back headlong. Then Rommel said, "That was unnecessary, I'll show you myself." We drove with his Kampfstaffel, his H.Q. and me, along the same stretch and came under heavy arty fire to right, ahead, left and to the rear. We had to disperse, hide and wait till nightfall. It was a final spurt.[33]

Not only did the Afrika Korps make little headway on July 3, but Rommel lost his most reliable Italian armored formation in the process. The Ariete Armoured Division, despite the shortcomings of Italian tanks, was regarded as the closest in effectiveness to the panzer divisions of Afrika Korps.[34] That morning, the Ariete Armoured Division, advancing to the south of Ruweisat Ridge, initially made good progress. But during its advance, the Division's guns and armored units became separated and its movement was "revealed by a chance air sighting."[35] As Ariete travelled parallel to the ridge, it was harassed by British armor and its progress suddenly halted by the guns of the New Zealand Division firing at close range from the Alam Nayil ridge. Ariete milled about in some confusion and was then attacked by a column of New Zealand infantry, which completed its rout. The New Zealanders captured 400 prisoners, forty-four guns, and a large number of vehicles. By noon of July 3, the Ariete Division was down to fewer than half a dozen tanks and almost no artillery. It was a serious blow to Rommel's plans. A Liaison Officer from 15 Panzer Division sent to find Ariete reported some devastating news:

Ariete has lost almost all of its artillery this morning, and now has 5 tanks and 2 guns available for the attack. The rest of Ariete is either weaponless or unfit for action.[36]

Rommel was shocked by the loss of the Ariete Division. "This reverse took us completely by surprise," he admitted in his diary. He also recorded that: "The attack had come to a standstill."[37] The next day, Rommel wrote a letter to his wife that reflected the condition of his forces:

> Unfortunately, things are not going as I should like them. Resistance is too great and our strength exhausted. However, I still hope to find a way to achieve our goal. I'm rather tired and fagged out.[38]

He decided to temporarily halt the offensive on July 4 in order to bring up more fuel, ammunition, and reinforcements.

Rommel was not the only Axis soldier feeling "fagged out." An Afrika Korps Medical Report recorded:

> With the lull in the fighting the number of wounded has decreased, but the number of sick is increasing . . . most noticeable are [cases of] diarrhoea, skin diseases, influenza, angina and exhaustion.[39]

A British intelligence summary of July 9 noted that after the last fortnight of military actions, there was "little doubt that the enemy forces are at the moment severely depleted and . . . that his casualties especially among officers have been extremely heavy." The summary noted that German prisoners of war were "conspicuous by their extreme tiredness."[40] An Australian battalion war diary noted on July 7 that the enemy forces were "tired and very under strength both in men and material."[41] Rommel would now wait for a few days, rest his troops, and refurbish his depleted forces. He would return to the attack when he felt his forces were strong enough to do so. For the moment, the initiative had passed to Auchinleck's Eighth Army.

*　*　*

Despite halting Rommel in early July, a strong strain of defeatism infected the higher echelons of Eighth Army. New Zealand Brigadier Howard Kippenberger was greatly disturbed by this and recorded a conversation with corps commander Lieutenant General "Strafer" Gott. General Gott showed Kippenberger a note from a senior staff officer that opened with the line: "The Chief has decided to save Eighth Army." Gott explained that this meant "a general retirement and evacuation of Egypt was in contemplation" and it was likely that the New Zealanders would soon be returning home. Kippenberger was shocked:

> I protested that we were perfectly fit to fight and that it was criminal to give up Egypt to 25,000 German troops and a hundred tanks (disregarding the Italians)—the latest Intelligence estimate—and to lose as helpless prisoners

perhaps 200,000 Base troops. Strafer [Gott] replied sadly that N.Z. Division was
battle-worthy but very few other people were and he feared the worst.[42]

Back in Cairo, there were visible signs of panic. Scraps of burnt paper
floated all over the city on July 1 as thousands of official confidential
documents were thrown on bonfires in the courtyards of various government departments. A pall of smoke hung over Cairo on a day dubbed
"Ash Wednesday."[43] Thousands of Cairo's British residents were being
evacuated in special trains to Upper Egypt and further afield to Palestine and the Sudan. "At G.H.Q. I'm afraid a pretty good 'flap' did occur
for a few days," admitted de Guingand.[44] Some dark humor was evident,
too. "Just wait till Rommel gets to Shepheard's—that will slow him up,"
was an often-repeated joke. The service in Cairo's premier hotel was
"notoriously slow."[45] The plan to evacuate Egypt during this great "flap,"
as it became known, was confirmed by another of Eighth Army's Corps
commanders. When Governor General of New Zealand after the war,
Lord Norrie, who had been a corps commander during this period, con-
fided to Kippenberger that the abandonment of Egypt to the advancing
Axis forces in early July 1942 "was the intention for a few days."[46] At the
time, the news left Kippenberger and other senior New Zealanders "both
sorely perplexed and depressed."[47]

They would have been even more depressed had they learned of the
true state of the Afrika Korps. The British official history of its intelligence efforts during the Second World War has claimed that from the
Gazala battle onwards, Eighth Army had superior intelligence over the
Axis forces in North Africa. It stated that, "the British forces in North
Africa were supplied with more information about more aspects of the
enemy's operations than any forces enjoyed during any important campaign of the Second World War – and probably, of any earlier war." It
also alleged that signals intercepts made "a significant contribution" to
Auchinleck's "greatest victory, the first battle of Alamein."[48] Despite being informed by Ultra radio traffic of the state and intentions of the enemy, at this stage the intelligence being gathered and assessed was often
wildly inaccurate. A document prepared by South African War History
Section was strongly critical of Auchinleck's tendency to "look over his
shoulder." It assessed the strength of the Afrika Korps on June 30, 1942,

as around 1,700 first line infantry, 330 guns of all types, just fifty-five tanks, and another fifteen armored cars. The document was scathing in its assessment: "This grave over-estimate had a serious effect in imposing undue caution on the British during the operations of the first ten days of July."[49] And, as mentioned above, many of the Afrika Korps soldiers were absolutely exhausted and in no fit state to fight a prolonged action.

Demonstrating the indecision that plagued Eighth Army at this time, on the morning of July 3, 6th New Zealand Infantry Brigade was ordered to "evacuate Box forthwith." It spent the early morning burying ammunition with bulldozers and preparing its food and water stores for demolition. The brigade departed from the Kaponga Box at 1000 hours that morning.[50] But after spending two days at Himeimat, where it was a prime target for Luftwaffe air attack, 6th Brigade was ordered back to the Kaponga Box on July 6. Three days later, the brigade abandoned Kaponga Box for good. One British military historian had discerned considerable tactical "deftness" in these moves, but it puzzled the New Zealanders why such a strong defensive position was given up without a fight.[51] It puzzled Rommel, too, who inspected the defenses of Kaponga on July 9. Rommel wrote that the box:

> Qaret el Abd itself lay in extremely favourable terrain and was fortified with well-built concrete strong-points, gun emplacements and extensive minefields. The New Zealanders had left behind quantities of ammunition and equipment, and we were at a loss to understand why they had given the position up.[52]

Spending so much energy and resources on a strong defensive position in such an important location and then abandoning it twice without a fight are not really indicators of tactical finesse. Rather they demonstrate considerable indecision and a lack of understanding of how such wasted effort affected the morale of those doing the digging and the fighting.

Mid July Actions

Auchinleck soon recovered his nerve no doubt helped by the arrival of another battle-worthy formation—the 9th Australian Division. Its first brigade, the 24th, arrived at the Alamein position on July 3 after a memorable journey. The Division's Operational Report recorded of it:

It was a journey that few will forget. The opposing traffic moved nose to tail in one continuous stream of tanks, guns, armoured cars and trucks all jammed, sometimes for hours, holding up the Divisional convoys at the same time.[53]

Auchinleck was keen to use the Australians immediately in the northern sector of the line. He wanted them there, as he was concerned about the state of the 1st South African Division. With the loss of the 2nd South African Division at Tobruk and a fractious relationship with Major General Dan Pienaar, Auchinleck now believed that the South Africans "could not be given any serious or difficult operational task in the future."[54] Instead, the Australians would be used in these roles, but as isolated brigade groups and even smaller detachments. Its commander, Lieutenant General Leslie Morshead, was not going to allow his Division to be split up like this, nor for it to pass from his command. On July 7, he outlined the situation to his superior in Australia, well aware that General Thomas Blamey had also been forced to fight this battle. Morshead informed Blamey that, "Since joining Eighth Army have twice had [to] plainly insist 9 Australian Division be kept intact under my command."[55]

Despite the weakness of their forces, neither Auchinleck nor Rommel was prepared to remain inactive for long. On July 7–8, Auchinleck deliberately weakened the southern sector of the position hoping to entice Rommel to commit his mobile German formations here. On the evening of July 9, Rommel, believing that the withdrawal of Eighth Army formations from some key positions indicated a general collapse and that a decisive breakthrough was within his grasp, launched an eastward thrust, committing most of his available force. In doing so, Rommel was forced to extend his formations across the whole Alamein position from the Depression to the sea while Eighth Army were concentrated in the center and to the north. Rommel wrote that "we planned to thrust on next day with all our strength . . . and thus bring about the fall of the Alamein line."[56] He was sure of success. Allied Enigma (Ultra) intercepts revealed that although desperately short of fuel, "Panzer Army Africa requires maps of CAIRO AREA showing road conditions." The day after this message, another intercept to the Wehrmacht's Map Depot in Munich revealed the extent of Rommel's confidence:

Immediate despatch required of 2000 sheets fet 500 CAIRO to Army (A) map station 575, Naples for the printing of additions. Please report despatch.[57]

But the morning of July 10 opened with a barrage of artillery fire in the north. The Afrika Korps War Diary recorded, "During the night particularly heavy artillery fire can be heard from the north. Veterans of the Great War say that it is even stronger than the Trommelfeuer [drumfire] of the Western Front."[58] Rommel recorded on hearing it: "I at once had an inkling that it boded no good."[59] Rommel's assessment was accurate and his dreams of marching on Cairo were abruptly ended that morning. The intense bombardment, the largest yet fired in the desert war, lasted several hours. It caused panic amongst the Italian defenders, mainly soldiers from the Italian Sabratha Division, many of whom soon took to their heels. At 1000 hours, the 26th Infantry Brigade of 9th Australian Division, supported by thirty-two Valentine tanks, attacked and captured the eastern part of the dominant feature of Tel el Eisa (The Hill of Jesus). On their left flank, the 1st South African Division, supported by eight Matilda tanks, also advanced to capture Tel el Makh Khad. But as well as capturing some key positions, the attack routed the Italian enemy in front of these positions. Rommel wrote of this disaster:

> Presently came the alarming news that the enemy had attacked from the Alamein position and overrun the Sabratha Division, which had been a line on either side of the coast road. The enemy was now in hot pursuit westwards after the fleeing Italians and there was a serious danger that they would break through and destroy our supplies.[60]

The Australians recorded of their successful night attack:

> Next morning the position had been cleared of all enemy and five disabled tanks could be seen inside the Battalion's FDLs [forward defensive lines]. In all, 1150 prisoners were captured including a German W/T [wireless telegraph] Intercept Unit with valuable documents, several guns were destroyed and 18 tanks knocked out or hopelessly bogged.[61]

Rommel soon discovered that the loss of his W/T Intercept Unit was as critical as his loss of tanks. This was the Nachrichten Fernsehsendung Aufsklärungs Kompanie 621 commanded by Captain Alfred Seebohm. Captain Seebohm had been killed in the Australian attack. Since April 1941, Kompanie 621, taking advantage of Eighth Army's lax signals security, had provided Rommel with "an unparalleled wealth of tactical intelligence."[62] As one of Rommel's senior intelligence officers, Generalmajor Friedrich von Mellenthin, stated after the war, "The best intelligence source, the reports of radio intelligence submitted by the intercept company, influenced his [Rommel's] decisions decisively."[63] It is little wonder that one German intelligence officer later wrote that the loss of Seebohm's company was "a catastrophe" of the most "serious consequences for Panzerarmee Afrika."[64] The officer who reported its loss described Rommel as being "absolutely furious" at the loss of this crucial asset.[65]

Rommel was now forced to abandon his own plan of attack in order to divert German forces north to seal the breach. Throughout the day came more alarming news that the Sabratha Division had been "nearly annihilated" and that the Italians, being attacked by the Australians and South Africans, had "left their line, many of them in panic, and with no attempt at defending themselves, sought the open desert, throwing away arms and ammunition as they ran."[66] During the morning of July 10, the Australians endured five separate Stuka attacks and then beat off two determined counterattacks by Afrika Korps that afternoon. According to Niall Barr, while it was "a very long day of fighting," the two battalions from the Australian 26th Brigade had performed "a fine feat of arms."[67]

The attack continued on July 11, making further progress. The Australians captured the rest of Tel el Eisa and struck south toward the Deir el Abyad. In the process, several battalions from the Trieste Division were mauled and hundreds of prisoners taken. The Australian attack on the Deir el Abyad was checked by the Axis defensive positions on the Miteiriya Ridge and they withdrew back to Tel el Eisa. But the damage had been done and Rommel lost more than thirty tanks against the Tel el Eisa positions in the next five days. His losses in tank crews were also "heavy."[68] After the second day of the Australian action, a chastened Rommel recorded in his diary:

> There could be no question of launching any large-scale attack in the immediate future. I was compelled to order every last German soldier out of his tent or rest camp to the front, for, in face of the virtual default of a large proportion of our Italian fighting power, the situation was beginning to take on crisis proportions.[69]

The successful attack at Tel el Eisa left the Australians brimming with confidence. One of the infantry battalions involved summarized the operation as two nights and a day of "hard fighting" but "the Bn with its supptg arms had shown itself more than equal to anything the Germans could produce."[70]

There was a telling feature in the Australians' defense of Tel el Eisa, one that Rommel must have noticed and would cost him dearly in his next large-scale attack at the end of August. An Australian operational narrative recorded of it:

> This was the first campaign in which 9 Australian Division was fully supported from the air. Co-operation between land and air forces was complete, and within an hour of calling for support Boston bombers and fighter bombers would be blasting enemy troops and positions.[71]

Prior to the attack, the war diary of 2/48 Battalion recorded that, "Our Air Force was conspicuous by its continued presence and tps warmly appreciate the news of air superiority." But such conspicuous support made the infantry soldiers complacent. They were "caught unawares" when four enemy planes bombed their positions, killing or wounding eleven soldiers. The war diary recorded a painful lesson:

> The tragedy of this small raid taught us our lesson and digging continued with renewed vigour. The false feeling of security has now gone and although the air superiority is definitely ours, all ranks now take the necessary precautions to make sure.[72]

The attack on July 9–10 marked an important transition in the battle. As a South African narrative noted, "Auchinleck had changed over finally to the offensive, and the Eighth Army was never again to know the anguish and humiliation of defeat."[73] While Niall Barr has written that "the importance of this attack has been overstated," there is no denying its effect on the fragile morale of Eighth Army.[74] Unfortunately, though, there was plenty of anguish and humiliation ahead for Eighth Army in this July battle.

* * *

Deeply concerned that the battlefront was coalescing into "rigid, static warfare" in which "the British were masters," Rommel decided to launch his own full-scale counteroffensive against the Alamein positions in the north on July 13. He would send 21st Panzer and "every gun and every aeroplane we could muster" to cut off the Alamein fortress in the north and then destroy it.[75] The attack was a dismal failure, not even getting beyond the start line. British artillery pounded the assembly points and 21st Panzer was exhausted and confused about what Rommel intended. Rommel summed up the results the next day in a letter to his wife: "My expectations for yesterday's attack were bitterly disappointed. It achieved no success whatever."[76] But Rommel was not finished with this attempt to break through. The next day the hard-pressed 21st Panzer Division was ordered to retake the position lost by the Sabratha Division three days earlier and now held by the Australians. After a heavy air bombardment, the 21st Panzer Division attacked the Australians, coming under air and artillery attack as they did so. 21st Panzer could make little headway against the Australians and that evening, threatened by the Eighth Army assault on Ruweisat Ridge, Rommel ordered the attack broken off.

The four days of July 10–14 had been crucial in the defense of the Alamein positions. They had been good days for the Eighth Army, disastrous for Rommel's Panzerarmee. Two Italian divisions had been all but destroyed and the Afrika Korps had also suffered heavy losses without getting close to breaking through the Alamein defenses. Rommel had been fought to a standstill and his fears of static, rigid, attrition-type operations were fully justified. He was desperately short of men and fuel. Intercepted German communications on July 10 revealed that to relieve the "strained fuel situation in Africa a long-range bomber gruppe is to be used to transport fuel from GREECE and CRETE."[77] Urgent reinforcements were to arrive by air, too, which included a reconnaissance unit and a mountain artillery regiment.[78] Eventually, a complete division, the 164th, would be sent by air from Crete.

But Eighth Army had its supply problems, too. It was so short of 25-pounder ammunition, the caliber of its standard field gun, that a proposal was made to limit firing to just 15,000 rounds per day. This amount was "completely inadequate" for an army engaged in a last-ditch defensive battle. There were severe shortages of many types of small arms ammunition too.[79] Despite these shortages, on the evening of July 14, the Eighth Army launched its own counter punches against the Axis forces.

They too would soon see their plans frustrated as Eighth Army incurred crippling losses amongst some of its best formations.

July 14–15, Ruweisat Ridge

After the capture of Tel el Eisa, General Auchinleck had been contemplating a significant blow against the Axis forces in the center of the Alamein position. He decided to capture the prominent feature of Ruweisat Ridge using two infantry and an armored division. The attack was codenamed Operation *Bacon*. The two infantry divisions, the 5th Indian Division on the right flank and the 2nd New Zealand Division to their west, were to capture the ridge in a silent night attack on the night of July 14. Critical to the success of the operation was the arrival of the tanks of the 1st Armoured Division in the early dawn of July 15. These tanks would be sorely needed, especially as the New Zealanders, after a six-mile advance, would be out of artillery range of their own 25-pounders and have an open, vulnerable left flank. The task of protecting this flank had been allocated to the 22nd Armoured Brigade, which had seventy-five tanks at its disposal, of which thirty-one were Grants. This was a strong force "well able to deal with whatever enemy armor was south of the ridge, *and* to protect the infantry during the inevitable period of disorganisation."[80]

The infantry attack commenced at 2300 hours on July 14. The New Zealanders on the left easily took their objectives, although one battalion went astray in the six-mile advance to the objective. At one stage, the New Zealanders were holding more than 20,000 Axis prisoners. But at first light, no British tanks were in position and an entire New Zealand brigade was overrun by German armor. New Zealand casualties were close to 1,500 and, of the six infantry battalions used in the attack, at the end of July 15 only one was fit for further action.[81] The War Diary of the 5th New Zealand Brigade summarized the dire situation of its battalions. Recording that one complete battalion, the 22nd, was reported as being taken prisoner, it logged:

> The attack had been a success and the objective occupied.
> Due to the tk attack our casualties appeared to have been heavy, and BNs were in need of reorganisation.[82]

On the right flank, the 5th Indian Division captured all of its objectives by noon of July 15, which also enabled the New Zealand portion of the ridge to be consolidated. It had been a fine feat of arms to carry out such a long advance through the positions of two Italian divisions and seize a vital feature of the Alamein position. Eighth Army achieved its objectives but coordination between various formations and arms had been abysmal and, as a result, casualties had been unnecessarily high. The 5th New Zealand Brigade recorded its battalion strengths on July 16 as just ninety all ranks in 21 Battalion, unknown in 22 Battalion, and 200 men in 23 Battalion.[83]

Missing the irony in his comment, one of the principal staff officers of Eighth Army later wrote that "a more prudent course" would have been to complete the capture of the ridge in two stages by designating an intermediate objective. That way, "proper artillery and armoured support could be provided to permit the advance to resume to Point 63." Years later, Major General Eric Dorman O'Gowan (Dorman-Smith in 1942), Auchinleck's Chief of Staff, wrote, "It is still a matter of surprise that the commander of the New Zealand Division does not appear to have protested at the difficulty of his task."[84] This statement revealed a fundamental difference in the mindset of British and Dominion officers. For Dominion commanders, orders from superior officers, especially the Army commander, were sacrosanct. They were to be fulfilled to the best of one's ability. But for many British officers in Eighth Army, these orders from the higher headquarters were seen as a starting point for discussion and debate. If things were considered too difficult, the orders could also be discreetly ignored. In keeping with this tradition, a recent British account of the debacle lays the blame for it squarely on the New Zealanders. According to Barr, New Zealand commanders had "wildly overestimated the capabilities of the two British Armoured Brigades" and they therefore expected "too much of the British armour."[85] It would seem that assuming the armored brigades would stick to the agreed plan was just too much to expect.

Certainly, the senior New Zealand commanders felt they had been allocated a difficult, if not impossible task. Both infantry brigadiers "made a special trip" to the Division's Headquarters upon receiving their orders on July 12. There they urged that the advance be done in two stages but "we were turned down."[86] The New Zealand commander, Lindsay Inglis, later claimed that he approached the corps commander about completing the advance in two stages, but "Gott would not let [Inglis] go any closer for fear of giving away our intentions."[87] Such an approach by Inglis seems unlikely and no record of it exists.

The New Zealand senior artillery officer later wrote:

> I feel quite certain in my own mind that it was beyond the strength of two Inf Bdes with one Bn in reserve, to advance 10,000 yards through defended country, capture a tactical objective at the end of it, clear the intervening country & hold it against a wide open left flank & a right flank which was only cleared on the objective.[88]

Despite Ruweisat Ridge being New Zealand's worst military disaster of the war, Strafer Gott regarded it as a limited success. He wrote to a recovering General Freyberg five days after the Ruweisat Ridge action, describing it as "a hard knock," but one that had captured more than 2,000 prisoners and a number of guns. He informed Freyberg that "we have great hopes of getting a more definite success soon."[89] While it could not be published in the New Zealand official history, Kippenberger's summation of the battle was more accurate. "The battle was a tragedy of misdirection and mismanagement," he informed the official historian.[90] Unfortunately, despite Gott's hopes for achieving more definite success soon, other tragedies were shortly to occur.

The capture of Ruweisat Ridge did alarm the Axis forces. An intelligence report of 15 Panzer Division recorded the sound of heavy fighting on the night of July 14, then the loss of three easternmost strongpoints "without a single report from the Italians." The report "was most astonished that the enemy could not exploit his penetration to a breakthrough by pushing his tanks forward."[91] Two German counterattacks on July 16 were driven off by the concentrated firepower of 13 Corps' artillery and the infantry's six-pounder guns. Rommel lost 24 tanks, six 88 mm anti-aircraft guns, and twenty other guns in these attacks and fell into a deep depression. He wrote to his wife on July 17:

> Things are going downright badly for me at the moment, at any rate, in the military sense. The enemy is using his superiority, especially in infantry, to destroy the Italian formations one by one, and the German formations are much too weak to stand alone. It's enough to make one weep.[92]

And according to General Fritz Bayerlein, the loss of Ruweisat Ridge on the heels of the Australian success near the coast was "devastating." Bayerlein later acknowledged that, "When Rommel lost Tel el Eisa and Ruweisat, he and all of us knew we were lost."[93]

On the day of the Ridge's capture, the Panzerarmee sent off an urgent signal outlining a deteriorating military situation. It read:

> The situation on the Alamein front became critical on 15/7 since, as a result of a night attack by the enemy in about brigade strength with individual light lorries (Kamionetten) and tanks, the main body of the Italian Brescia and Pavia Divs. was routed, that is to say they were either taken prisoner or they abandoned their positions.
>
> Several times lately Italian troops under the influence of artillery fire have abandoned their positions, and could not be persuaded even by their officers to offer resistance to the enemy. These symptoms of panic make it imperative to send further German forces, particularly lorried infantry and anti-tank troops, to Panzer Army as quickly as possible.[94]

The capture of Ruweisat Ridge had clearly taken Rommel by surprise. It could have been turned into a greater reversal for Rommel had the armored brigades been able to protect the isolated infantry on the Ridge and use the position for further exploitation of the exposed Axis forces. The fleeting opportunity was lost and, overall, Operation *Bacon* was a disappointment. Worse still it further eroded confidence in Eighth Army's leadership. Eighth Army seemed incapable of mounting a sustained offensive operation if it required detailed planning, shared doctrine and tight coordination.

The Later Attacks in July

Auchinleck was determined to keep Rommel off balance and from mid-July, he mounted several attacks using primarily the Australian and New Zealand infantry formations. These followed a depressingly familiar pattern in that they were poorly coordinated and were unnecessarily costly for those infantry units at the sharp end. Nor did they achieve the desired breakthrough of the Axis positions. In fact, they seldom achieved the attainment of their first specified objective.

In the north, the 9th Australian Division, the freshest formation in the Eighth Army, made three of these attacks against a section of the Miteiriya Ridge named Ruin Ridge. Miteiriya Ridge was ten miles to the

north of Ruweisat Ridge and ran almost parallel to it. Although difficult
to see from a distance, Miteiriya offered a valuable observation site, especially as it ran east to west for a considerable distance. While named after
the remains of a building on its crest, the part of the ridge named Ruin
Ridge proved a most apt name for the Australian attacks here. The first
action to capture Ruin Ridge was made on July 17 by just one Australian
battalion when at least a brigade attack was required. The 2/32nd Australian Infantry Battalion initially succeeded in capturing Ruin Ridge,
but vigorous German counterattacks were made and took their toll. Reinforced by 2/43rd Battalion, the third German counterattack drove the
Australians back. The 9th Division's War Diary recorded of it:

> Between 1630 and 1730 hrs intense enemy arty fire and pressure from enemy tks
> on front and flanks forced the withdrawal of our tps to telegraph line south and
> SW of ry [railway] causing substantial casualties to personnel tks and equip-
> ment. Our front was firm by 2030 hrs.[95]

One battalion diarist recorded how the change from "comparative triumph to gloom was startling."[96] The moment 2/43 Battalion moved forward to join 2/32 Battalion on the ridge, "Bn. Came under severe shelling
from enemy batteries which continued until final objective was reached."
With their ammunition stocks "almost exhausted," with no communication with its artillery support, and with several large enemy counterattacks looming, the "CO ordered withdrawal."[97] Given the unfavorable
circumstances, there was little else the battalion could do. The attack was
very similar to that launched by the New Zealanders on Ruweisat Ridge,
but this time the feature could not be held. Casualties in both battalions
were high and numbered 317.[98]

Such a swift reversal of fortune was repeated twice more at this location on July 22 and again on July 27. An Australian infantryman summarized the attack of July 22, part of Operation *Splendour*, as "a balls-up
altogether."[99] The plan, which Morshead had tried to have altered, involved three battalions of the Australian Division all attacking in different directions. The planned attacks "resembled a bomb burst, going
out in all directions with none of sufficient strength to deal properly
with the opposition."[100] It was a recipe for disaster. The Division's War
Diary recorded that its infantry had been "heavily counter attacked causing substantial casualties during the morning."[101] Armored support was

provided to the Australians but it was poorly coordinated and overshot the objective. When ordered back, half of the 50th Royal Tank Regiments tanks were casualties, with 23 of them left "burning in the desert."[102] Some Australian soldiers had been impressed with the courage of the tank crews. Sitting on a Valentine tank, Bill Loffman of 2/28 Battalion remarked to a crew member that the tank's gun was very small. "Yes, we know," was the reply. "It's only a two-pounder and we do know what we are up against." To Loffman, the tank crews were "bloody heroes." He stated that, "British armour was crap taken into action by heroes."[103]

Lieutenant Colonel Bernard Evans, commanding the 2/23 Battalion, recorded sadly in his report on the action that his casualties had been "very heavy." He wrote:

> In the past week, the fighting has been so hy [heavy], that I have had all Coy Comds killed and all their replacements made casualties too. In all, 19 offr casualties and 270 wounded and dead, and 50 (roughly) missing.

Evans noted that most of his battalion's casualties had been caused by concealed machine gun and mortar positions. He lamented that, "In this respect, the absence of tk [tank] support was sorely felt."[104]

*   *   *

If possible, the Australian attack on July 27 was even worse. This was part of Operation *Manhood* and it would be Auchinleck's final offensive. Restricted just to 30 Corps because 13 Corps was played out, *Manhood* involved the Australians, the South Africans, and a British Brigade. This latter formation was the 69th Infantry Brigade, which had been detached from the 50th Division. As expected, the attack was a complete disaster. It never recovered from a faulty plan involving two infantry brigades attacking in different directions, making adequate artillery protection impossible.[105] While the objectives were captured, battalions were left isolated and unsupported, just ripe for the enemy counterattacks that soon came. Three battalions, including the Australian 2/28th were "virtually destroyed, killed or captured."[106] It took some time for the full extent of the disaster on Ruin Ridge to become known. The 9th Australian Division's Headquarters knew the 2/28th was in grave danger by the urgent messages being received at regular intervals. "We are in trouble," "We need help now," "We need armour," they informed the headquarters. An operations report recorded of the tragedy: "The full story of 2/28 Bn's resistance on the Ridge is not known for not one man who was with them when the counter-attacks began got back." The report concluded: "After this unfortunate action no further operations were undertaken before the end of the month."[107] The Division's War Diary tried to find some solace in a disastrous military action:

> Reported missing from 2/28 Bn were 21 offrs and 470 OR, but it is considered that, although the main operation did not succeed, considerable casualties were inflicted on the enemy mainly by our intense and accurate arty fire.[108]

The reconstructed war diary of 2/28 Battalion recorded a depressing situation. Formed into two echelons, A Echelon consisted of "98 all ranks" organized into two skeleton infantry platoons. Neither platoon possessed an automatic weapon. B Echelon consisted of 105 all ranks, mainly Q Staff and drivers. Of these survivors, 75 percent were under treatment for minor ailments, particularly the ever-present desert sores. Treatment was provided at an RAP by a medic sergeant as the Battalion's RMO had been captured on Ruin Ridge. Despite these hardships, the war diary recorded that "their spirit is amazingly good."[109] Most were probably grateful to be alive.

Since July 10, the Australians had suffered more than 2,500 casualties and had only 100 immediate reinforcements available. Morshead sent an urgent telegram to Australia on July 29 asking, "What is earliest we can expect reinforcements from Australia and how many?"[110] For the time being, the Australians had had enough disasters.

Two British battalions of the 69th Brigade were also lost later that morning. Both the Durham Light Infantry and East Yorks Battalions had reached their objectives, suffering heavy casualties in doing so. There, in depressingly similar circumstances they were isolated, short of ammunition and support arms and their wireless communication had broken down. Once 2/28th Battalion had been overwhelmed, the German panzers turned their attention to the two British battalions. These were soon surrounded and subjected to tank fire. They had no choice but to surrender. As Barr has written, "All three battalions involved in the attack had been overrun and captured in a disastrous replay of Ruweisat and El Mreir."[111]

El Mreir and "another Balaclava": July 22

A similar fate was experienced by the only intact infantry brigade left in the New Zealand Division after the Ruweisat disaster. On July 22, as the Australians made their second attempt on Ruin Ridge in the north, the 5th Indian Division attacked Deir el Shein while the 6th New Zealand Brigade captured the eastern rim of the El Mreir Depression. These moves were part of the hastily mounted, poorly coordinated, ill-named Operation *Splendour*. Planning and coordination for these actions was "more of the same." While close cooperation was required to make the plan work, no combined training had been undertaken nor was there even a corps conference for the senior commanders. Armored commanders were adamant that their tanks would be on the objective in support of the infantry at first light. But despite being pressed to do so, they refused to move their tanks into position during the night. As predicted by all the infantry commanders, British tank support arrived late for both attacks with tragic results. Three New Zealand battalions were on the edge of the El Mreir depression on the morning of July 22 after making another long night march. One battalion, with German tanks immediately in front of them, wisely withdrew before first light. The other two battalions held their positions and awaited the arrival of the British tanks. They were soon overrun by the tanks of two Panzer Regiments. The New Zealand Division lost a further sixty-nine officers, including the brigadier, and 835 ORs from its one complete brigade.[112] The promised armored support moved off at 0630 hours that morning, an hour and a half after the New Zealand 6th Brigade had been overrun.

The commander of the New Zealand 6 Brigade was, quite naturally incensed, at the failure of the British armor to appear. Brigadier George Clifton, who would be captured later in the day trying to salvage what remained of his command, sought to have it out with his armored counterpart. Clifton's diary recorded:

> Failure due entirely to 2 Armd Div NOT carrying out their orders. Told GOC and other people that Bgdr was either a cold footed bastard or not competent to command a sanitary fatigue. Went over to his HQ to tell him personally but unfortunately he was out.[113]

Clifton's feelings regarding the armored commanders were common amongst many of the senior infantry commanders. Writing to General

Freyberg to explain the two disasters that had crippled the New Zealand Division, Inglis's letter captured his sense of frustration and his blanket refusal to do more military actions of this kind.

> Our people did their stuff, but the armour, so we feel, let us down very badly on both occasions so that we got a severe handling both times, not in the attacks but in the aftermath. For the next show [El Mreir] I took every step I could think of to ensure that there should be no repetition . . . Anyway the result is that I have flatly refused to do another of the same kind while I command. I have said that the *sine qua non* is my own armour under my own command.[114]

It wasn't only the Dominion forces who suffered on July 22, either. Rushed to the Alamein position after barely two weeks in theater, 23 Armoured Brigade's first military action was a harsh introduction to desert warfare. Two regiments of the brigade were sent off on "a latter day Balaclava charge with guns to the right, left and in front of them and the further striking parallel of a mistake in orders."[115] This foolish action, hastily conceived on the spot by Gott and Gatehouse after a brief, early-morning consultation, achieved nothing but heavy casualties. The tank charge to nowhere cost 23 Armoured Brigade most of the tanks involved. Some 106 tanks had commenced the charge at 0800 hours that morning. That evening, only seven remained.[116] The 23rd Armoured Brigade had been annihilated.

Lieutenant Geoffrey Giddings, a British engineer serving with the 23rd Armoured Brigade, saw first-hand the price of inexperience, poor planning, and lack of desert training:

> The Tanks of the 40th RTR [Royal Tank Regiment] had driven forward to the West through gaps in a marked minefield opened up by engineers of the 5th Indian Division. They came under heavy fire from German positions and—it being <u>their</u> first day of action came racing back to our lines and (?) safety (?). Our troop was sent up to the minefield to shepherd them through the gaps. The Tanks swept back panic stricken and despite waving, running towards them, and other futile attempts to attract them, they carried on blindly—and one after another we saw those Tanks, brought all the way from England and their crews trained over months and years, blown up, engulfed in flames or killed outright. We felt so helpless, frustrated and angry. Some, of course, got back, but the fighting strength of that Regiment was thrown away in a fruitless "swan-up" over the desert.[117]

This "swan-up" left the 40th RTR with just four of its new Valentine tanks. Giddings reported the losses in person to Brigade Headquarters through "bitter tears." It had been his "first day of action."[118] In little more than four hours, 23 Armoured Brigade had lost thirty officers, 173 other ranks, and almost 100 tanks. Enemy losses were claimed as just seven tanks.[119] Tank losses across Eighth Army numbered more than 120 on that day, although German sources claimed that the figure was as high as 140.[120]

The Intelligence Diary of 15 Panzer Division, the formation that had shattered the 6 New Zealand Brigade at El Mreir, contained a neat summary of the day's events:

> The enemy lost heavily, and our defence held firm in most places, with the result that the enemy was thrown into some confusion . . . and seemed to be fighting with no sure plan of action.[121]

That evening, an elated Rommel sent a congratulatory message to his troops:

> I send all ranks my special appreciation of their gallant action during our victorious defence of 22nd July. I am positive that any further enemy attack will meet with the same reception.[122]

Surprisingly, Auchinleck issued a similar statement to his army just three days later. In a Special Order of the Day sent on July 25, Auchinleck informed the soldiers of his Army that:

> You have done well. You have turned a retreat into a firm stand and stopped the enemy on the threshold of EGYPT. You have done more. You have wrenched the initiative from him by sheer guts and hard fighting and put HIM on the defensive in these last weeks . . . You have borne much but I ask you for more. We must not slacken. If we can stick it, we will break him. STICK TO IT.[123]

Coming immediately after the debacles of Ruweisat and Ruin Ridges, El Mreir, and the destruction of 23 Armoured Brigade, such an order must have had an especially hollow ring.

The July battle, the First Battle of El Alamein, had peculiar results. It began well, halting Rommel's advance in its tracks and thereby saving the situation in Egypt. As one German staff officer later wrote, "And to Auchinleck fell the honour of being the general who succeeded in checking Rommel's advance into Egypt, an honour that every German *Afrikasoldat* who knows what happened does not hesitate to award to him."[124] Rommel's chief operations officer, Colonel Siegfried Westphal, always believed that it was this July battle of El Alamein that was the critical one in North Africa. Many years later he told an interviewer that:

> You succeeded in summer 1942 finally to stop the exhausted rest of the German Army that reached Alamein, and that was absolutely the deciding point. I think the German Army in the desert has never fully recovered from this exhausting campaign, which did begin on 26th May and ended in El Alamein. Besides, it was absolutely unknown to us that you had built up a strong position at Alamein.[125]

However, the military actions of Eighth Army deteriorated after the early days of July to become "often messy, confused and seemingly random to the troops who took part."[126] The British official history of its intelligence activities is correct to describe these attacks as having a "heavy cost in men and material" while "rarely [being] properly prepared." By mid-July, "Eighth Army's losses had now reached an alarming level," but still Auchinleck persisted in making them.[127] The poorly coordinated, clumsy offensive actions in mid- and late July all but destroyed the unity of Eighth Army and squandered much of the fighting power of its very best formations. Lieutenant Colonel Bernard Evans recorded a neat summary of the month's fighting in his battalion's war diary:

> The month has been fast moving. The approach into the desert, my own dash from PALESTINE to resume command, and then the ever increasing momentum of moves, orders, counter orders, more moves—action and still more action—and heavy casualties.

This frantic tempo, with its inevitable heavy casualties, denuded the battalion of its junior leadership and imparted hard, painful lessons "too numerous to mention." While Evans was confident that his men had the measure of the "Bosch," the numerous lessons and the newly appointed officers meant that "I shall need a period of intensive training to bridge these gaps in knowledge."[128]

Another Australian battalion commander recorded that from the moment his battalion arrived at the El Alamein position, "there was little rest for weary men." As a result of the actions of July, described as a "fine show," [. . .] "Many old faces had disappeared from the unit ranks."[129]

The soldiers of Eighth Army also needed rest and a chance to recover their physical condition. An Australian medical report noted of its men's general condition:

The men, due to a very tiring trip from Syria, and continued moves and digging in after arrival in Egypt, were not as physically fit as they might have been, and hy [heavy] engagements plus continued digging in, took toll of the men's physical condition.

Very hy [heavy] arty fire and air attacks caused a severe mental strain on the men. Several were evacuated and others relieved from front line for a few days.

Some men who were able to get about during the day, were able to get to the beach for a swim and this was a great help. Desert sores continue to be a source of worry and there seems to be no quick method of healing them.[130]

According to Howard Kippenberger, at a time when Eighth Army was in "dire need" of nursing back to health, Auchinleck "undertook a series of unnecessary and unsuccessful counter-offensives very badly coordinated and costing . . . 14000 casualties." Kippenberger did not think "that a single one of these was necessary."[131] Brigadier George Clifton echoed Kippenberger's view. The *Bacon* and *Splendour* attacks were "regrettable" and cost the Eighth Army thousands "of the best Inf[antry] in the world to no purpose whatever."[132] Even senior staff officer de Guingand thought that the later offensive operations "were a mistake." The troops undertaking them were either too tired and "it was difficult to see the object, as . . . no large scale exploitation was possible."[133] These failed attacks thoroughly undermined any confidence in the Army's senior commanders.

This lack of confidence in the way Eighth Army was fighting its battles stretched all the way down to the private soldier. Letters of New Zealand soldiers submitted for censorship revealed a strong condemnation of the British High Command, a deep distrust of armored formations and a general belief that the Dominion soldiers were being allocated the hardest fighting. While morale of the New Zealanders was generally good, "There is however a tendency to think 'The German War Machine is just about perfect compared with the British Army Mess Up.'"[134] Regarding the distrust of the British armor, Kippenberger caught the mood in *Infantry Brigadier*. He wrote:

At this time there was throughout Eighth Army, not only in New Zealand Division, a most intense distrust, almost hatred, of our armour. Everywhere one heard tales of the other arms being let down; it was regarded as axiomatic that the tanks would not be where they were wanted in time.[135]

This mistrust and lack of confidence in Eighth Army's abilities originated with its commander, Auchinleck. Major General Douglas Wimberley, who had arrived in Egypt ahead of his 51st (Highland) Division, was at Eighth Army headquarters during the debacle of July 27. There he witnessed Auchinleck "pacing up and down in front of the mess," a worried and anxious man. His brief time at Eighth Army Headquarters "was not one at that time to give great confidence."[136]

Auchinleck's reputation and fate is reminiscent of the Gallipoli commander General Sir Ian Hamilton. Both are often portrayed as tragic, lonely figures; men who, despite their considerable military skills, could not bring these to change the military circumstances they faced. Both ended up being overwhelmed by events and were then ignominiously replaced. In Auchinleck's case, this is misleading. Hamilton never had the same resources allocated to Auchinleck and never outnumbered the opponents he faced. Most of Auchinleck's problems were of his own making and he was not placed in an unwinnable position from his campaign's inception. As early as March 1942, "Chink" Dorman-Smith had warned Auchinleck in a written report that Eighth Army, with its amateur tactics, widespread desert jargon, and old-boy network was "more of a club than a strictly disciplined entity."[137] Auchinleck had ignored this sound assessment.

The South African historian J.A.I. Agar-Hamilton certainly had Auchinleck's measure when he wrote that:

> Auchinleck as a commander was hopeless, but not because he was a fool. He possessed in fact both a first class military brain and good fighting spirit. What he lacked was leadership. He never seemed to be able to get anyone to obey him.[138]

It was an astute assessment. In confirmation of Agar-Hamilton's last point, Howard Kippenberger confirmed Auchinleck's lack of leadership skills. According to Kippenberger, "I myself heard him say—'It is like everything else in this Army, if I want a thing done I have to do it myself.'"[139] British author and wartime press officer in Cairo, Lawrence Durrell, thought that Auchinleck was "absolutely charming." But Durrell also recalled that Auchinleck "had no real personality" and, as a result, "he just could not inspire men to action."[140] To this, Freyberg would add that Auchinleck was "one of the finest characters imaginable but he was stubborn and one of the worst judges of men." Freyberg believed that until the appointments of Montgomery and Alexander in August 1942, "the prestige of British generalship was at its lowest possible point."[141]

Auchinleck was certainly not helped by his choice of corps commanders, either, which reflected his inability to judge their qualities. The six-foot, former army boxing champion, Strafer Gott, for example, had strong leadership skills and, because of his calm courage in the face of so many crises, he had become "an almost legendary figure to the officers and men of the Eighth Army."[142] While Gott was universally admired, he was content to follow his own path rather than implement Auchinleck's orders. Freyberg thought that Gott was "a likeable man and a brave one. But there was something very wrong with the way he worked."[143] Agar-Hamilton's view was that Auchinleck was continually undermined by Gott. He wrote shortly after the war that "The Auk was undoubtedly unlucky in having to deal with one with such outstanding qualities of leadership, a legendary personality, and a complete absence of military sense."[144] This applied to most of Auchinleck's key appointments. Kippenberger thought that the armored commanders were "wretched fellows" who never read military history and consequently "evolved practices contrary to the experience of war."[145] Auchinleck's decision to relieve the reasonably competent corps commander Lieutenant General Charles Willoughby Norrie on July 7 and replace him with Major General William Ramsden from 50th Division caused "extreme surprise and consternation" throughout Eighth Army. Kippenberger explained why: "The British officers at that period spoke of [Ramsden] as a notorious bonehead and he certainly looked like one."[146] Auchinleck never explained why he relieved Norrie of command, but it is probable that he blamed Norrie for much of the Gazala debacle. Norrie was liked and respected by many in Eighth Army and his sacking was just another indicator of "the division and friction amongst its higher commanders."[147]

In the July battle, Auchinleck was fortunate that the DAF had air superiority over the battlefield. Without this, Eighth Army's casualties would have been much higher than they were. Robin Neillands wrote, "In this continual July fighting, much of the credit on the British side must go to the Desert Air Force."[148] It had been the DAF's busiest month of the war to date. During July, its squadrons had flown more than 15,000 sorties, which was "an average of over 500 attacks a day."[149]

In the summer months of 1942, Eighth Army had incurred a staggering 80,000 casualties.[150] In July 1942, it had suffered more than 13,000 casualties during this First Battle of El Alamein. Most of these were experienced by the infantry divisions doing the hard fighting. The 2nd New Zealand Division had suffered just over 4,000 casualties, the Australian 9th Division 2,552, and the 5th Indian Division some 3,000.[151] Niall Barr wrote a summary of Operation *Splendour*, which is apt for the First Alamein battle. Barr wrote, "The soldiers of Eighth Army had once again displayed courage and determination but had been let down by faulty tactics, poor planning and a fundamental failure of command."[152] The constant activity and heavy losses resulting from the poorly planned and ill-coordinated operations had brought Eighth Army "close to exhaustion."[153]

There was overwhelming evidence to suggest that Eighth Army suffered "a morale crisis in the summer of 1942 and that it severely affected Eighth Army's performance."[154] This was caused by the effects of both the Gazala battle and First Alamein. Gazala was a serious defeat with heavy casualties; First Alamein was a victory, but casualties had been needlessly excessive and attempts to drive Panzerarmee off key features in late July had also failed. This crisis of morale was evident in the incidence of NYD (N) (Not Yet Diagnosed (Nervous)) or battle exhaustion, which was "disturbingly high."[155] Also "disturbingly high" were all the other indicators of low morale: sickness, desertion, absenteeism, and surrender. This morale crisis can be directly attributed to Eighth Army's leadership.

Auchinleck was aware of how serious the morale and discipline problem had become. His solution was to request the British War Office to reinstate of the death penalty for "desertion in the field" and for "misbehaving in the face of the enemy in such as a manner as to show cowardice."[156] Desertion and cowardice had been military crimes punishable by death during the First World War, but capital punishment for such offenses had been abolished in 1930. That Auchinleck now wanted it reinstated as "a salutary deterrent" was an indication of his poor leadership skills. Rather than relying on his personal and expert powers,

Auchinleck "was forced to turn to policies of coercion to maintain his troops' willingness and discipline to fight."[157] Auchinleck's request also indicates how little he understood the men he was commanding. The reintroduction of the death penalty for desertion and cowardice would have further eroded the Army's fragile morale. Its implementation would have had dire consequences too. One of New Zealand's most respected and able military commanders made this clear after the war. Howard Kippenberger wrote to a friend in 1949 that he was "very distressed" to learn that the death penalty was being considered for desertion and cowardice in Eighth Army. Kippenberger wrote:

> I don't know what justification there is for execution for cowardice. There were four men executed in 1st NZEF.... We had, of course, no death penalty, and I think if men belonging to the 2nd [New Zealand] Division had been executed the morale of the whole show would have been ruined.[158]

Kippenberger was certainly correct in his assessment. The crisis in Eighth Army's morale and the request to reinstate the death penalty were clear evidence that Auchinleck was failing in his task of commanding Eighth Army. He could not provide the leadership it needed to win a decisive battle.

It was certainly apparent to those at the sharp end of the fighting in the Western Desert that there was a crisis of confidence in Eighth Army. Fortunately for the soldiers and junior commanders of the Army, the political and military authorities in London also had grave concerns with how Eighth Army was being used. Some new brooms were being readied for use.

NOTES

1. Major General Alfred Toppe, "Desert Warfare: German Experience in World War II," FMS D739, 21, Army Heritage and Education Center, Carlisle PA (AHEC).

2. The 16 divisons was Norrie's estimate. See Barr, *Pendulum of War*, 70.

3. Ibid., 71.

4. Auchinleck's Despatch, p.328, WO 32/10160, The National Archives of the UK. (TNA).

5. Pugsley, *A Bloody Road Home*, 286.

6. Mohamed Awad and Sahar Hamouda, "Alexandrians Tell Their Story: Oral Narratives of the War in North Africa 1940-43," in *El Alamein and the Struggle for North Africa: International Perspectives from the Twenty-first Century*, ed. Jill Edwards. (Cairo: The American University in Cairo Press, 2012), 223.

7. Barr, *Pendulum of War*, 69.

8. South Africans Crisis in the Desert, May-July 1942, CAB 44/20, TNA, 50.

9. War Diary, 6 New Zealand Infantry Brigade, 28 June 1942, WA II, I 1660, DA 58/1/21, ANZ.

10. War Diary, 6 New Zealand Infantry Brigade, 30 June 1942, WA II, I 1660, DA 58/1/21, ANZ.

11. Barr, *Pendulum of War*, 72.

12. Ibid., 74.

13. Eric Dorman O'Gowan, "Battle of First Alamein," in *History of the Second World War*. Vol. 3. No. 7, ed. Barrie Pitt. (London: Purnell & Sons and Imperial War Museum, 1967), 1068.

14. Dorman O'Gowan, "Battle of First Alamein," 1070.

15. Barr, *Pendulum of War*, 75.

16. Generallietnant Fritz Herman Bayerlein," German Experience in Desert Warfare During World War II. Supplement," FMS D739 Sup 1, AHEC, 52.

17. Toppe, "Desert Warfare," 14.

18. Hinsley, *British Intelligence in the Second World War: Volume 2*, 392.

19. War Diary, 6 New Zealand Infantry Brigade, 1 July 1942, WA II, I 1660, DA 58/1/22, ANZ.

20. Anon, *The Tiger Kills*. (Bombay: HMSO Government of India, 1944), 230.

21. Ibid., 231.

22. Ibid., 232.

23. Barr, *Pendulum of* War, 80.

24. War Diary, 90th light Division, 2 July 1942, WA II 11/23 German Army Documents on Operations in North Africa 1942-43, ANZ.

25. Bierman and Smith, *Alamein: War without Hate*, 136.

26. Holland, *Together We Stand*, 204.

27. Barr, *Pendulum of War*, 88.

28. Rommel, diary entry, 1 July 1942, in Liddell Hart, *The Rommel Papers*, 246.

29. Ibid., 248.

30. Ibid., 248.

31. Hinsley, *British Intelligence in the Second World War: Volume 2*, 395.

32. Barr, *Pendulum of War*, 91.

33. General Krause, "Rommel's abortive pushes against the Alamein line, 16/5/43," El Alamein Miscellaneous Papers, WO 106/2286, TNA.

34. Carrier, *War in History*, 505.

35. AIR 41/26, TNA, 34. Quoted in Hinsley, *British Intelligence in the Second World War: Volume 2*, 396.

36. 15 Panzer Division, 1230 hours, 3 July 1942, Afrika Korps Messages In, 25 June–2 August 1942, GMDS Files 22926/8 and 9, WA II 11/23 Afrika Korps Records, ANZ.

37. Rommel, diary entry, 3 July 1942, in Liddell Hart, *The Rommel Papers*, 249.

38. Rommel to Dearest Lu, 4 July 1942, in Liddell Hart, *The Rommel Papers*, 250-251.

39. Extracts Afrika Korps Medical Report March-August 1942, WA II 11/23 Afrika Korps Records, ANZ.

40. Weekly Intelligence Summary No.92. 9 July 1942, GHQ Middle East Forces, WA II 11/2 ANZ.

41. War Diary, 2/13 Australian Infantry Battalion, 20 Aust Inf Bde Gp OO No.16, 7 July 1942, Item 8/3/13, AWM 52, AWM.

42. Kippenberger, *Infantry Brigadier*, 139.

43. Barr, *Pendulum of War*, 69.

44. de Guingand, *Operation Victory*, 126.

45. Bierman and Smith, *Alamein without Hate*, 199.

46. Howard Kippenberger, letter to J.L. Scoullar, 29 March 1949, 181/32/1, Correspondence of Howard Kippenberger 1947-1955, WA II 11/2, ANZ.

47. Kippenberger, *Infantry Brigadier*, 139.

48. Hinsley, *British Intelligence in the Second World War: Volume 2*, 380.

49. South Africans Crisis in the Desert, May–July 1942, p. 56, CAB 44/20, TNA.

50. War Diary, 6 New Zealand Infantry Brigade, 3 July 1942, WA II, I 1660, DA 58/1/22, ANZ.

51. Barr, *Pendulum of War*, 104.

52. Rommel, diary entry, 9 July 1942, in Liddell Hart, *The Rommel Papers*, 252.

53. 9 Australian Division Operations in the El Alamein Area July 1942, Morshead Papers 3 DRL 2632, AWM.

54. Barr, *Pendulum of War*, 90.

55. Morshead, message to AUSFORCE (Blamey) 7 July 1942, 3 DRL 2632, AWM.

56. Rommel, diary entry, 9 July 1942, in Liddell Hart, *The Rommel Papers*, 252.

57. CX/MSS/1177/T23, 8 and 9 July 1942, HW 1/723, German Records, TNA.

58. Quoted in South Africans Crisis in the Desert, May-July 1942, CAB 44/20, TNA, 120.

59. Rommel, diary entry, 10 July 1942, in Liddell Hart, *The Rommel Papers*, 252.

60. Ibid.

61. 9 Australian Division Operations in the El Alamein Area July 1942, 3 DRL 2632, AWM.

62. Barr, *Pendulum of War*, 112.

63. Generalmajor Friederich von Mellenthin,. Supplement to "Reasons for Rommel's Successes in Africa 1941-42," D-084, Foreign Military Studies, AHEC, 4.

64. Behrendt, *Rommel's Intelligence in the Desert Campaign 1941-1943*, 168.

65. Ibid., 170.

66. Rommel, diary entry, 10 July 1942, in Liddell Hart, *The Rommel Papers*, 252-253.

67. Barr, *Pendulum of War*, 109.

68. 9 Australian Division Operations in the El Alamein Area July 1942, 3 DRL 2632, AWM.

69. Rommel, diary entry, 11 July 1942, in Liddell Hart, *The Rommel Papers*, 253.

70. War Diary, 2/48 Australian Infantry Battalion, 10 July 1942, 8/3/36, AWM 52, AWM.

71. Narrative of Operations, Miscellaneous Papers Item 13/2, 3 DRL 2632, AWM.

72. War Diary, 2/48 Australian Infantry Battalion, 6 July 1942, 8/3/36, AWM 52, AWM.

73. South Africans Crisis in the Desert, May-July 1942, CAB 44/20, TNA, 120.

74. Barr, *Pendulum of War*, 109.

75. Rommel, diary entry, 11 July 1942, in Liddell Hart, *The Rommel Papers*, 254.

76. Rommel to Dearest Lu, 14 July 1942, in Liddell Hart, *The Rommel Papers*, 255.

77. CX/MSS/1177/T28, 10 July 1942, HW 1/723, German Records, TNA.

78. CX/MSS/1177/T20, 9 July 1942, HW 1/723, German Records, TNA.

79. Barr, *Pendulum of War*, 117.

80. Dorman O'Gowan, "Battle of First Alamein," 1074.

81. Harper, *Kippenberger*, 161.

82. War Diary, 5 New Zealand Infantry Brigade, 15 July 1942, WA II, I 1652, DA 52/1/31, ANZ.

83. War Diary, 5 New Zealand Infantry Brigade, 16 July 1942, WA II, I 1652, DA 52/1/31, ANZ.

84. Dorman O'Gowan, "Battle of First Alamein," 1074.

85. Barr, *Pendulum of War*, 123.

86. Howard Kippenberger, annotation on Weir letter dated 14 April 1948, WA II 11/2, ANZ.

87. Inglis, quoted by Howard Kippenberger, letter to J.L. Scoullar, 2 July 1952, WA II 11/2, ANZ.

88. Brigadier C.E. Weir, letter to Kippenberger, 14 April 1948, WA 11/2, ANZ.

89. Gott, letter to Freyberg, 20 July 1942, WA II 8/24 Minqar Qa'im and Ruweisat Ridge, ANZ.

90. Howard Kippenberger, comment on an early draft of Scoullar's history, November 1953, WA II 11/2, ANZ.

91. 15 Panzer Division Intelligence Diary, 15 July 1942, GMDS File 24442/3, WA II 11/23 German Army Documents on Operations in North Africa 1942-43, ANZ.

92. Rommel to Dearest Lu, 17 July 1942, *The Rommel Papers*, 257.

93. Quoted in Dorman O'Gowan, "Battle of First Alamein," 1074.

94. CX/MSS/1201/T21, 15 July 1942, HW 1/723, German Records, TNA.

95. 9 Australian Division General Staff Branch War Diary, 17 July 1942, 1/5/20, AWM 52, AWM.

96. Quoted in Mark Johnston and Peter Stanley, *Alamein: The Australian Story*. (Melbourne: Oxford University Press, 2006), 85.

97. War Diary, 2/43 Australian Infantry Battalion, Operations, 17 July AWM 52, AWM.

98. Barr, *Pendulum of War*, 149.

99. Quoted in Johnston and Stanley, *Alamein: The Australian Story*, 94.

100. Barr, *Pendulum of War*, 155.

101. 9 Australian Division General Staff Branch War Diary, 22 July 1942, 1/5/20, AWM 52, AWM.

102. Johnston and Stanley, *Alamein: The Australian Story*, 95.

103. Bill Loffman, quoted in Thompson, *Forgotten Voices*, 164.

104. Report on Action—22 Jul 42, 2/23 Infantry Battalion War Diary, AWM 52, AWM.

105. Barr, *Pendulum of War*, 176.

106. Johnston and Stanley, *Alamein: The Australian Story*, 107.

107. 9 Australian Division Operations in the El Alamein Area July 1942, 3 DRL 2632, AWM.

108. 9 Australian Division General Staff Branch War Diary, 27 July 1942, 1/5/20, AWM 52, AWM.

109. War Diary, 2/28 Australian Infantry Battalion, 28-29 July 1942, Item 8/3/28, AWM 52, AWM.

110. Morshead, message to AUSFORCE (Blamey) 29 July 1942, 3 DRL 2632, AWM.

111. Barr, *Pendulum of War*, 180.

112. Harper, *Kippenberger*, 164.

113. George Clifton, diary entry, 23 July 1942, Personal Diary of Brigadier George Clifton, DSO, MC, WA II 11/9 Miscellaneous Papers, ANZ.

114. Inglis, letter to Freyberg, 27 July 1942, copies of Extracts from official papers of GOC 2NEF, Series 24 Minqar Qa'im and Ruweisat Ridge, WA II 11/2, ANZ.

115. J.L. Scoullar, *Battle for Egypt: The Summer of 1942*. (Wellington: War History Branch, 1955), 339.

116. Ibid., 360.

117. Geoffrey Giddings, "Oppa's War Years 1939-46," 93/4/1, IWM, 32.

118. Ibid.

119. Scoullar, *Battle for Egypt*, 360.

120. Scoullar, *Battle for Egypt,* 365. Rommel, diary entry, 22 July 1942, *The Rommel Papers*, 258.

121. 15 Panzer Division Intelligence Diary, 22 July 1942, GMDS File 24442/3, WA II 11/23 German Army Documents on Operations in North Africa 1942-43, ANZ.

122. Rommel, diary entry, 22 July 1942, in Liddell Hart, *The Rommel Papers*, 259.

123. Auchinleck's Special Order of the Day, 25 July 1942, messages to 9 Australian Division, Series 2, Item 2/7, 3 DRL 2632, AWM. The order is recorded in most of the Australian battalion and brigade war diaries.

124. Behrendt, *Rommel's Intelligence*, 163.

125. Colonel Siegfried Westphal, in Holmes, *The World at War*, 263.

126. Barr, *Pendulum of War*, xxxix.

127. Hinsley, *British Intelligence in the Second World War: Volume 2*, 399, 406.

128. CO's Report and Comments on Month, 2/23 Infantry Battalion War Diary, AWM 52, AWM.

129. War Diary, 2/48 Australian Infantry Battalion, "A brief account of 2/48 battalion's move from Syria to Egypt and of the fighting around TELL El EISA in July 42," 8/3/36, AWM 52, AWM.

130. Monthly Report July 1942, A.D.M.S. 9 Aust Div, 2/23 Infantry Battalion War Diary, AWM 52, AWM.

131. Howard Kippenberger, letter to J.L. Scoullar, 8 July 1949, WA II 11/2, ANZ.

132. George Clifton to Kippenberger, letter, 14 July 1949, WA II 11/2, ANZ.

133. de Guingand, *Operation Victory*, 125.

134. W.G. Stevens, Memorandum to Freyberg, 9 August 1942, General Papers 1942, WA II 8/26, ANZ.

135. Kippenberger, *Infantry Brigadier*, 180.

136. Douglas Wimberley, "A Scottish Soldier, Vol II," unpublished memoir, PP/MCR/182 Wimberley MSS 430, Imperial War Museum, (IWM), 30.

137. Lavinia Greacen, *Chink: A Biography*. (London: MacMillan London, 1998), 192.

138. J.A.I. Agar-Hamilton, letter to Kippenberger, 2 July 1951, WA II 11/2, ANZ.

139. Kippenberger, letter to Freyberg, 11 August 1955, WA II 11/2, ANZ.

140. Lawrence Durrell, in Holmes, *The World at War*, 260.

141. Freyberg, letter to Kippenberger, 5 November 1947, WA II 11/2, ANZ.

142. Barr, *Pendulum of War,*118.

143. Freyberg, letter to Kippenberger, 23 July 1951, WA II 11/2, ANZ.

144. J.A.I. Agar-Hamilton, letter to Kippenberger, 2 July 1951, WA II 11/2, ANZ.

145. Kippenberger, letter to J.L. Scoullar, 23 December 1953, WA II 11/2, ANZ.

146. Kippenberger, letter to J.L. Scoullar, 29 March 1949, WA II 11/2, ANZ.

147. Barr, *Pendulum of War*, 103.

148. Neillands, *The Desert Rats: 7th Armoured Division*, 146.

149. Ibid.

150. Fennell, "Steel my soldiers' hearts," 25.

151. Scoullar, *Battle for Egypt*, 387. Mark Johnston, *That Magnificent 9th: An Illustrated History of the 9th Australian Division*. (Sydney: Allen & Unwin, 2003), 86. Barr, *Pendulum of War*, 184.

152. Barr, *Pendulum of War*, 174.

153. Hinsley, *British Intelligence in the Second World War: Volume 2*, 406.

154. Fennell, "Steel my soldiers' hearts," 5.

155. Ibid., 8.

156. Jonathan Fennell, "Courage and Cowardice in the North African Campaign: The Eighth Army and Defeat in the Summer of 1942," in *War in History*, (Vol.20, Number 1, November 2013), 100. Auchinleck made this request to the British War Office on 7 April 1942.

157. Fennell, "Courage and Cowardice," 116.

158. Kippenberger, letter to Air Commodore J. Findlay, 9 November 1949, IA 77/35, WA II 11/2, ANZ.

THREE

"DRASTIC AND IMMEDIATE" CHANGES

Waging war in the Egyptian desert was never easy. But campaigning during the peak of summer—in July and August—was a torment for those who were forced to do it. The fierce sun beat down from a cloudless sky at a location where no natural shade was to be found. This was a land well-suited for war. There were no farms or crops to ruin, no cities or towns to pound to rubble. One British soldier poet expressed the landscape succinctly:

> This land was made for war. As glass
> Resists the bite of vitriol, so this hard
> And calcined earth rejects
> The battle's hot, corrosive impact. Here
> Is no nubile, girlish land, no green
> And virginal countryside for War
> To violate. This land is hard,
> Inviolable.[1]

Fighting in this hard land had its challenges. The lack of water was a serious problem. It had to be pumped in from distant locations and then carted on transport vehicles to the forward positions. There was never enough of the precious liquid. Eighth Army's water came via a pipeline from Alexandria to various distribution points. From there, they were taken forward by water trucks. The ration for soldiers in the Eighth Army was usually a one-liter bottle a day. It tasted flat and had been chemically treated. This small ration had to be used for all purposes: "half a mugful for a wash and shave and the rest for drinking."[2] The Germans and Italians took most of their water from old wells and cisterns along the coast. Much of the water was brackish, polluted with oil, and had also been chemically treated. It tasted foul. However, the Germans also shipped quantities of salty or brackish water, with an issue of salt water soap, to be used only for washing.[3]

The fierce sun and lack of good water were hard enough to endure, but there were other torments, too. Constant vehicle traffic had ground the surface into a fine, powdery dust. The slightest breeze distributed this dust everywhere so that "all food and drink contained some dust."[4] The dust clung to weapons which, as a result, had to be cleaned several times a day. Swarms of flies added to the anguish, as did the fact that the slightest scratch could turn into a suppurating desert sore. Sometimes as large as a slice of lemon, these sores took weeks and sometimes months to heal and they left a scar lasting more than a year.[5]

Enduring these conditions, the men of British Eighth Army and the German-Italian Panzerarmee Afrika faced one another across the ill-defined no-man's-land of the Alamein position. Neither army was capable of renewing the offensive at the end of July 1942. The soldiers of Panzerarmee Afrika had a distinct advantage, though. They still maintained faith in the higher leadership of their army. In Eighth Army, this faith had been steadily eroded from mid-July on. As the New Zealand official history noted:

> It could be said with some justice for a time Eighth Army had ceased to be an army, so that plans of army action made by the commander, General Ritchie, and later by General Auchinleck, had little value. Even corps' control was uncertain, as the stories of Matruh and Minqar Qaim make evident. It was hardly an army, but rather individual units and formations acting with little concert, that finally, at El Alamein, stopped an enemy exhausted by victory.[6]

As identified in chapters one and two, Auchinleck had failed to grip Eighth Army sufficiently and he lacked the leadership skill required of a senior field commander. But he was intelligent and well aware that his army had significant problems. In late July, he made an attempt to address the most pressing of these: his disobedient corps commanders and the failure of the armored formations to be where they were most needed. "Indiscipline at the top" was "a recurrent theme" in Eighth Army's recent defeats. Auchinleck's orders "were received, doubted, questioned, discussed" and seldom acted upon with alacrity.[7] The soldier/historian David Fraser believed that an overriding cause of Eighth

Army's defeat in the Gazala battle "lay in the leisurely and questioning way in which orders were treated."[8] On July 28, Auchinleck called in his two corps commanders, Gott and Ramsden, to discuss his plans for going on the defensive in the short term with the hope of renewing the offensive sometime in September. Two days later, he held another conference with them, which set out their main tasks for the weeks ahead. Then Auchinleck turned to address the problem of his unreliable, disobedient armored formations.

On July 29, Auchinleck had a meeting with Major General Richard McCreery, his senior armored advisor, and Major General John Harding, the Director of Military Training. Both men had flown in from Cairo at Auchinleck's request. At the meeting, Auchinleck outlined a radical plan to change the organization of the armored formations in Eighth Army. With the gulf between armor and infantry seemingly "unbridgeable," Auchinleck, on the advice of Dorman-Smith, now believed that the best solution was to "abolish the distinction" and combine the two.[9] That is, every division in Eighth Army would have its own armored and infantry formations. This would usually be one armored and two infantry brigades but the mix could vary according to the allocated mission. It was a radical proposal and McCreery was horrified by it. The meeting was stormy, with a tired and irritated Auchinleck informing McCreery that if he "would not obey orders he could consider himself relieved of his appointment."[10] There was considerable merit in Auchinleck's proposal, but substantial naivety, too. Barr notes, "Auchinleck did not realise the depth of feeling that his proposal engendered amongst the officers of Eighth Army."[11] It also caused consternation amongst senior officers in the United Kingdom. This inventive approach to a serious shortcoming in Eighth Army shows that not only was Auchinleck well aware of the problem, but he was prepared to take radical steps to solve it. In the end, only one division in Eighth Army adopted this proposal. Lieutenant General Freyberg, sickened by what had occurred at Ruweisat Ridge and El Mreir, concluded that he needed an armored brigade operating under his command. One of the New Zealand infantry brigades would be converted to an armored formation. If offensive operations were necessary during the conversion process, as occurred during the October Alamein battle, Freyberg insisted on having a British armored brigade under his direct command and integrated within the 2nd New Zealand Division. This structure made a considerable difference to the Division's strike power.

At the end of July and in the first few days of August, three military Appreciations were written by senior officers of Eighth Army. All three were used to develop a blueprint for Eighth Army's defensive positioning in August and outlined plans to counter Rommel's next offensive, which was expected to happen later that month. The first, prepared by Brigadier "Chink" Dorman-Smith on July 27, was the most important of these. Often blamed unfairly for many of the problems afflicting Eighth Army at this time, Dorman-Smith's Appreciation was to be the most influential of the three. In fact, due to its clarity of thought and the logical framework it contained, it was used as a model appreciation at the British Command and Staff College for many years after the war. Determined to prevent more failures like the attacks at Ruweisat and Ruin Ridge, Dorman-Smith's Appreciation "led to three main conclusions."[12] The first was that Eighth Army was in no fit state to carry out further offensive operations. The reason for this was clear:

> None of the formations in Eighth Army is now sufficiently well-trained for offensive operations. The Army badly needs either a reinforcement of well-trained formations or a quiet period in which to train. [13]

Eighth Army therefore needed to "adopt the tactical defensive until we are strong enough to attack." This could not be until "mid-September at the earliest."[14] Rommel, however, could not afford to wait that long, and was likely to attack in the southern sector around mid- to late August. Rommel would "certainly try to attack before the end of August," avoiding the strong defensive positions to "seek success in manoeuvre." Eighth Army should encourage Rommel to "strike prematurely" but rely on its defensive strengths to counter this.[15] Finally, Eighth Army needed to build up its strength, train its troops hard, and prepare to launch its own offensive in the northern sector but not before "the latter part of September."[16]

At first, Auchinleck dismissed Dorman-Smith's Appreciation as being "insufficiently aggressive." Dorman-Smith then challenged his general to read it again and list the military mistakes made in it. Auchinleck could find none and had to reluctantly accept its logic. On the evening of July 30, Whitehall was informed that Eighth Army was going on the defensive while it built up and trained for an offensive later in the year. This message probably sealed Auchinleck's fate as commander in the Middle East.

But on August 1, Auchinleck produced his own Appreciation, which was much more offensively minded than Dorman-Smith's earlier one. Accepting that Eighth Army could not mount a large-scale offensive until at least mid-September, there were ways it could carry the fight to the enemy and maintain the initiative. The Object spelled out in Auchinleck's Appreciation made this clear:

> OBJECT
> While Eighth Army is on the defensive, to cause the greatest possible loss to the enemy and to disturb his plans.[17]

Auchinleck envisioned this pressure being applied to Panzerarmee Afrika through a series of raids mounted by mobile elements of Eighth Army, but also using the Long Range Desert Group, the Royal Navy, and the Desert Air Force. As Auchinleck made clear:

> Our policy should be to harass the enemy by all possible means (moral as well as physical), so as to keep him stretched and impede his preparation for attack. All this while keeping ourselves concentrated.[18]

This Appreciation has often been ignored by military historians. It is important, though, as it shows that Auchinleck, while obviously tired, had not lost the offensive spirit. Barr wrote:

> Even taken in isolation, this appreciation proves that Auchinleck and the senior commanders of Eighth Army were certainly not "looking over their shoulder" to consider further retreat but instead were planning to cause as much damage and disruption to the Panzerarmee Afrika as possible.[19]

The commander of 13 Corps, Lieutenant General Strafer Gott, also produced an Appreciation on August 1. Drafted by Gott's two talented principal staff officers, Brigadier "Bobby" Erskine and Major Freddy de Butts, Gott's Appreciation predicted the likely shape of Rommel's next offensive and how it could be countered. The Alam el Halfa Ridge was the key:

> ALAM EL HALFA and GEBEL BEIN GABIR point like fingers to SW and provide all the observation and the good going to the coast road. These features

and particularly ALAM EL HALFA are vital for any advance down the Coast to
Alexandria—they are also vital to us for holding our present positions.[20]

Gott's Appreciation predicted that Rommel would attempt to capture
the Alam el Halfa Ridge before cutting the coast road and driving for
Alexandria. Gott, who knew the terrain better than any other serving
British officer, was certain that this would be Rommel's only viable
course of action:

> There are many possible variations in the details of such a plan but it is the only
> one which he could carry out with his present shortage of infantry if he is mak-
> ing ALEXANDRIA his objective.[21]

Barr has called Gott's Appreciation "a vital document" that "predicted almost exactly" the scale, scope, and objective of Rommel's
next attack in late August 1942. Barr concluded that "Gott and his
staff, rather than Dorman-Smith or Auchinleck—or any other British
commander—should be given the full credit for this."[22] This is certainly
true, but all three documents were important. Dorman-Smith's Appreciation prevented any more half-baked attacks that squandered precious
trained infantry and convinced Auchinleck that a defensive posture best
suited Eighth Army in August 1942. Auchinleck's document showed
how a defensive posture could still keep the enemy off-balance and re-
tain some semblance of initiative. Gott's Appreciation accurately predicted Rommel's next attack and how best to counter it. All three, and
another Appreciation prepared by Auchinleck on August 2, provided a
solid foundation for Eighth Army's future success. Despite what Montgomery would write about developing a "master plan" for the next two
battles of El Alamein, these "actually originated with Auchinleck and his
corps commanders."[23] Some of Auchinleck's senior staff officers deserve
a share of the credit too.

To counter Rommel's next attack, Eighth Army altered its positions
in the southern sector. In the north, the positions remained unchanged,
with the 9th Australian Division holding the coastal section including
the El Alamein railway station and the newly won sector of Tel el Eisa. To
their south, the 1st South African Division occupied the El Alamein Box,
while the 5th Indian Division held Ruweisat Ridge. These three infantry
divisions made up 30 Corps under the command of Lieutenant General

W.H. Ramsden. To the south of Ruweisat Ridge, the 2nd New Zealand Division began the construction of the New Zealand Box. The western edge of this box covered the five miles from Ruweisat to the Alam Nayil feature and it constituted the southern end of the Alamein position.[24] To the south of the New Zealand Box, the armored cars and mobile gun-columns of the 7th Armoured Division patrolled the broken desert as far as the impassable Qattara Depression. The New Zealanders and 7th Armoured formed 13 Corps under Lieutenant General Gott. Close behind the center of the line, where it could assist either corps, was the bulk of the British armored formations. These were being reorganized by Auchinleck and classified according to the types of tank available. The 22nd Armoured Brigade, with all of the Grant and some Crusader tanks, was the "heavy" formation. The Valentine tanks were placed in 23 Armoured Brigade, while 4 Light Armoured Brigade was equipped with all the Stuart (Honey) tanks and the leftover Crusaders. Some 300 Sherman tanks were on their way, but would not arrive before the end of August.

Facing Eighth Army across the no man's land of El Alamein was the Panzerarmee Afrika under the command of the now Field Marshal Erwin Rommel. It consisted of one German and three Italian corps. Down to just 150 German and fifty Italian tanks at the beginning of August, Rommel interspersed his German units amongst the Italian formations while holding the static position around El Alamein. The strike power of his Panzerarmee always remained the Afrika Korps consisting of 15 and 21 Panzer Divisions and the 90th Light Division. In August, Rommel received some much-needed reinforcements. These included the remainder of 164 Light Division, which had been arriving by air since June, the Ramcke Parachute Brigade and the Italian Folgore Parachute Division. As Rommel built up his strength for another attempt to break through to Cairo, the Army that blocked his way was going through a clean sweep of its senior commanders.

* * *

On August 3, Winston Churchill and the Chief of the Imperial General Staff (CIGS), General Sir Alan Brooke, arrived in Cairo clearly determined to "fix" the problems in Britain's only active field army. Brooke had been appointed CIGS only in December 1941. So far he had little pleasure in the job. Described as hardworking, perceptive, strong, "utterly professional" and ruthless, Brooke knew that Eighth Army had serious problems and that these began the top.[25] Auchinleck and other senior officers were anxious about the visit as indeed they should have been. After a year in command under Auchinleck, Eighth Army "had suffered over 100,000, mostly Commonwealth casualties—100 per cent of its original strength."[26] There was little to show for these heavy casualties: a string of defeats, two sacked army commanders, and an army that had lost its confidence after finally halting Rommel on the Alamein position. As the New Zealand official history colorfully described the visit, it was known Churchill had "brought a supply of bowler hats" and was here to decide "on their allocation."[27] On learning of the pending visit on July 31, "Chink" Dorman-Smith wrote to his mistress in Cairo that: "I feel the Auk's time is numbered."[28] It was an astute assessment.

Even before arriving in Egypt, Churchill had reached the staggering conclusion that Strafer Gott was the man to command Eighth Army. This decision ran counter to that of Brooke, who wanted someone more energetic "to instil a new spirit of self-confidence in the Eighth Army." For Brooke, that person had to be Bernard Montgomery, who was "bounding with self-confidence." Brooke reflected after the war that "It is interesting to note that Winston was already selecting Gott without having seen him."[29] Churchill's explanation for selecting Gott demonstrated some sensitivity, but it reflected how little he knew of the mood of Eighth Army. Churchill felt that if a clean sweep of the higher commanders was imposed, it might be taken as a slur on the reputation and performance of the entire army. What he needed was a fighting commander who commanded loyalty and respect: "Here General Gott seemed in every way to meet the need."[30]

So, Eighth Army was to have a new commander in Strafer Gott. Auchinleck's fate as commander in the Middle East now hung in the balance. It was essential to his survival that he created a good impression when he briefed Churchill on the state of Eighth Army and his future plans. That meeting took place on August 5, and for Auchinleck, it went very badly. Churchill was hostile from the beginning and the atmosphere during the briefing by Auchinleck and Dorman-Smith degenerated to what the latter described as an "icy chill." Churchill insisted on an August or early September offensive, which both Auchinleck and Dorman-Smith "were compelled to resist." Churchill's displeasure was "obvious."[31] Churchill stormed out after the meeting to stand alone in the desert, deep in thought. Barr has written, "Auchinleck and Dorman-Smith's fates were sealed by this disastrous briefing."[32]

The decision was made. Churchill informed the Deputy Prime Minister and Cabinet on August 6 that, "after prolonged consultations . . . I have come to the conclusion that a drastic and immediate change is needed in the High Command."[33] This started at the very top. Auchinleck, who was never part of the "prolonged consultations," was to go although he was offered a smaller, inactive command, which he refused. To add further to his humiliation, neither Churchill nor Brooke informed Auchinleck that he was being relieved of command. Instead Churchill's military secretary, Colonel Ian Jacob, was sent with a letter from Churchill informing him of the decision and demanding a reply whether he would accept the new command being offered. Jacob, carrying the fatal letter, felt "as if I were just going to murder an unsuspecting friend." Jacob was deeply impressed with the calm manner with which Auchinleck received the news that ended his military career as a field commander. For Jacob, Auchinleck remained "a great man and fighter."[34] But both Churchill and Brooke had lost faith in Auchinleck, and the New Zealand official history records that "there is no record of a single voice being raised on [Auchinleck's] behalf."[35] Brooke, for whom August 6 had been "one of the most difficult days of my life with momentous decisions to take," never forgave Auchinleck for refusing the lesser Iraq-Persia command, either, as a new commander for the position still needed to be found.[36] He wrote in his diary on learning that Auchinleck had refused it: "I am not certain that we are not better off without him." After the war, Brooke reflected that:

> I still think he was wrong not to accept the Iraq-Persian Command. . . . it was a vital strategic point at that time. It would also have been a more "soldierly" act to accept what he was offered in war, instead of behaving like an offended film star.[37]

In early 1943, when Wavell wanted to appoint Auchinleck to an Army command in Burma, Churchill vetoed the appointment. His explanation was a damning indictment: "As a result of our conference with

General Montgomery and the reports received from him on the state of the Eighth Army, C.I.G.S. and I have both lost confidence in General Auchinleck as a military commander in the field."[38] Auchinleck's replacement as the Middle East theater commander was General Harold Alexander, who had recently impressed Churchill with his "magnificent conduct" in the ill-fated Burma campaign.[39] On August 10, Churchill handed Alexander a hand-written, two paragraph directive. The first paragraph was "considered paramount in His Majesty's interests." It was clear in what Alexander was expected to do:

> Your prime and main duty will be to take or destroy at the earliest opportunity the German-Italian Army commanded by Field-Marshal Rommel together with all its supplies and establishments in Egypt and Libya.[40]

* * *

Auchinleck was not the only casualty of the Churchill/Brooke visit in early August 1942. Also relieved of their appointments and leaving Egypt were the Chief of General Staff Middle East, Lieutenant General Thomas Corbett; 30 Corps commander Lieutenant General W.H.C. Ramsden; and Deputy CGS, Major General Eric Dorman-Smith. The changes were "drastic and immediate," but it was not quite a "clean sweep." The old desert warrior Strafer Gott had been appointed as the new commander of Eighth Army.

As stated above, Churchill had decided on appointing Gott to the command of Eighth Army prior to actually meeting him. It was not an appointment the CIGS Brooke endorsed and he warned Churchill that Gott was "very tired and needed a rest."[41] Meeting Gott in theater did nothing to change Brooke's view. Indeed, it was reinforced when Gott admitted to Brooke in a private interview on August 5 that he was out of ideas on how to defeat the Germans and, as a result, he lacked self-confidence. Brooke wrote that this meeting "confirmed my opinion that [Gott] was probably not the man to lead the 8th Army in an offensive to turn the tide of the war."[42] Yet Churchill, who shared a car ride with Gott that afternoon, had come to the opposite conclusion. Churchill was impressed with Gott's calm manner, magnetic personality, and above all, "his calm blue eyes."[43] The announcement that Gott was to be the new commander of Eighth Army was made the next day.

Churchill's choice of Army commander was impetuous and wrong. It caused considerable consternation in many parts of Eighth Army. That the man whom many held responsible for the debacles of the Gazala stakes, Mersa Matruh, Deir el Shein, Minqar Qaim, Ruweisat Ridge, El Mreir, and more should now be the Army commander seemed like a bad joke. One of the New Zealand official histories was frank in its assessment that Gott's appointment "may seem astonishing in the light of his record."[44] The South African historian J.A.I. Agar-Hamilton was scathing in his assessment of this appointment:

> Gott was impossible.... It has not been unknown for a commander to pass from disaster to disaster, but it is quite without precedent for any commander to pass from promotion to promotion as a reward for a succession of disasters.[45]

But Strafer Gott never assumed command of Eighth Army. One day after the announcement of his promotion to Army commander, Gott was killed when his transport plane was shot down. He was on his way to Cairo to celebrate his new appointment and the air space was considered relatively benign. However, two German Me 109 fighters had been forced down to ground level after a dogfight with British fighters when they spotted the lumbering Bombay transport plane. Rapid bursts of cannon fire damaged the plane, wounded the pilots, and forced a crash landing. Gott and fifteen other passengers died when the crippled Bombay suddenly burst into flames.[46] The New Zealand brigadier Howard Kippenberger reached the crash site just an hour later. He was haunted by what he saw. "There were," he recalled, "about 14 burnt bodies lying around."[47]

Despite the horrific nature of his death, some in Eighth Army regarded the event as fortunate. Freyberg wrote to Inglis soon after that while Gott's death had been tragic and that Gott himself had "great personal qualities," nevertheless "the change of regime here has been drastic and I think necessary."[48] The South African general Dan Pienaar is alleged to have said, on learning of Gott's death: "Now I know that Heaven is on the side of the British."[49] Ironically, General Pienaar would also be killed in an air crash traveling back to South Africa in December 1942. But even someone as sensitive as the CIGS, Alan Brooke, could see divine intervention in Gott's fate. Brooke later wrote:

> It seemed almost like the hand of God suddenly appearing to set matters right where we had gone wrong. Looking back on those days with the knowledge of

what occurred at Alamein and after it I am convinced that the whole course of
the war might well have been altered if Gott had been in command of the 8th
Army.[50]

There is little doubt that Gott as Eighth Army commander would surely
have been a disaster leading it to even more defeats. As Bierman and
Smith aptly surmised, "The scene was surely now set for another disastrous failure of British leadership in the Western Desert."[51] With Gott's
demise, the path had been cleared for Brooke's preferred candidate for
the job: Lieutenant General Bernard Law Montgomery.

*   *   *

Montgomery's positive impact on Eighth Army was immediate. But at
first Montgomery's appointment as commander of the Eighth Army
caused considerable trepidation, especially amongst some senior British
officers. He was not regarded as a "good chap" or one of "the team." In
fact, his biographer described Montgomery during the interwar period
as "the most unpopular general in the British army."[52] Freyberg wrote
to Kippenberger of this: "he was very unpopular and was criticised by
British officers for no reason other than they said he was not a 'good fellow.'" This, however, gave Freyberg "a certain feeling of confidence."[53]
Kippenberger recalled the news of Montgomery's appointment:

> No New Zealanders had heard of him and our English friends were unenthu-
> siastic. One English Brigadier told me he was understood to be mad and, more
> cheerfully, that he would certainly get rid of some of the dead wood.[54]

The "mad" new commander assumed command two days ahead
of time and visited Freyberg and other commanders on that day. He
arrived at Kippenberger's headquarters unannounced, spoke "sharply
and curtly, without any soft words, asked some searching questions, met
the battalion commanders and left me feeling very much stimulated."[55]

Freyberg had also found the new commander stimulating. Upon
their first meeting Freyberg outlined to Montgomery the independence
permitted by his charter and stressed his determination to keep the 2nd
New Zealand Division together and not be part of the British "mania
for breaking up military organisations."[56] Freyberg also informed Montgomery that he had now witnessed the demise of two full generals, eleven

lieutenant generals, and numerous major generals all because they had put their trust in Jock columns, Brigade Groups, and the Crusader tank.[57] To his pleasant surprise, Montgomery was in complete agreement and Freyberg never had to refer to his charter for the rest of the North African campaign. A very relieved Freyberg cabled to the New Zealand Government:

> It makes position here much easier as for two-and-a-half years I have striven to prevent New Zealand Division being divided into Brigade Groups, being convinced that by fighting as a Division maximum power is developed.[58]

The era of the brigade group or "cowpat" battle was over.

One of Montgomery's immediate actions was to send the troop carrying vehicles seventy miles to the rear of the Alamein position to stress that there was to be no withdrawal from where the army now stood. Freyberg passed on Montgomery's message to the New Zealand senior officers and informed them of a "completely new outlook. . . . This looking over your shoulder and cranking up to get back to the position in the rear is to cease." There was also to be a change in terminology. "Consolidating," which was army speak for "sitting down and doing nothing" was to be replaced with "reorganisation." From now on, the term "Box" was "something with a lid on it," not a defended position. Finally, regarding "Battle Group": "We do not want to hear this word again. We are a Division fighting as a Division."[59] It was a refreshing change and one that had a huge impact on Eighth Army. "We were delighted," recalled Kippenberger, "and the morale of the whole Army went up incredibly."[60]

Equally delighted were the Australians, whom Montgomery visited on August 14. There at the 9 Australian Division's Headquarters, he informed them of "three principal points." These were that Eighth Army would cease "looking over the shoulder" and would "stand and fight in its present position." Next the "formation of battle groups was to cease." Lastly, although the Australians looked "brown and fit," this was deceptive. They, like every other unit in the Eighth Army, "required toughening and hardening and units required training." Every opportunity was to be taken to "harden the men and to raise the standard of training in units." The Australians recorded how Montgomery's message was received:

The effect of the new policy was quickly apparent. General relief and satisfaction were felt when it became known that the enemy was to be met and fought in the prepared positions then held. Confidence and morale increased rapidly. From the first day of its arrival in the desert, the breaking up of the division and its formation into battle groups with inadequate fire resources and lacking the advantage of the normal system of command and control had been strenuously and continuously opposed. For these reasons the new policy was most welcome.[61]

It was not only the Dominion formations that experienced and welcomed Montgomery's changes. The newly appointed army chief of staff, Freddie de Guingand, while a great admirer of Auchinleck, admitted that Eighth Army in July 1942 was "craving guidance and inspiration. There was no stability of outlook, and no great confidence in the outcome of a fresh encounter."[62] Montgomery's arrival provided this missing guidance, confidence, and inspiration. And it happened almost immediately. De Guingand recalled that Montgomery's first address to his senior staff officers was "electric—it was terrific." That night, he recalled that all who heard the address slept "with a new hope in our hearts and a great confidence in the future of our Army."[63] De Guingand had been pleased too that Montgomery had ended his talk by stating he would permit no "bellyaching." To de Guingand, this "grand word . . . so aptly describes the type of in-discipline that prevailed amongst commanders in the Army at this time." Montgomery made this cease, and those who persisted with it soon paid the price.[64]

Montgomery's speech had not started well. He was thirty minutes late after his escort officer had accidently led him into a minefield. It took some time to extract themselves. Then Montgomery, small, slight, pale skin and speaking in a high-pitched voice, certainly lacked Auchinleck's commanding presence. But his words made a lasting impression. Indeed, it has become one of the most famous speeches in British military history:

> Here we will stand and fight; there will be no further withdrawal. I have ordered that all plans and instructions dealing with further withdrawal are to be burnt, and at once. We will stand and fight here. If we can't stay here alive, then let us stay here dead . . . Now I understand that Rommel is expected to attack at any moment. Excellent. Let him attack. I would sooner it didn't come for a week, just give me time to sort things out. If we have two weeks to prepare we will be sitting pretty; Rommel can attack as soon as he likes after that and I hope he does . . . Meanwhile, we ourselves will start to plan a great offensive; it will be the beginning of a campaign which will hit Rommel for six right out of Africa . . . He is definitely a nuisance. Therefore we will hit him a crack and finish with him.[65]

Geoffrey Giddings, who had witnessed the heartbreaking destruction of a newly arrived armored brigade in the July battle, noted that "Monty" brought "a sense of purpose and organisation" to an otherwise demoralized Eighth Army.[66] Captain Charles Kennedy Craufurd-Stuart, serving in the 1st King George V's Own Gurkha Rifles, welcomed Monty's "ruthless and magnetic personality."[67] In mid-August, Winston Churchill was back in Egypt on a return journey from the Soviet Union. He was "so uplifted" by the changes he witnessed, he could not sleep. Meeting with as many soldiers as possible, Churchill sensed "the reviving ardour of the Army." He cabled to his War Cabinet on August 21 that "a complete change of atmosphere has taken place." No longer was Eighth Army "oppressed by a sense of bafflement and uncertainty" or "heading for disaster." Churchill concluded his report with a ringing endorsement of the Army's leadership: "I am satisfied that we have lively, confident, resolute men in command, working together as an admirable team under leaders of the highest military quality."[68]

Montgomery had taken little time to outwardly transform a defeated and bewildered army. Touring around the front line in mid-August, General Alexander "paid particular attention to the morale and bearing of the troops." He concurred with Churchill's assessment that Eighth Army had been "brave but baffled" before Montgomery's arrival.[69] In just over two weeks, after taking command, Montgomery's Eighth Army would be put to the test of battle. It remained to be seen whether Montgomery's impact had been deep enough to shake Eighth Army out of its sense of inferiority and befuddlement.

NOTES

1. Jocelyn Brooke, RAMC, "Landscape Near Tobruk," in *Poems of the Second World War: The Oasis Selection*, ed. Victor Selwyn. (London: J.M. Dent & Sons Ltd, 1985), 59. Only the first seven lines have been quoted. These were read by Sir Lawrence Olivier to introduce Episode 8 of the television documentary series *The World at War*.

2. Scoullar, *Battle for Egypt*, 371.

3. Ronald Walker, *Official History of New Zealand in the Second World War: Alam Halfa and Alamein.* (Wellington: Historical Publications Branch, Department of Internal Affairs, 1967), 4.

4. Scoullar, *Battle for Egypt*, 372.

5. Peter Llewellyn, *Journey towards Christmas: Official history of the 1st Ammunition Company Second New Zealand Expeditionary Force, 1939–45* (Wellington: Historical Publications Branch, Department of Internal Affairs, 1949), 249.

6. Walker, *Alam Halfa and Alamein*, 5.

7. Fraser, *And We Shall Shock Them*, 225.

8. Fraser, *Knights' Cross*, 333.

9. Barr, *Pendulum of War*, 187.

10. Quoted in Barr, *Pendulum of War*, 187.

11. Ibid., 187.

12. Greacen, *Chink*, 227.

13. Appreciation of the Situation in the Western Desert, 27 July 1942, in Greacen, *Chink*, 363.

14. Ibid., 366–367.

15. Ibid., 367–368.

16. Ibid., 370.

17. Appreciation by C in C. in C, M.E. at Eighth Army at 0800 1st August 1942, WO 201/556, TNA.

18. Ibid.

19. Barr, *Pendulum of War*, 188.

20. Appreciation by Comd 13 Corps, 1 August 1942, WO 201/556, TNA.

21. Appreciation, 1 August 1942, WO 201/556, TNA.

22. Barr, *Pendulum of War*, 188–189.

23. Ibid., 192.

24. Walker, *Alam Halfa and Alamein*, 8.

25. Fraser, *And We Shall Shock Them*, 84.

26. Nigel Hamilton, *The Full Monty: Montgomery of Alamein 1887–1942*. (London: Allen Lane, 2001), 477.

27. Walker, *Alam Halfa and Alamein*, 25. The bowler hat, an expression of speech, signified an immediate transition from soldier to civilian. That is, the soldier was sacked.

28. Quoted in Greacen, *Chink*, 229.

29. Alex Danchev and Daniel Todman (eds.), *War Diaries 1939–1945: Field Marshal Lord Alanbrooke*. (London: Weidenfeld & Nicolson, 2001), 290.

30. Churchill, *The Second World War Volume IV*, 413.

31. Eric Dorman O'Gowan, "Alamein: the Aftermath," in *History of the Second World War*. Vol. 3. No. 7., ed. Barrie Pitt. (London: Purnell & Sons and Imperial War Museum), 1080.

32. Barr, *Pendulum of War*, 201.

33. Churchill to Deputy Prime Minister, 6 August 1942, quoted in Churchill, *Vol. IV*, 415–416.

34. Sir Ian Jacob, diary entry, 8 August 1942, quoted in Arthur Bryant, *The Turn of the Tide: A Study based on the Diaries and Autobiographical Notes of Field Marshal the Viscount Alanbrooke*. (London: The Reprint Society, 1958), 374.

35. Walker, *Alam Halfa and Alamein*, 25.

36. Bryant, *The Turn of the Tide*, 369.

37. Danchev and Todman, *War Diaries 1939–1945*, 296.

38. Churchill, Secret Signal to Secretary of State for India, M102/3, 2 March 1943, PREM 3/1837, TNA.

39. Churchill, *Vol. IV*, 413.

40. North, *The Alexander Memoirs*, 10.

41. Churchill, *Vol. IV*, 413.

42. Danchev and Todman, *War Diaries 1939–1945*, 292.

43. Churchill, *Vol. IV*, 414.

44. Scoullar, *Battle for Egypt*, 380.

45. J.A.I. Agar-Hamilton, letter to Howard Kippenberger, 19 April 1949, WAII 11/2, ANZ.

46. Barr, *Pendulum of War*, 203.

47. "Death of Gott," Kippenberger's Personal Wartime Reminiscences, Private Collection of W.A. Glue, Stoke, Nelson (Glue Papers).

48. Freyberg, letter to Inglis, 21 August 1942, WA II 8/Part V GOC Personal Private Correspondence, ANZ.

49. J.A.I. Agar-Hamilton, letter to Howard Kippenberger, 19 April 1949, WAII 11/2, ANZ.

50. Notes to diary entry 2 August 1942, in Danchev and Todman, *War Diaries 1939–1945*, 295.

51. Bierman and Smith, *Alamein: War without Hate*, 218.

52. Hamilton, *The Full Monty*, 126.

53. Freyberg, letter to Kippenberger, 5 November 1947, WAII 11/2, ANZ.

54. Kippenberger, Draft of *New Zealand Listener* Article, July 1947, Glue Papers.

55. Kippenberger, *Infantry Brigadier*, 196.

56. Freyberg to War History Branch, 5 November 1957, quoted in Walker, *Alam Halfa and Alamein*, 230.

57. Freyberg, letter to Kippenberger, 5 November 1947, WAII 11/2, ANZ.

58. Freyberg to Fraser, cipher message, p.130, 3 October 1942, GOC's Papers "Lightfoot" and "Supercharge," WAII 8/25A, ANZ.

59. Freyberg, notes of GOC's address to CO's, 16 August 1942, WAII 11/2, ANZ.

60. Kippenberger, *Infantry Brigadier*, 196.

61. 9 Australian Division, Report on Operations, WO 201/2826, TNA.

62. de Guingand, *Operation Victory*, 133.

63. Ibid., 136–137.

64. Ibid., 138.

65. Western Desert Copy of address to officer of Headquarters 8th Army by General B.L. Montgomery on taking over command, 13 August 1942, Cabinet Office Historical Section 106/703, TNA.

66. Geoffrey Giddings, "Oppa's War Years 1939–46," 93/4/1, IWM, 34.

67. Charles Kennedy-Craufurd-Stuart, "Return to Ardmillan," ARMY 042 John I. Kennedy Craufurd-Stuart, Liddle Collection, Brotherton Library, University of Leeds (Liddle Collection).

68. Churchill, *Vol. IV*, 464, 465, 467.

69. Alexander's Despatch, Supplement to *The London Gazette*, 5 February 1948, CAB 106/613, TNA. See also Churchill, *Vol. IV*, 415. Churchill used the term "bewildered."

FOUR

ALAM HALFA: ROMMEL'S
LAST ATTEMPT

On August 30, a cacophony of engine noise broke the silence of the desert night. It came from the massed vehicles of the Panzerarmee Afrika, which included more than 500 tanks. At 10:00 p.m., in bright moonlight, the lead tanks surged eastward to begin what was hoped would be the complete encirclement of the Eighth Army positions around Alamein. In the early morning of August 31, the word "Twelvebore" was flashed around to the formations of Eighth Army indicating an attack was imminent. "The expected big party was on!" a New Zealand War Diary recorded.[1] Rommel's last German-Italian offensive in Egypt was underway and it soon ran into problems even he could not resolve.

Surprisingly, for someone with such a strong belief in his own destiny, Rommel was not confident of success. There were several reasons for this. First, he was as exhausted as his men, and he was also ill. A signal sent to Berlin by Rommel's Chief of Staff and his principal medical advisor wrote:

> Field Marshal Rommel suffering from chronic stomach and intestinal catarrh, nasal diphtheria and considerable circulation trouble. He is not in a fit condition to command the forthcoming offensive.[2]

He had become so sick that, prior to renewing the offensive, Rommel requested that the only commander he thought up to the task, General Heinz Guderian, should be sent out to command it. When Rommel received the short reply from Berlin that "Guderian unacceptable," Rommel felt compelled to remain and see it through.[3]

Then Rommel had recently lost his best sources of intelligence. No longer was he in receipt of the "little Fellers" from Cairo, nor had he

been able to replace his wireless intercept unit, which had been captured by the Australians on Tel el Eisa. This left him blind as to his enemy's strengths and plans. Most seriously of all though, Rommel was
well aware of the perilous logistical situation his army faced, especially
its inadequate reserves of fuel. As Christopher Pugsley has written, the
battle of Alam Halfa, the designation assigned to this six-day offensive,
was "a desperate gamble conducted on a logistical shoestring with fuel
supplies dependent on ships yet to arrive."[4] Being stranded so long in the
desert at the gates of Egypt had created a "quartermaster's nightmare."[5]
It had proved difficult to keep this army supplied with its daily require-
ments, let alone build up a stockpile for an offensive. And in August, a
third of Rommel's supplies and 41 percent of his fuel was destroyed en
route to North Africa.[6] Rommel's letter to his wife on the eve of this renewed offensive reflected the logistical weakness of his army, and, for the
first time, doubts whether his offensive would succeed. Rommel wrote:

> To-day has dawned at last. It's been such a long wait worrying all the time
> whether I should get everything I needed together to enable me to take the
> brakes off again. Many of my worries have been by no means satisfactorily
> settled and we have some very grave shortages. But I've taken the risk, for it will
> be a long time before we get such favourable conditions of moonlight, relative
> strength, etc., again. I, for my part, will do my utmost to contribute to success.
>
> As for my health, I'm feeling quite on top of my form. There are such big
> things at stake. If our blow succeeds, it might go some way towards deciding
> the whole course of the war. If it fails, at least I hope to give the enemy a pretty
> thorough beating. Neurath has seen the Fuehrer, who sent me his best wishes.
> He is fully aware of my anxieties.[7]

In relation to his health, Rommel was lying and attempting to reassure
a worried spouse. He was a long way from feeling "on top of my form."
Rommel's medical advisor Professor Horster saw Rommel leave his
quarters on the morning of the attack "with a very troubled face." Rommel approached Horster and spoke to him:

> "Professor," he said, "the decision to attack to-day is the hardest I have ever
> taken. Either the army in Russia succeeds in getting through to Grozny and we
> in Africa manage to reach the Suez Canal, or . . ." He made a gesture of defeat.[8]

Given the state of his health, his lack of military intelligence, and the
logistical shortcomings of Panzerarmee, it is little wonder that Rommel
lacked his usual optimism and drive in this last throw of the dice.

But Rommel knew time was not on his side. A senior German staff officer recalled: "It was clear to Rommel that time was working against him and that as soon as the enemy had brought forward sufficient reinforcements he would launch a powerful counteroffensive."[9] To counter this, Rommel strengthened his own defenses, making particular use of "mine gardens." But his best form of defense was to attack first: "As soon as the supply situation permitted, Rommel intended making another effort from the other end of the line to break through to Alexandria."[10] At the end of August, taking the gamble that enough fuel would arrive to sustain it, Rommel launched what would be his last offensive in Egypt.

Rommel planned to make a powerful thrust against the southern portion of the Alamein position using the bulk of his armored formations. Here he believed:

> Only small British forces lay in the southern part of the front. Our reconnaissance had consistently reported that only weakly defences existed in the south, which would be comparatively easy to penetrate. These positions were to be taken in a night attack by the German and Italian infantry, and the enemy thrown back by armoured formations following immediately behind.[11]

Once sufficient depth to this eastward thrust had been made, somewhere between twenty-five to thirty miles, the armored formations were to wheel north to the coast and then continue east into the British rear areas. Such a deep penetration of their defenses would either send the British forces rearward in panic or force them to give battle in the open. Rommel's armor and mobile forces would "encircle and destroy Eighth Army in a repeat of Gazala."[12] He expected a clear-cut decision in the first two days and warned that "The decisive battle was on no account to become static."[13]

Reinforcements had recently landed in theater by Ju 52 transport aircraft. While lacking vital equipment, the arrival of the German 164th Division, the Italian Folgore Parachute Division, and the German Ramcke Parachute Brigade had given the Panzerarmee some reason for optimism. The War Diary of the Afrika Korps recorded on the night of August 30:

> After a pause of about three weeks Afrika Korps once more advanced to the attack. During this time the strength of the Korps had considerably increased. Morale was good and confident. The Panzer Regts had a total of 237 runners.

The infantry regiments, which had had heavy casualties, were not yet up to full strength again.[14]

On the eve of the offensive, Rommel's forces numbered 84,000 German and 44,000 Italian personnel. Panzerarmee contained 237 German and 281 Italian tanks. Most of the German tanks outmatched anything Eighth Army could field. They included 170 "Specials" with a long-barreled 50 mm gun and additional frontal armor. Another twenty-six German tanks were the new Mark IV "Special," which, with their long-barreled 75 mm guns, were "the most formidable tanks in the desert."[15] Its gun was effective at 3,000 yards, which was "three times further than any British tank or anti-tank weapon."[16] The quality of the Italian tanks "was the most serious weakness of the Italian army during the North African campaign."[17] The M 13 and its upgraded variants, the M 14 and M 15, were "the backbone" of the Italian armored formations. The M 13 and its variants mounted an effective gun but the tanks were defective in armor protection and underpowered.[18] The M 13 could not match the new Eighth Army Grant and Sherman tanks. Rommel's "critical problem" was not the number or quality of his tanks, though. As always, it was the fact that Panzerarmee "remained desperately short of fuel."[19]

Unfortunately for Rommel and the "confident" Afrika Korps, Rommel's intelligence reports were wildly inaccurate and through Ultra, Eighth Army knew the attack was coming. It had been anticipated in both Dorman-Smith's and Gott's Appreciations, which had been accepted though seldom acknowledged by Montgomery. Also, Rommel's plan for the offensive was well known to Montgomery, having been intercepted by signals intelligence on August 15. This decrypt "was perhaps the most important single item of information that the Enigma had yet contributed to the desert campaign."[20] Further Enigma (Ultra) decrypts gave Rommel's precise tank strength on the eve of the attack, indicating that by August 28, Rommel had 234 German and 281 Italian tanks ready for action.[21] Alexander's Despatch makes it clear that Rommel's Alam Halfa attack was anticipated and that Eighth Army was well prepared to meet it. Alexander wrote:

> This intention [Rommel's plan] was no surprise to me and, as has been seen, our dispositions had been made to meet just such an attack, facing west and south with a strong armoured force disposed centrally. . . . We had the advantages of

ground and prepared defensive position while the enemy's advantage of the initiative had been diminished by the loss of surprise.[22]

For Montgomery's chief of staff, Freddie de Guingand, Alam Halfa was "a heaven sent event." It provided "the whole Army, its commander, staff and the fighting troops a great opportunity of running themselves in."[23] This "running in" would be at Rommel's expense.

* * *

The critical ground was the Alam el Halfa Ridge, which was "about ten miles from and ran roughly parallel to, the coast."[24] Alam el Halfa's highest point was 132 meters (433 feet) above sea level and for some kilometers, either side of the ridge was more than 100 meters (328 feet) above sea level.[25] The Alam el Halfa Ridge "formed one of the principal keys to the whole defensive system."[26] It was "the obvious key!—to the whole of our defensive system," recalled General Alexander.[27] Its height dominated a considerable part of the Alamein position. As long as the British held it, Rommel "could have no freedom of action."[28]

Around this vital feature, four divisions of Eighth Army's 13 Corps were ready to meet the enemy strike force of six divisions. The July battles had shown that Eighth Army's strengths were its determined infantry, its artillery assets, and the DAF. Conversely, its weaknesses were the armored formations, and its inability to coordinate arms during an attack.[29] Montgomery's plan for this Alam Halfa battle had taken these factors into account. 13 Corps consisted of two infantry divisions, the veteran 2nd New Zealand Division, and the newly arrived 44th Division. The 7th and 10th Armoured Divisions provided the armor. They could also call on a further 100 tanks of 23 Armoured Brigade, which was designated the Corps' reserve.[30] Two brigades of armor and the 44th Division were positioned on Alam el Halfa itself. The 22nd Armoured Brigade was in hull-down positions at the foot of the ridge. In this brigade were concentrated ninety-two of 164 Grant tanks on which heavy responsibility lay. The Grants were "known for their 75-mm guns as the E.L.H., Egypt's Last Hope."[31] A further armored brigade in the open desert blocked the path around the ridge. The 2nd New Zealand Division held the Alam Nayil Ridge, a smaller feature immediately west of Alam el Halfa and directly in the path of Panzerarmee's advance. Such a strong

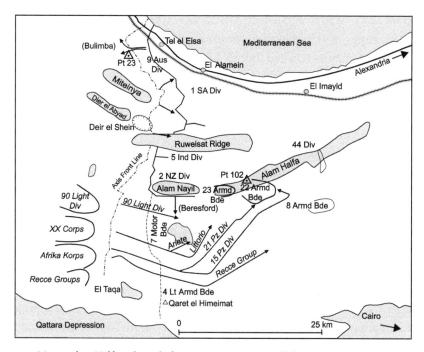

Map 2. Alam Halfa at the end of August 1942 was Rommel's last attempt to break through the El Alamein position. While the battle was Montgomery's first victory in North Africa, the two counter-punches of *Bulimba* and *Beresford* showed how weak Eighth Army was in an attack role. It was still a turning-point battle, one General Alexander said was far more important than it would appear.

defensive force in thoroughly prepared positions was not going to be easily thrust aside. Lieutenant General Brian Horrocks, the corps commander, was under strict instructions from Montgomery. According to Horrocks, Montgomery "ordered me to defeat the Germans *but not under any condition to become mauled in the process*."[32] For this reason, the tanks of Eighth Army would be used as an anti-tank gun. They would remain in hull down, defensive positions and not maneuver against Panzerarmee. To move out and engage with the Afrika Korps risked being beaten again as had happened so often in the past.[33]

The two sides would be evenly matched in both armor and artillery. Initially, it was the dense minefields and the intervention of the DAF that blunted Rommel's attack. From June, the DAF had been joined by units of the US Army Air Force. Panzerarmee never recovered from its poor start. At first, as the German tanks reached the British minefields, their hopes of achieving a tactical surprise were high. But just before midnight, reports reached the 7th Armoured Division that Panzerarmee was on the move and held up at the minefields. An immediate request was sent to the DAF to commence bombing the areas west of the British minefields. The DAF was "tensed for maximum effort" and immediately executed a three-pronged air campaign.[34] This planned to cause maximum damage to enemy concentrations, sever their lines of communication, and control the air space above the battle. Montgomery, according to Horrocks, was "the most air-minded general I ever met." He was determined that Eighth Army and the DAF would fight the one battle "hand in hand."[35] Alam Halfa would be the first test of this partnership. At 0030 hours on August 31, Fairey Albacore aircraft from the Fleet Air Arm began dropping flares across the southern sector minefields illuminating the targets trying to get through them. Following the Albacores were the Wellington Bombers of No. 205 Group, whose bombs caused havoc on those below. In total, thirty-eight tons of bombs and incendiaries fell on Panzerarmee that night and the bombing was accurate. Added to this were the anti-tank guns of 7th Armoured Division, which had no trouble picking out targets lit up by the magnesium flares. Carrier patrols constantly harassed the German engineers trying to clear pathways through the minefields.

Made aware that a large offensive was underway at last, de Guingand felt that he should inform the Army Commander. De Guingand walked over to Montgomery's caravan and woke him. Informed that Rommel was on the move, Montgomery uttered two words: "Excellent, excellent." He then went back to sleep and appeared at breakfast the next morning "at his usual hour."[36] It was an impressive display of confidence.

In Cairo, General Alexander sent Churchill a "monosyllabic signal," which said, simply, "Zip." It was a prearranged code, based on an item of clothing Churchill wore, and it indicated that Rommel's much-anticipated offensive was underway. Churchill immediately informed Stalin and Roosevelt of Rommel's attack and that "an important battle may now be fought."[37]

It was not until 0500 hours that the first gap through the minefields was made and the panzer regiments moved cautiously through it. Rommel's advance was well behind schedule. The Afrika Korps War Diary told a depressing story:

> The minefields and the enemy opposition had delayed the advance more than anticipated. Our plan to surprise the enemy by getting opposite his deep flank and rear by first light and then swinging north have not succeeded.... In view of this appreciation he [Rommel] gave orders to continue the attack and change direction.[38]

On this opening night of the offensive, 21 Panzer Division led the advance and recorded that enemy night bombers had attacked them eighteen times.[39]

Rommel had other serious problems too. Two Wellington bombers of No.104 Squadron struck the jackpot while searching for targets. The tented camp on which they scored a direct hit was the battle headquarters of the Afrika Korps. Two staff officers were killed and General Walther Nehring, the DAK commander, was seriously wounded. Staff Colonel Fritz Bayerlein took over temporary command of the Korps. Twenty minutes later, Generalmajor Georg von Bismarck was killed by mortar fire and his chief staff officer badly wounded. Bismarck was the talented commander of 21 Panzer Division and he had gone forward that evening in order to get the stalled advance moving again. Niall Barr wrote of these losses: "The command and control of the Afrika Korps was thus disrupted at the very moment it was needed most."[40]

Added to this was Panzerarmee's critical fuel shortage. This was known before the attack commenced, but the delay getting through the minefields aggravated it. A senior German staff officer recalled a dire situation:

> The attack actually soon began to move forward but already in the evening of 31 August the shortage of gas began to make itself seriously felt. Furthermore, a sandstorm which had been blowing continuously, stopped after several hours and enemy air attacks commenced with an intensity that had not been experienced before.... Kesselring had promised to deliver 400 tons of fuel per day by air if necessary, but only a fraction of this quantity reached the troops. The reason for this was that the transporting planes consumed most of the fuel themselves on the long trip.[41]

By 0800 hours on August 31, both panzer divisions of Afrika Korps were through the minefields and had advanced about four kilometers (2.4 miles) east of it. The original plan had been for them to drive much further east, almost forty kilometers (twenty-four miles), before turning north to the coast road. But Rommel's plan was in tatters. He wrote of it: "The assault force had been held far too long by the strong and hitherto unsuspected mine barriers, and the element of surprise, which had formed the basis of the whole plan, had been lost."[42] For a time, Rommel contemplated calling off the attack. After conferring with Colonel Bayerlein, "we decided the attack should go on."[43] But instead of driving deeper into the British positions, the loss of surprise and the growing fuel shortage compelled Rommel "to decide on an earlier turn to the north than we had intended."[44] Once the Afrika Korps had refueled and replenished its ammunition stores, the turn to the north commenced at 1300 hours. The new objective was Point 102, a small feature on the western edge of the Alam el Halfa Ridge. This was just twelve kilometers (7.5 miles) from the minefields that had caused him so much trouble. As Rommel anticipated, "From our experience in similar situations we knew that the battle for the [Alam el Halfa] ridge, which was the key to the whole El Alamein position, would be very severe."[45]

The decision to continue the fight was hardly surprising, given Rommel's personality. But this new direction of attack was precisely what Dorman-Smith, Gott, and others had anticipated and Eighth Army was well prepared to meet it. Alexander issued a Special Order of the Day. It stated that the enemy were attacking but that Eighth Army must "stand firm." Alexander stated that, "The results of the whole war may well depend on how we conduct ourselves in this great battle." He called on the troops to be determined to "win or die. This is the fighting spirit which will give us victory." He then ordered: "SOLDIERS: DO YOUR DUTY."[46] Montgomery issued a similar call to arms. He stated that there would be no withdrawal and no surrender and that "Every officer and man must continue to do his duty as long as he has breath in his body."[47] Rommel's prediction of a "severe fight" ahead was certainly on the mark.

The New Zealand Box on the Alam Nayil Ridge was "a solid doorpost on which Rommel's Panzer Army Afrika will swing in its right hook onto the Alam Halfa Ridge."[48] But as they did so, the New Zealand artillery took a heavy toll. With its artillery concentrated and reinforced to a total of eight field and two attached medium regiments, the guns in the New Zealand Box harassed the Panzerarmee constantly. Brigadier

"Steve" Weir, the New Zealand CRA, wrote after the battle: "With this [10 regiments of artillery] and a plentiful supply of ammunition we slogged it out for the next week."[49]

On the afternoon of August 31, more than 120 tanks of 21 Panzer Division advanced in three waves toward Point 102. There they "met a wall of dug-in steel and their troubles really began."[50] With their new Panzer Mk IV tanks armed with a long-barreled, high-velocity 75 mm gun that outranged anything the British had, the tanks defending Alam el Halfa were soon knocked out. But the anti-tank guns, primarily the six-pounders, were a different matter. These, organized in a defensive screen, held their fire until the German tanks were just 300 yards away and then took a heavy toll. All the while, heavy concentrations of artillery fire, much of it from the New Zealand Box, were directed against the advancing panzers. 21 Panzer reported a dire situation to Afrika Korps:

> The enemy seemed to be firing heavy DF [Defensive Fire] forward of the whole PZ Regt from a strong system of field positions. Enemy tanks were firing from reverse slope positions in little hollows mainly on the left flank. The PZ Regt's left-hand unit had faced left and was in action against an enemy force in well-built and camouflaged positions.[51]

This opposition was unexpected and 21 Panzer could make no headway against it. As darkness fell, the Division withdrew towards the Ragil Depression in the south and assessed its options, having lost around thirty tanks that day. Barr writes, "The action had been short but sharp."[52] It had also been decisive. That evening, the weather cleared after a day of driving sandstorms and the DAF bombers added to the Panzerarmee's misery by pounding 21 Panzer Division, laagered in the Ragil Depression. The Axis transports trying to get additional fuel and supplies forward were also hammered.

In normal circumstances, this would have been a minor setback to the Afrika Korps. It would have regrouped, refueled, and driven further east, then swung around to take Point 102 from the flank and rear. Indeed, Bayerlein suggested this course of action to Rommel that evening. But there was one overriding factor that made this maneuver impossible. The combination of the delay at the minefields, the soft sand encountered, and the unexpected opposition had drained the Afrika Korps of what little gasoline had been available. The turn north had consumed "abnormally large amounts of fuel."[53] This made a wide outflanking move impossible. An exasperated Rommel recorded his problems:

> Meanwhile, the promised petrol had still not arrived in Africa, added to which our supply traffic through the lanes in the enemy minefields was being seriously disturbed by the British armour south of our salient (7th Armoured Division). Consequently, on the morning of the 1st September, I found myself compelled to give up any attempt at major action for the moment; all large-scale movement of the motorised forces had to be avoided, and the most we could permit ourselves was a few local, limited objective attacks.[54]

These local attacks on September 1 were carried out by 15 Panzer Division, which attacked the defenses at Alam el Halfa and shot up some British tanks. Then, "with their petrol almost exhausted, they were forced to call off even this local advance."[55] In fact, the fuel tanks of the panzers were almost empty "and, indeed placed the whole of the Afrika Korps in a very precarious situation."[56] A tank without fuel was vulnerable, and worthless as a fighting armored vehicle. The Afrika Korps War Diary recorded on September 1:

> The petrol situation at present would not allow the attack to be continued, and so Army intended to replenish supplies in the present area . . . Army intended to pull out reserves and go over to the defensive in its present area.[57]

Throughout the day the DAF kept up its bombing attacks which Rommel admitted caused "severe casualties." The next day, in the space of two hours traveling across the battlefront, Rommel was bombed from the air "no less than six times."[58]

It was a situation that could not be resolved. On the evening of September 1, Rommel again considered breaking off the battle. On the morning of September 2, the tanks of Afrika Korps attempted another frontal attack on the Ridge, and then tried to work around the flanks of the defenders there. After two hours and making no progress, the tanks withdrew south to refuel. One more probe that afternoon met with no success and the tanks pulled away without staging an attack. This now convinced Rommel he had no option but to call off this offensive. It was a painful, but necessary decision. Rommel recorded his reasons for making it:

> I decided to call off the attack and retire by stages to the line El Taque-Bab el Qattara. My reasons were the serious air situation and the disastrous state of our

supplies. Our offensive no longer had any hope of success, partly because we had no petrol and insufficient fighter cover and partly because the battle had now reached a stage where material strength alone would decide the issue.[59]

Just after midday on September 2, the order was issued to the Afrika Korps:

(1) The enemy's air superiority and the petrol shortage and that of other supplies compel us to cancel the offensive.
(2) Afrika Korps will withdraw west in several bounds.[60]

The battle, though not over, had been won in these first two days. As General Alexander recorded in his Despatch:

The first two days of the battle had ended without any decisive success for the enemy and this was already a decisive success for us. . . . It was the nearest the Germans ever got to the Delta.[61]

The time had come for Eighth Army to try some limited offensive action of its own.

* * *

The first of these actions occurred in the morning of September 1, when the Australian 9th Division launched a one battalion raid from Tel el Eisa. The 9th Australian Division was rated the best division in Eighth Army by many German staff officers. It was "a not undeserved accolade in view of our experiences with the Australians," one German intelligence officer later wrote.[62] Any offensive action by the Australians was bound to make the Germans nervous. The raid was codenamed Operation *Bulimba*, named after a brand of Australian beer. The plan was for the 2/15 Battalion, supported by a squadron of Valentine tanks from 40th Royal Tank Regiment, to seize Point 23. This Point was a small rise some two-and-a-half miles south west of Tel el Eisa. The plan was very similar to those mounted by the Australians and New Zealanders in July. It was for the infantry, with their armored support, to seize the feature and form a bridgehead for further exploitation by a follow-up force of two squadrons of Crusader tanks and troops of field and anti-tank guns. The force committed to Operation *Bulimba* "was far too small to have any real effect."[63]

Initially, the operation went well. At 0535 hours, the two leading companies of 2/15 Battalion crossed the start line on the way to the objective. Fifteen minutes later, the Division's artillery opened up on the German and Italian positions and the first objectives were soon taken. From this point, the situation rapidly deteriorated. The Battalion's Commanding Officer was severely wounded when his carrier ran over a mine and, once again, the armored support failed to appear. The lead tanks had been destroyed by anti-tank gunfire and two more had been destroyed by mines when they sought an alternative passage through the cleared minefields. Despite these setbacks, by 0835 hours the 2/15 Battalion had captured Point 23 but their position there was precarious. Without tank support, suffering heavy casualties, low on ammunition, and lacking heavy weapons, the Australians could not hold Point 23 in the face of counterattacks from the German 164 Light Division. At 0845 hours, the Battalion's senior officer, Major C.H. Grace, knowing that his force was now too weak to hold Point 23, made the difficult decision to leave.[64] The withdrawal commenced at 0900 hours and went smoothly, although the seriously wounded had to be left behind. The Battalion's War Diary records a succinct summary of the action:

> Previously planned Bn raid (code word "BULIMBA") carried out. ZERO 0535 hrs. CO, Lt-Col OGLE wounded. casualties – killed 2 Offrs and 24 ORs, missing 2 Offrs and 31 ORs, wounded 5 Offrs and 108 ORs. PW taken 1 Offr and 107 ORs. Estimated over 150 enemy killed.
> During the afternoon Bn moved back to bivouac area, near EL ALAMEIN rd hunc (88812946) and came under comd 24 Aust Inf Bde.[65]

The end result was that "2/15th Battalion had suffered 36 per cent casualties and Bulimba had failed."[66]

It must have been some comfort when General Sir Harold Alexander visited the 2/15th Battalion four days later and "very highly praised Bn on the BULIMBA OP, said the Bn did all that was asked to do. Op caused the desired diversion."[67] It was "exactly the result desired," Alexander assured the battalion.[68] But once again the armored support had been "disappointing to infantry," with the infantry believing the tank crews were "extremely nervous particularly after loss of comds."[69] Major A.S. Gehrmann, the engineer officer who commanded the 2/13th Field Company during the raid, wrote a scathing indictment of Operation Bulimba. According to Gehrmann:

It is my firm opinion, frequently voiced prior to the operation, that the action
was doomed to failure before it started because:
1. The force was too small.
2. The front was too narrow.
3. The flanks were insecure.
4. The proposed penetration was too narrow.
5. The information was too scanty.
6. The operation was unsuitable for tanks.[70]

The Australian official history concluded that Operation *Bulimba* was
"not in vain, for the knowledge gained and lessons learned were utilized
when the next attack was planned."[71] This knowledge and "lesson" were
already well known from the July action. The 2/15th Battalion's Report
was correct to conclude that: "Few new lessons, if any, emerged from
the operation."[72] The 9th Division's War Diary recorded that "the initial attack shows that we can by surprise and vigorous assault capture a
position."[73] Holding onto captured positions and exploiting them was
a different matter. The failure of the raid and the problems experienced
in carrying out combined offensive operations were all too depressingly
familiar. The situation was not about to improve either when Eighth
Army launched its next minor offensive aimed at disrupting the Axis
forces as they withdrew to their start lines. This was codenamed Operation *Beresford*.

It had been relatively quiet in the New Zealand Box since the start of
Rommel's attack, but this was about to change. Rommel's withdrawal so
early into the offensive had taken Eighth Army by surprise, so it was not
until September 3 that Montgomery ordered an infantry counterattack:
Operation *Beresford*. The Afrika Korps found the lack of vigorous pursuit
strange and recorded in its War Diary that "The enemy pursued Afrika
Korps half-heartedly during the day."[74] Despite his objections, Freyberg
was ordered to undertake the counterattack with only two brigades. Two
infantry brigades could do very little but probe the enemy's defenses
when a hammer blow by at least two divisions seemed warranted. Once
again, and for the last time, the infantry brigade advance was to be a
silent, night attack, although each infantry brigade would be supported
by a squadron of tanks—the only assistance received from the armored
corps. And yet again there was no effective liaison with other formations
of Eighth Army.

The 2nd New Zealand Division had learned much since Ruweisat, however, and Freyberg, still recovering from his wound at Minqar Qaim, was back in charge. This was very evident in the progress made by the two infantry brigades used in the counterattack—Kippenberger's 5 New Zealand Brigade and 132 Brigade of the inexperienced British 44 Division.

Kippenberger's 5th Brigade was to attack down a narrow corridor between two minefields and secure the northern ridge of the Munassib depression. The attack was timed for 2230 hours on the night of September 3. This final objective was to be taken by 28 (Maori) Battalion with 21 Battalion holding the northern and western edge of a smaller rim of a smaller depression immediately behind 28 Battalion. One battalion, the 22nd, was held in reserve. Kippenberger later commented:

> We were learning by experience and there were several differences between our plans for Ruweisat and for this battle. All the preparations were made without hitch or misunderstanding, with very minor exceptions.[75]

Even so, things still went seriously wrong during the attack. Signals broke down, companies got lost and were late moving off, the gap between the minefields was shelled heavily, and, most seriously of all, the lead battalion did not follow orders and effective control was lost. As Kippenberger learnt from the 28 (Maori) Battalion CO:

> It appeared that the objective had been reached after violent and most bloody fighting. Most of the two companies had then carried on into the Munassib depression directly contrary to their orders and were slaughtering the transport drivers and burning the trucks there.[76]

The dispersal and withdrawal of most of the Maori Battalion left Kippenberger with no choice but to leave the depression next morning and bring forward his reserve battalion to link up with 21 Battalion. This meant that most of the ground taken could be held. To ward off the inevitable German counterattack, Kippenberger had the front of both battalions bristling with anti-tank weapons, both six- and two-pounders. His front was also protected by the New Zealand artillery. When the counterattacks came at midday on September 4, they were easily beaten off.

The hard-won experience of the New Zealanders was very evident in this assault. 21 Battalion had accomplished its relatively easy task "neatly and efficiently," while 22 Battalion had been "quick and businesslike." The Māori, who had suffered most of the Brigade's 120 casualties, had made "a brilliantly successful attack" and, according to Kippenberger, had inflicted more than 500 casualties. This claim of 500 casualties was recorded in the Brigade's War Diary.[77] It is disputed by other historians and by German sources.[78] The Afrika Korps War Diary does not support it. Afrika Korps recorded:

> Our casualties were 38 officers and 533 [ORs], and 145 MT and 9 guns were total losses. Our heavy casualties were mainly caused by the enemy air force.[79]

Kippenberger was not happy with the Māoris' "fit of over-enthusiasm."[80] He wrote, somewhat gently, in *Infantry Brigadier*:

> They had, however, got badly out of control and were lucky to have got out without disaster. Splendid troops as they were and easy for a hard commander to handle, the Maoris needed an iron hand. It was the stern George Dittmer, their original commander, who made them a battalion, and throughout the war, the sterner and firmer their commander, the better they responded.[81]

The failure of the Māoris at Alam Halfa explains why they were allocated a "mopping up" role in the next large battle, a decision that still puzzles Māori historians.[82] For propaganda purposes, the Māori attack on September 3–4 was transformed into a great victory and widely publicized in New Zealand. The attack was so effective "that they swept all before them at the point of the bayonet right past the objective set for them into the enemy B echelon." The Axis casualties were inflated to 600 killed and 150 POWs.[83]

The experience of the New Zealand brigade was especially evident when its achievements were compared with the disastrous advance of 132 Brigade on 5 Brigade's right flank. The commander of 132 Brigade, Brigadier Robertson, rejected Kippenberger's sound advice to establish a Tactical Headquarters well forward with good communications and reserves and support weapons close at hand. Instead, Robertson moved his HQ up too close behind his lead infantry battalions and he was one of the first people wounded by enemy shell fire. The New Zealand writer John Mulgan, an officer in 132 Brigade, recalled prior to Operation *Beresford*:

> Nobody in the battalion felt very comfortable about this attack. We were all of
> us too new to desert fighting to have any confidence or exact knowledge as to
> what we should do, and everything was very hurried. There was very little time
> for preparation and our commander had always believed that fighting spirit can
> redeem any lack of minute planning.[84]

The 132nd Brigade suffered that night from enemy bombing and then stumbled onto one of Eighth Army's minefields. They set off an hour late, out of contact with their armored support squadron and completely bunched up to make the night traveling easier. A half-hour after midnight, heavy enemy artillery fire rained down on the compact units of the brigade, wounding the Brigadier and stopping the advance of the brigade in its tracks. The brigade did not penetrate beyond the line on which it came under fire. Rather, it halted on a forward slope of a ridge totally exposed to the enemy fire from three sides: "long enough to collect a bitter quota of casualties."[85] The next morning, only one battalion of 132 Brigade was intact and near its final objective. The other two battalions were thoroughly disorganized and completely disoriented. Mulgan wrote of moving forward at dawn on September 4 to locate the brigade and observed the Brigade Major trying to reorganize the shambles— "the only coherent man we met all that day."[86]

Operation *Beresford* ended on the morning of September 5, when the New Zealand Battalions were withdrawn into the New Zealand Box and the gaps in the minefields closed. The 132nd Brigade had suffered more than 700 casualties during its brief advance and Freyberg felt himself to be very much responsible for the disaster because he had used such an inexperienced brigade for this type of operation.[87] The Corps commander, Horrocks, experiencing "the most difficult period I had in the whole war" because of Freyberg's ungenerous behavior toward him, was "pierced with remorse" after the war over the use of 132 Brigade.[88] The fault really rested, though, with 132 Brigade and more particularly with its commanders. The commanders of the brigade rejected all of the sound advice offered by the New Zealanders as, "there was a resistance to suggestions that the brigade was inexperienced in anything except the terrain."[89] The tactics used by 132 Brigade were totally inadequate for desert fighting and the brigade seemed determined to learn by its mistakes rather than from the experience of other formations.

The New Zealanders, and Freyberg in particular, have been accused of being primarily responsible for the failure of Montgomery's counterattack at Alam Halfa. This is especially true of British writers. Lord Carver, for example, wrote of Montgomery's plans:

> He had planned to cut off Rommel's thrust with a counter-attack by Freyberg's New Zealanders, reinforced by brigades of the 44th, and then launch Lumsden's *corps de chasse* in a wide sweep round Rommel's rear but the New Zealand attack petered out ineffectively and Montgomery, the realist, saw that his army needed more thorough training before it would be able to respond to his demands.[90]

Nigel Hamilton, Montgomery's sympathetic biographer, is probably the most damning of the British writers. To him, Operation *Beresford* was "the New Zealand Division's failure," a failure that provided "an illuminating insight into the disastrous lack of offensive skill in the 8th Army."[91] Not only does Hamilton mistake which New Zealand brigade was used in the attack, but all the disasters are laid entirely at the feet of the New Zealand brigade while any success obtained is credited to 132 Brigade, hardly an accurate description of the action. Niall Barr's assessment of 132 Brigade's performance as "a bloody shambles" and "probably the worst debacle suffered by a British brigade in the course of the desert war" is much nearer the mark.[92] One British writer, however, has hit upon the real reason for the failure of Operation *Beresford*. Correlli Barnett believed that Rommel's withdrawal should have been met with "annihilating counter-stroke in the grand style." Such a decisive knock-out blow did not fit in with Montgomery's plans or his cautious command style in which "unexpected opportunities, however great, were embarrassing." The counterattack, when it was made, was "a half-hearted attempt, carried out by the New Zealand Division alone, and it was too late."[93]

The failure of the counterattacks at Alam Halfa then can be put down to four factors. These were the cautious command style of Montgomery, who let the opportunity pass; the small force used in each attack; the poor coordination; and the total inexperience and inflexibility of one of the two infantry brigades used in Operation *Beresford*. Howard Kippenberger, however, was pleased that a larger counterattack had not been attempted. He wrote in 1955:

> My own feeling is that battle was never really joined. Montgomery was rightly
> determined not to be defeated and Rommel's plan had become impracticable
> and he only half-heartedly attempted a modification of it within a few hours. I
> remember quite clearly that Horrocks told us that the main object was not to
> be beaten, and that I was delighted that the Army commander had not been
> tempted into launching a general counter-attack.[94]

With Eighth Army recovering from a state of despair in August 1942,
and still poorly trained and lacking adequate doctrine, Montgomery's decision not to launch a massive counterattack was probably the
correct one.

As mentioned above, on September 4, the Panzerarmee attacked
the new lodgments established during Operation *Beresford*. These were
easily beaten off, but during the night the New Zealand infantry withdrew from their exposed positions back into their original perimeter.
On September 4 and 5, Rommel's "slow and stubborn withdrawal" continued all the time while being harassed by the DAF and mobile units of
7 Armoured Division.[95] On September 5, the Panzerarmee reached the
British minefields that had imposed a fatal delay on their advance. Here,
Rommel turned to face his pursuers determined to hold at least this thin
stretch of ground. When it became clear that Rommel's withdrawal had
ended, at 0700 hours on September 7, Montgomery called the battle
off. Rommel's advance captured a thin strip of territory of which only
the peak of Himeimat, offering superb observation over the battlefield,
could be considered valuable. Alam Halfa cost Panzerarmee 53 tanks,
almost 700 vehicles, 70 guns, and 4,500 men. Eighth Army's losses were
68 tanks, 19 guns, and 1,640 men killed, wounded, or missing.[96]

The battle of Alam Halfa was a significant turning-point battle in the
North African campaign. The reasons for Rommel's failure here were
astutely assessed by one of his intelligence officers. Rommel's Alam
Halfa offensive failed "because of the minefields, because of the stubborn defence put up by the British, and ultimately—and *this* really was
decisive—because of the lack of fuel."[97] Of the stubborn British defense,
the DAF and Eighth Army's artillery had been key to its success. Certainly, Rommel and other German commanders recognized the significance of Alam Halfa. On September 4, Rommel could not conceal his
bitterness in a letter to Lucie-Marie. Rommel wrote:

Dearest Lu,
Some very hard days lie behind me. We had to break off the offensive for supply reasons and because of the superiority of the enemy air force—although
victory was otherwise ours. Well, it can't be helped. Made a quick call at H.Q.
for the first time to-day, even had both my boots off and washed my feet. I'm
still hoping that the situation can be straightened out. All my wishes to you and
Manfred.
        P.S.—Bismarck killed. Nehring wounded.[98]

Despite the severity of the artillery and air attacks, Panzerarmee's tanks
losses had been light: just thirty-six German and eleven Italian tanks
were total losses. Its losses in guns and motor transport had been heavier,
but it had abandoned the offensive "less on account of battle losses than
of supply difficulties."[99] Ever the realist, Rommel recognized that the
fortunes of war had turned against him and Germany. He wrote shortly
after the battle:

With the failure of this offensive our last chance of gaining the Suez Canal had
gone. We could now expect that the full production of British industry and,
more important, the enormous industrial potential of America, which, conse-
quent on our declaration of war, was now fully harnessed to the enemy cause,
would finally turn the tide against us.[100]

Rommel's gamble, unlike his earlier risk taking, had failed. The price
would be much higher than he perhaps realized.

General Alexander, in his post-war Despatch of the North African
campaign, wrote that Alam Halfa "was far more important than would
appear." It was the last chance for a German victory there and the beginning of the turn of the tide against the Axis. More significantly, it also
restored a lost faith in British leadership and a confidence in their own
fighting abilities. One veteran wrote that the importance of this victory
was "in the proof it gave that British tanks and infantry could stand up
to the Germans and inflict a crushing defeat." As a result, "morale rose to
great heights and confidence was re-established."[101] As Alexander wrote,
reflecting the views of many fighting in Eighth Army: "I now felt sure that
we should be able to defeat the enemy when we were ready to take the
offensive."[102] As another veteran of the battle stated, "it was our first obvious victory and a tremendous morale booster. At last a plan that actually
worked!"[103]

Montgomery may not have taken the opportunities presented to him in this battle, but he had achieved his main objective. Alexander was correct when he wrote that Montgomery handled "his first battle in the Western Desert with skill and care."[104] As Horrocks stated above, this was to meet the Panzerarmee head on and not be beaten or make any major mistakes that could lead to defeat. This would have produced a further fatal erosion of morale. While Operations *Beresford* and *Bulimba* were poorly executed, with their failure resulting in unnecessary and heavy casualties for the units involved, they did not lead to defeat. It was Rommel who had been decisively beaten in what would be the last Axis attempt to reach Cairo. Montgomery's first success in North Africa was critical. It set Eighth Army on the road to recovery from its bewilderment and from the many disasters of May through July 1942. It was "the beginning of something new" as air-ground cooperation "now went up a gear" and "paid extra dividends."[105] It left Montgomery free now to plan and prepare his own battle of El Alamein, where these dividends could be fully exploited. As the British official history noted, with their forces growing stronger every day, "the initiative was theirs for the taking."[106] Montgomery was determined to seize it. When he felt his army was ready, Montgomery would strike against Rommel's Panzerarmee with all the considerable force at his disposal.

NOTES

1. War Diary 2 NZ Divisional Staff, 0119 hours 31 August 1942, DA 21/1/32, WA II 1, ANZ.

2. Note by General Bayerlein, in Liddell Hart, *The Rommel Papers*, 271.

3. Ibid.

4. Pugsley, *A Bloody Road Home*, 326.

5. Barr, *Pendulum of War*, 218.

6. Levine, *The War Against Rommel's Supply Lines*, 27.

7. Rommel to Dearest Lu, 30 August 1942, in Liddell Hart, *The Rommel Papers*, 275.

8. Note by General Bayerlein, in Liddell Hart, in Liddell Hart, *The Rommel Papers*, 271.

9. Toppe, "Desert Warfare," 45.

10. Ibid.

11. The New Break-through Plan, in Liddell Hart, *The Rommel Papers*, 273.

12. Barr, *Pendulum of War*, 221.

13. The New Break-through Plan, in Liddell Hart, *The Rommel Papers*, 274.

14. War Diary, DAK, 2200 hours 30 August 1942, GMDS File 2586/1, WA II 11/23 Afrika Korps Records, ANZ.

15. Hamilton, *The Full Monty*, 582.

16. Ibid., 598.

17. Carrier, *War in History*, 512.

18. Ibid., 513.

19. Barr, *Pendulum of War*, 222.

20. Hinsley, *British Intelligence in the Second World War: Volume 2*, 408.

21. Ibid., 412.

22. Alexander's Despatch, Supplement to *The* London *Gazette*, 5 February 1948, 845, CAB 106/613, TNA.

23. de Guingand, *Operation Victory*, 144.

24. Walker, *Alam Halfa and Alamein*, 19.

25. Ibid.

26. Verney, *The Desert Rats*, 123

27. North, *The Alexander Memoirs*, 4.

28. Verney, *The Desert Rats*, 123

29. Jonathan Fennell, "Air Power and Morale in the North African Campaign of the Second World War," *Air Power Review* (Vol.15, Number 2, Summer 2012), 9.

30. Alexander's Despatch, Supplement to *The London Gazette*, 5 February 1948, CAB 106/613, TNA, 845.

31. North, *The Alexander Memoirs*, 23.

32. Quoted in Hamilton, *The Full Monty*, 553. Italics original. See also Brian Horrocks, *A Full Life*. (London: Collins, 1960), 125

33. Fraser, *And We Shall Shock Them*, 236.

34. Barr, *Pendulum of War*, 225.

35. Horrocks, *A Full Life*, 122.

36. de Guingand, *Operation Victory*, 146.

37. Churchill, *Vol. IV*, 489.

38. War Diary, DAK, 31 August 1942, GMDS File 2586/1, WA II 11/23 Afrika Korps Records, ANZ.

39. Barr, *Pendulum of War*, 227.

40. Ibid.

41. Toppe, "Desert Warfare," 46.

42. Liddell Hart, *The Rommel Papers*, 277.

43. Ibid.

44. Ibid.

45. Ibid.

46. H.R. Alexander, Special Order of the day, 31 August 1942, Series 2 Item 2/10, PR 3 DRL 2632, Papers of Lt Gen Sir Leslie Morshead, AWM.

47. Montgomery, Special Order of the day, 31 August 1942, Series 2 Item 2/10, PR 3 DRL 2632, Papers of Lt Gen Sir Leslie Morshead, AWM.

48. Pugsley, *A Bloody Road Home*, 328.

49. Brigadier "Steve" Weir, letter to Scoullar, 9 June 1948, WA II 11/2 ANZ.

50. Bierman and Smith, *Alamein: War without Hate*, 235.

51. 21st Panzer Division War Diary, 31 August 1942, WA 11/23 Afrika Korps Records, ANZ.

52. Barr, *Pendulum of War*, 231.

53. Hinsley, *British Intelligence in the Second World War: Volume 2*, 416.

54. Liddell Hart, *The Rommel Papers*, 279.

55. Ibid.

56. Barr, *Pendulum of War*, 231.

57. Afrika Korps War Diary, 1 September 1942, WA 11/23 Afrika Korps Records, ANZ.

58. Liddell Hart, *The Rommel Papers*, 279.

59. Ibid., 280.

60. Korps Order, 1230 hours 2 September 1942, Afrika Korps War Diary, WA 11/23 Afrika Korps Records, ANZ.

61. Alexander's Despatch, Supplement to *The London Gazette*, 5 February 1948, CAB 106/613, TNA, 846.

62. Behrendt, *Rommel's Intelligence*, 189.

63. Barr, *Pendulum of War*, 232.

64. 2/15 Aust Inf Bn Report of 'BULIMBA' 1 Sep 42, War Diary 2/15 Infantry Battalion, 8/3/15, AWM 52, AWM, 4.

65. War Diary 2/15 Infantry Battalion, 1 September 1942, 8/3/15, AWM 52, AWM.

66. Barr, *Pendulum of War*, 233.

67. War Diary 2/15 Infantry Battalion, 5 September 1942, 8/3/15, AWM 52, AWM.

68. Summary of BULIMBA, War Diary 2/15 Infantry Battalion, 8/3/15, AWM 52, AWM.

69. Ibid.

70. Quoted in Barton Maughan, *Australia in the War of 1939–1945: Tobruk and El Alamein*. (Canberra: William Collins in association with the Australian War Memorial, 1987), 634.

71. Ibid.

72. 2/15 Aust Inf Bn Report of 'BULIMBA' 1 Sep 42, War Diary 2/15 Infantry Battalion, 8/3/15, AWM 52, AWM, 5.

73. War Diary 9 Australian Division General Staff Branch, 1 September 1942, 1/5/20, AWM 52, AWM.

74. Afrika Korps War Diary, 3 September 1942, WA II 11/23, ANZ.

75. Kippenberger, *Infantry Brigadier*, 209.

76. Ibid., 213.

77. 5 Bde War Diary lists the casualties inflicted by 28 Battalion as 475 Germans and 40 Italians killed and 108 POWs, WA II 1 DA 52/1/33 ANZ.

78. See, for example, Michael Carver, *El Alamein*. (London: Fontana Books, 1973), 71.

79. Afrika Korps War Diary, 4 September 1942, WA II 11/23, ANZ.

80. Carver, *El Alamein*, 70.

81. Kippenberger, *Infantry Brigadier*, 217–218.

82. Wira Gardiner, *Te Mura O Te Ahi: The Story of the Maori Battalion*. (Auckland: Reed Books, 1992), 103.

83. *The Dominion*, Wellington 16 October 1942, Interviews and Speeches November 1939-December 1944, WA II 2/16, ANZ.

84. John Mulgan, *Report on Experience*. (Auckland: Blackwood and Janet Paul, 1967), 57–58.

85. Ibid., 59.

86. Ibid., 61.

87. Walker, *Alam Halfa and Alamein*, 165.

88. Nigel Hamilton. *Monty: The Making of a General 1887–1942*. (London: Hamish Hamilton Ltd., 1981), 463, 693.

89. Walker, *Alam Halfa and Alamein*, 165–166.

90. Quoted in John Keegan, ed., *Churchill's Generals*. (London: Weidenfeld & Nicolson, 1991), 154.

91. Hamilton, *Monty. The Making of a General*, 714, 688.

92. Barr, *Pendulum of War*, 247.

93. Correlli Barnett, *The Desert Generals*. (London: Pan Books Ltd., 2007), 265–266.

94. Kippenberger to Scoullar, letter, 6 October 1955, WA II 11/2, ANZ.

95. Alexander's Despatch, Supplement to *The London Gazette*, 5 February 1948, CAB 106/613, TNA, 846.

96. Ibid., 845.

97. Behrendt, *Rommel's Intelligence*, 192.

98. Rommel to Dearest Lu, 4 September 1942, in Liddell Hart, *The Rommel Papers*, 282.

99. Panzerarmee Report QT 941 of 8 Sept 19142, CX/MSS/1378/T19, quoted in Hinsley, *British Intelligence in the Second World War: Volume 2*, 417.

100. Liddell Hart, *The Rommel Papers*, 283.

101. Verney, *The Desert Rats*, 125.

102. Alexander's Despatch, Supplement to *The London Gazette*, 5 February 1948, CAB 106/613, TNA, 847.

103. Neillands, *The Desert Rats: 7th Armoured Division*, 136.

104. North, *The Alexander Memoirs*, 24–25.

105. Bungay, *Alamein*, 143

106. Playfair et al., *Volume IV*, 2.

FIVE

PREPARATIONS AND PLANS

In September 1942, Winston Churchill was desperate for a British victory. He craved it above anything else. As Churchill explained in his history of the Second World War, "I had now been twenty-eight months at the head of affairs, during which we had sustained an almost unbroken series of military defeats." These defeats, commencing with the fall of France in 1940 and including the recent loss of Tobruk, "all these were galling links in a chain of misfortune and frustration to which no parallel could be found in our history."[1] Churchill later admitted to his doctor that September and October 1942 were "the most anxious months of the entire war."[2]

It is hardly surprising, then, that Churchill put considerable pressure upon his new command team in North Africa to deliver him the victory in battle he so anxiously wanted. On September 11, Churchill wrote to Alexander demanding to know when Eighth Army would launch its next offensive. He added a chiding note that, "I had hoped to have heard from you before."[3] Six days later, he sent a similar message. Churchill informed Alexander that:

> I am anxiously awaiting some account of your intentions. My understanding with you was the fourth week in September. Since then you have stated that the recent battle, which greatly weakened the enemy, has caused delay in regrouping, etc. I do not wish to know either your plan or the exact date, but I must know which week it falls in, otherwise I cannot form the necessary judgements affecting the general war.[4]

This pressure from Churchill caused some concern for Alexander, as Montgomery was adamant that he could not launch his offensive until

late October. It was just not possible to reorganize and train Eighth Army
to the required standard for an offensive in September 1942. Also, a full
moon would be required for a night attack, which would occur around
October 24. But this was more than a month later than Churchill wanted.
This was precisely the reason Alexander had not communicated this
intention to Churchill, but Churchill's two messages forced his hand.
The Eighth Army Chief of Staff, Major General Freddie de Guingand,
recalled years later how Montgomery solved the problem for Alexander.
According to de Guingand:

> Alex showed Montgomery a signal he'd just had from the Prime Minister
> saying we must attack in September and that it was absolutely essential. Alex
> said to Monty, "What shall I answer?" and Monty said, "I'm not going to attack
> in September." So he said to me, "Freddie, give me your pen." He wrote in his
> very clear handwriting and said, "Send this to the Prime Minister." The first
> point he made was that Rommel was attacking on 31st August and it would
> cause delay in our preparations, secondly that training and getting used to
> the new tanks and equipment would take longer than September before we
> were ready and he finished up saying if we are forced to attack in September it
> will probably fail. If we wait until October then it will be a complete success.
> And he said, "Alex, send that off to Winston," and Alex read it and said, "Yes,
> I will," which he did. Any Prime Minister getting a document like that from
> the military commanders, he couldn't go against it. If he forced us to attack in
> September and it failed then there it was on record that the principal military
> authority said it would fail.[5]

Churchill received this decision from Alexander on September 19 and
it was "unwelcome news."[6] He expressed his displeasure to Alexander,
stating that he was "greatly distressed to receive such bad news for which
I was not prepared having regard to your strength compared with the enemy."[7] Churchill also expressed his displeasure to the CIGS, General Sir
Alan Brooke, interrupting Brooke's brief grouse shooting holiday in the
country to do so. Churchill was a bit nonplussed when Brooke informed
him that he thought Alexander's reasons for delaying the offensive "were
excellent."[8] But Montgomery was correct. Having recently replaced the
senior command team and with this team having just repelled the latest
German offensive in North Africa, Churchill had no choice but to accept
their decision to delay the offensive until late October. On September 23,
Churchill informed Alexander that:

> We are in your hands, and of course a victorious battle makes amends for much
> delay. Whatever happens we shall back you up and see you through.[9]

It was the CIGS General Sir Alan Brooke who was responsible for
Churchill's last sentence offering his full support. Brooke had been concerned that Alexander would feel that Churchill was losing confidence
in him, which was "a most disconcerting thing before a battle." After an
unpleasant hour-long harangue from Churchill about the problems with
British generalship, Brooke "succeeded in getting a very definite tem-
pering of the message."[10] Montgomery now had a free hand and, more
significantly, the time to plan and train for his first offensive as Eighth
Army commander.

* * *

There were three essential tasks Montgomery needed to achieve in the
space of just over seven weeks. First, Eighth Army needed to be condi-
tioned to desert fighting. This would entail a period of intensive training designed to harden the men for battle in this inhospitable terrain.
This training also needed to focus on offensive action and, in particular,
the infantry needed to become adept in weapon handling and in mine-
clearing activities. Second, the armored formations needed to be trained
to be part of a combined arms team and for their new role as a *corps
de chasse*. Third, Montgomery's plan for the offensive needed to be explained to all those taking part so that every individual knew his place in
it. These tasks meant that the weeks of September and October 1942 were
filled with frantic activity. Montgomery also used this period to get rid of
senior commanders in whom he had no confidence. Lieutenant General
W.H. Ramsden, 30 Corps commander and one-time acting Army Commander, was one of the first to go. He was replaced by the newly arrived
Oliver Leese, who "had never had a major field command."[11] Several
more replacements, including a new commander for 7th Armoured Division, soon followed.

Montgomery was renowned as a trainer of formations and this new
command was to be no exception. He took personal responsibility for
training in Eighth Army. He later admitted that prior to the battle, the
low standard of training in Eighth Army was "my great anxiety."[12] As
soon as the battle for Alam Halfa was over, Montgomery drafted and

issued Eighth Army Training Memorandum No. 1, which contained his training instructions. More than this though, he "saw personally that all three Corps of 8th Army acted upon them."[13] Montgomery's Training Memorandum was comprehensive. It contained fundamental doctrinal principles of all arms cooperation in battle. It addressed the fundamental importance of morale and fighting spirit and the necessity of good junior leadership. It addressed the various roles of armor, artillery, engineers, signallers, and infantry. It gave practical advice on the formation of tactical headquarters, night movement, bridging minefields, medical arrangements, passing on vital information, and the importance of troops' mental and physical fitness. He even included advice on maintaining personal hygiene in the desert. As Montgomery's biographer records, in these training instructions, "nothing was left to chance." Hamilton wrote:

> Certainly no successful British field commander had ever evinced the genius for training that Montgomery did; and the victory of Alamein would result not from simple superiority of arms, but from an army which was capable of using them. Every detail of the Training Instructions would play its part in preparing 8th Army for the battle of Alamein only six weeks away; and every technique ignored would be paid for in blood.[14]

That blood would be spilt primarily by Eighth Army's infantry formations. For them, as was to be expected, the weeks before the final battle of El Alamein was a frantic period of hard realistic training. This training culminated in full-scale rehearsals for their role in the attack. These were designed to simulate the exact conditions the soldiers would face during the battle. The full-scale rehearsals undertaken by each infantry division was critical to the development of Montgomery's plan. At long last the infantry divisions, and Eighth Army as a whole, were fully tailoring their training exercises to the plan of attack. It was a critical change. As Niall Barr has commented, these full-scale rehearsals "ensured that each of the infantry was properly trained and prepared to achieve the ambitious objectives set for them."[15]

The Report on Operations prepared by 9 Australian Division outlined the purpose of this training period. It stated that:

> Training was directed to –
> (a) Further toughening and hardening of troops;
> (b) Developing battle drills suited to the operation;

(c) Making the exercises so similar to the initial attack that every man and officer unwittingly became familiar with the part he was to play.[16]

The battle drills stressed all-arms cooperation and effective weapon handling. Considerable time was spent practicing methods of clearing minefields. These needed to be clearly marked, the cleared lanes visible at night. A training exercise conducted by the Australian 2/43rd Battalion overnight on September 23 "was completed in a satisfactory manner," according to its War Diary. The exercise, however, had produced twenty-six separate learning points on infantry and tank cooperation so that the exercise was immediately repeated with better results. However, the War Diary noted that "much more trg [training] is required."[17] Over the next weeks, the men of 2/43 Battalion received much more training, especially "gradually lengthening route marches" as a way of "hardening" the men.[18]

The Commander's Summary in the War Diary of the Australian 2/17th Battalion neatly outlined what was achieved in a very short space of time:

> For the three weeks preceding operations the bn trained continuously to fit itself for the job that everyone knew was ahead. Div exercised No 2 based on the plans for the initial attack on night 23/24 OCT was done three times in all.[19]

The full-scale rehearsals for the operation were taken very seriously. For example, the Australian 9th Division carried out a full-scale rehearsal of their role in the attack on the night of October 18. The very next morning, they did it again. The War Diary of 2/24 Battalion recorded of this rehearsal:

> Preparations for exercise, though hurried, had been made in great detail. An actual section of the GERMAN front was reproduced on the ground complete in every detail with wire, mines and booby traps. This embodied all known details of the section to be later attacked. Patrol infm, aerial photographs and OP observations were all collated and the disposns as reproduced were, as was later proved, an almost exact replica of the enemy front.
>
> Many lessons were learned to be put into practical use at a later date. 2 ORs evacuated to hosp.[20]

The War Diary of 2/48 Battalion recorded the strain of repeating the exercise:

The bn returned to the leaguer area and after breakfast the exercise was repeated in daylight to give all ranks a clearer picture of what had been done at night and to show the necessity for accurate pacing and the difficulty of maintaining direction in the dark. This second exercise was very strenuous because of the fact that very little sleep had been had during the night and because of the hy [heavy] man loads which all ranks carried.

The War Diary also noted that the Divisional commander, Lieutenant General Sir Leslie Morshead, "witnessed both the day and night exercise."[21] The end result of this training was that by October 22, "the men were fit and keen for their job and each man knew his part. There was a definite feeling of confidence in the bn."[22]

In an effort to bring the men of the recently arrived 51st Highland Division up to the standard required, some of the units of this division were attached to the Australians for training. Taking part in the exercise with 2/43 Australian Infantry Battalion on September 23, the one that had produced the twenty-six learning points on infantry/tank cooperation, were thirty soldiers from 5/7 Gordon Highlanders.[23] The Australian 2/28th Battalion had a party from the Black Watch arrive on September 21 and these men were distributed amongst its rifle companies. The 2/28th War Diary recorded that the Scots visitors were received "with interest and pleasure."[24] Members of the Black Watch remained with 2/28 Battalion until the end of September, when they were replaced with men from the 5th Seaforth Regiment.[25] On September 14, 1942, the Australian 2/48th Battalion dispatched yet another of its Rifle Companies to attend Eighth Army's Mine School. The next day, the Commanding Officer and Adjutant of the 5th Camerons Regiment arrived to inspect the Battalion's defenses and to discuss "attachments of offrs and ORs from 5 Camerons for experience."[26] The 5th Cameron soldiers arrived a week later.

These attachments were part of an intensive training period for 51 Highland Division. An officer in the 1st Gordon Highlanders recalled that for "five months since our arrival in North Africa . . . we had been training for this action and in the last month unbeknown to us, specifically for this Night Attack."[27] Royal Engineer officer John Laing recalled years later how the engineers had devoted most of their training to the essential task of mine clearance. Laing wrote of this time:

> Not knowing the exact date of the start of the attack, we kept on a high state
> of alert. A method of clearing minefields had been worked out over the past
> few months, known as the Eighth Army gapping drill, and this we practised
> assiduously making sure that every officer, NCO and Sapper knew his place and
> function.[28]

Corporal E.G. Waggett of the Royal Army Service Corps managed to rejoin his unit at Berg el Arab after a long journey with another unit through the Nile Delta. This diversion had been "an extraordinary wasteful journey since it accomplished nothing." But back with his unit in 13 Corps, Waggett had a pleasant surprise. He recorded at the time:

> Following that, one day we had a visit from Genl. Horrocks, G.O.C. 13 Corps,
> who told us in an address all about it and what they were planning to do in the
> coming great battle. It has been the policy of the Army Commander in this cam-
> paign to keep the troops well informed, which appears to be a good idea judging
> by the results.[29]

Engineer officer Geoffrey Giddings also commented on the "good results" of keeping the men informed. He wrote that knowing Montgomery's battle plan was "most important of all." It meant that "We all knew the part we were to play—and what a sense of confidence and purpose that gave to us all."[30] As an engineer, Giddings' main task would be to clear a path through the minefields. Issued with new "Polish" mine detectors, the engineers devised a gap-clearing drill that was effective at locating, marking, and lifting both enemy and British mines. As Giddings recalled, "We practised and practised by day, blind folded and at night so that we became proficient at it."[31]

Prior to commencing their training, after the strains of First Alamein and Alam Halfa, Lieutenant General Freyberg insisted that the New Zealanders have a period of rest prior to preparing for this next battle. After a very eventful fortnight of leave, which saw "a record number of cases of bad behaviour" reported, 2 New Zealand Division moved twenty miles south of the Burg el Arab rest area to begin an intensive period of hard training.[32] The Division was now reinforced by the inclusion of 9 Armoured Brigade and by additional regiments of field and medium artillery. Training was very tough, with live firing exercises used on many occasions, which resulted in some casualties. Brigadier Kippenberger commented on this training:

It was not going to be easy and we spared no pains. I have never worked or
thought harder than in these weeks, nor have I ever worked troops so hard; and
all commanders and staff did the same.[33]

Freyberg recorded:

Time being short, we started our training with a full scale Divisional rehearsal
under conditions as similar as possible to the actual attack we were to carry out
later to capture Miteiriya Ridge. Complete plans and preparations were made
for the "attack" which we carried out by moonlight on 26 September. Minefields
had been laid in the positions we expected to find them.[34]

The simulated attack involved the infantry brigades "laying up" during
the day and crossing live minefields under an artillery barrage in conditions as close to the reality of battle as possible. The lessons derived from
the rehearsal and the brigade and battalion that followed "formed the
basis of our planning for the attack." Freyberg wrote, "The operation
required a high degree of training of all arms and most careful timing."[35]

Part of this "all arms" training of the New Zealanders involved working closely with its embedded armored brigade. The 2nd New Zealand
Division was to have a dual role in the battle, being part of the infantry
attack during the break-in phase and then being part of the *corps de chasse*
during the pursuit. Its unique structure made it more suitable for the
mobile role, but its experienced infantry was needed for the break-in, too.
Before the battle commenced, Freyberg explained the Division's new
structure to the New Zealand Government. He assured them that, with
its three tank regiments, the 2nd New Zealand Division was now "more
powerful than a Panzer Division." Freyberg commented further that the
days of New Zealand infantry being overrun by enemy armor "are I hope
past."[36] Freyberg was more forthright with a former colleague, writing:

In my opinion we will be the most formidable fighting force in the world . . . I
do trust that the days of being overrun by German tanks are over—there they
should be. We have had a very difficult two-and-a-half years fighting tanks with
inadequate weapons.[37]

More occurred with the New Zealanders than just training. Freyberg took every effort to see that the British 9 Armoured Brigade, with
its new Sherman and its obsolete Crusader tanks, was fully integrated
within the 2nd New Zealand Division. Each infantry brigade carried out

brigade and battalion exercises with the armored regiments and social events were held wherein officers of all brigades mixed freely. The regiments of 9 Armoured Brigade put the New Zealand Division's distinctive fern-leaf emblem on their tanks (and it is still used by some of the regiments), mixed ceremonial parades were held, and joint exercises and Tactical Exercise Without Troops (TEWTS) were conducted so that members of all the formations got to know one another well. As Kippenberger recorded:

> Both they and we were resolved that there was going to be no more nonsense about tanks and infantry failing to cooperate.... The result was that throughout the battle 9 Armoured Brigade gave us magnificent support regardless of their terrible losses. No formation can have made greater sacrifices for the victory.[38]

In fact, 9 Armoured Brigade was the only armored formation consistently to follow directives in the forthcoming battle and take all its stated objectives throughout. Kippenberger recalled after the war that while the New Zealanders were "moderately confident of much better things" from the British armor before El Alamein, in 9 Armoured Brigade, they had "complete and justified confidence."[39]

9 Armoured Brigade was well suited for its role with the New Zealanders. The three regiments were all Yeomanry cavalry regiments that had been sent to Palestine in 1939. They had seen action during the Syrian campaign in 1941, but had not fought in the Western Desert. Their commander John Currie was both open minded and had "a reputation for fearlessness in action."[40] He would be killed by shellfire in Normandy on June 26, 1944. Not being part of the armored clique of Eighth Army meant that 9 Armoured Brigade "had few ingrained prejudices about tank-infantry cooperation."[41] But the Brigade had some hurdles to overcome. It was inexperienced in desert warfare and had only just received the latest Sherman tanks. Freyberg and Currie had just on six weeks to prepare this fresh armored brigade for the largest set piece battle to be fought in North Africa.

* * *

Most of Eighth Army's armor was placed in the newly created 10 Corps. This was Montgomery's *corps de chasse*, the Army's armored spearhead which was modeled on Rommel's famed Afrika Korps. It consisted initially of two armored divisions, the 1st and 10th Armoured Divisions.

Once the breakthrough had been made, the 2nd New Zealand Division was to join 10 Corps, providing its motorized infantry. This Corps was Montgomery's concept and it was meant to provide Eighth Army with formidable strike power. Montgomery regarded it as his *"corps d'elite."*[42] But from its inception, the *corps de chasse* caused Montgomery considerable headaches. The first problem was to find a suitable Corps commander. Montgomery wanted Brian Horrocks for the job, but Horrocks, an infantry officer, was averse to take the command. Horrocks had already experienced considerable friction with armored commanders during the Alam Halfa battle and was not keen for more. Reluctantly, Montgomery appointed Lieutenant General Herbert Lumsden to this critical role. Lumsden had commanded the 1st Armoured Division in previous desert campaigns and, despite repeatedly letting down infantry formations, he was "highly spoken of in Middle East circles." Montgomery had his doubts about Lumsden, but was prepared to give him the chance to prove himself. He later wrote of Lumsden, "I hardly knew him and so could not agree with complete confidence; but I accepted him on the advice of others."[43]

The second problem occurred during 10 Corps' training for the battle ahead. Much time was devoted to moving at night, something British tanks had not tried before. While it was recognized that such movement and the fighting that followed would entail working alongside the infantry divisions of 30 Corps, "at no point did the rehearsals actually include training with those divisions."[44] While all the rehearsals conducted resulted in a considerable number of learning points to be addressed, rather than find solutions to the problems being encountered, these convinced the senior armored commanders that Montgomery's plan couldn't be done. Therefore, they would not follow it. Lumsden expressed this view at several planning conferences, much to the alarm of the senior infantry commanders. He described armor as being "very brittle" and being prone "to break very easily." Therefore, he had no intention of "breaking" his armor on minefields, which the infantry should clear first. This would destroy the *corps de chasse* before it even got started. Major General de Guingand recalled an incident that he felt compelled to report to Montgomery:

> Monty had been called away to give a lecture at the Staff College, Haifa. Lumsden was commander of 10 Corps, and I thought I'd better go over and

listen to what he'd got to say. And he got up: "Monty's plan—there's one point I don't agree with: that tanks should be used to force their way out of the minefields. Tanks must be used as cavalry: they must exploit the situation and not be kept as supporters of infantry. So I don't propose to do that." So after the conference I went up to Herbert and I said: "Look here, my dear boy, you can't do this, you know Monty. You must know him well enough—he won't permit disobedience to his orders." And he said: "Oh, leave that to me." "Well, I warn you," I made clear. Monty came back the next day and I repeated to him this conference. He said: "Whistle in Lumsden . . ."[45]

Montgomery's biographer labels the attitude of Lumsden and the senior armored commanders as "tantamount to mutiny" and believes it showed that Eighth Army was still very much a prisoner of its past defeats and failures.[46] He goes further and describes the creation of the *corps de chasse* as "a mistake, for rather than promoting a really true professional armoured formation of the calibre of the Afrika Korps it encouraged the amateur independence that characterised British armoured units."[47] Despite this "rebellion," Montgomery had no choice but to stick with Lumsden and 10 Corps as his *corps d'elite*. But despite his cajoling and direct orders, 10 Corps never achieved its objectives in the break-in or dog fight phase of the battle ahead. After the battle, Montgomery replaced Lumsden with Horrocks and abandoned his *corps de chasse* concept.

* * *

While the armored formations balked at their part in Montgomery's plan, the artillery formations relished the opportunity to demonstrate what concentrated firepower could do. The officer in charge of Eighth Army artillery was Major General Sidney Kirkman, a Montgomery appointment. At his initial meeting with Kirkman, Montgomery had outlined his battle plan and told Kirkman to see that "the gunner plan is absolutely as good as it can be—it's one of the most important factors." Kirkman replied, "Yes sir, I understand" and "that was that."[48] Montgomery never had to speak to Kirkman again about the importance of artillery in the coming battle.

A detailed artillery plan was prepared that would protect the infantry moving forward and destroy known German artillery positions and strong points. Eighth Army had some 850 field and fifty medium guns in its arsenal. In addition, it had more than 1,000 anti-tank guns, of which

753 were the effective six-pounder. Ammunition supplies were abundant. "These were riches which Eighth Army had never seen before," recalled de Guingand.[49] Eighth Army's artillery "was formidable indeed" and they would give it a cutting edge in the battle ahead.[50] On the opening night of the battle, the artillery would fire the heaviest bombardment used by the British Army in the war to date. Much of the artillery was sited within 1,000 yards of the frontline so as to offer maximum protection to and beyond the final infantry objective. The artillery would fire a concentrated barrage on a particular location known as a "stonk." They would also provide a thin creeping barrage for two of the four attacking infantry divisions on the night of the attack. Tracer shells from 40 mm Bofors anti-aircraft guns would be used to mark brigade and divisional boundaries. All of these innovations had originated with the 2nd New Zealand Division, whose CRA, Brigadier Steve Weir, was regarded by many as "the best gunner in Eighth Army."[51] In scientific gunnery, Eighth Army had a qualitative edge over Panzerarmee. Freyberg explained in his secret report on operations how the artillery plan worked:

> All artillery on the Corps front was under command C.C.R.A., 30th Corps. The New Zealand Division had four field regiments plus one medium battery, or 104 guns, covering a front of 2,500 yards at the first objective and opening out to 4,800 yards on the final objective, which meant a gun to every twenty-four yards on the first objective and a gun to every forty-six yards on the final objective. As this was not really sufficient for an artillery barrage, the programme provided for twenty-five per cent of the guns, or one gun per hundred yards of front, to fire on a barrage line to keep the infantry on the proper line of advance, and seventy-five per cent of the guns to fire timed concentrations on known enemy defences.[52]

On the eve of the offensive, many senior commanders delivered stirring speeches to the men they commanded. Montgomery was no exception, speaking to all officers in Eighth Army down to lieutenant colonel over the two days of October 19 and 20. His Chief of Staff, de Guingand, recalled that these speeches were "a real *tour de force*" and believed they were the best Montgomery ever delivered.[53] Montgomery also sent a personal message to all members of Eighth Army assuring them that they were now fully ready for battle. He informed them that:

> The battle which is now about to begin will be one of the decisive battles of history. It will be the turning point of the war. The eyes of the world will be on us, watching anxiously which way the battle will swing. We can give them their answer at once: "it will swing our way."[54]

It was certainly inspirational.

One of the most moving and often quoted speeches was delivered by the Australian commander Lieutenant General Sir Leslie Morshead on October 10. Speaking at a meeting of officers of the 9th Australian Division down to lieutenant colonel level, Morshead impressed on all the officers present "the necessity for all ranks to fight to the last man and the last round in order to destroy the enemy."[55] Then Morshead told them:

> I cannot stress too greatly the value and necessity for <u>determined</u> leading, and it will apply in this battle as never before.... We must all apply ourselves to the task that lies ahead, work, think, train, prepare, enthuse. We must regard ourselves as having been born for this battle.[56]

* * *

Montgomery's plans were relatively simple. Essentially it was to "blow a hole in the enemy positions" and then dispatch a corps strong in armor through that hole.[57] The battle was codenamed Operation *Lightfoot,* which displayed a staff officer's dark humor given the density of the minefields to be crossed. Montgomery divided the battle neatly into three phases. In the north, the cream of Eighth Army's infantry was concentrated in 30 Corps commanded by Lieutenant General Oliver Leese. The four infantry divisions of the corps were to achieve the break-in. This break-in had to be achieved on the opening night of the attack. Once the break-in had occurred, the two armored divisions of 10 Corps, under Lumsden, would pass through 30 Corps' positions. They would move along two cleared laneways in the minefields and deploy immediately to their front. This also had to happen on the opening night. Both 30 and 10 Corps would then engage with Panzerarmee during the dogfight phase. This was the attritional stage of the battle, during which Eighth Army would "slowly 'eat the guts' out of its enemy."[58] The Axis infantry would be "crumbled" away in their static positions and when Rommel's armor sought to intervene, it would be destroyed in the pitched armored battle that followed. This phase of the battle would be a deadly "killing match" and Montgomery made it clear in a Memorandum on October 6 that this would no easy victory. Montgomery explained:

> This battle will involve hard and prolonged fighting.... Our troops must not think that, because we have a good tank and very powerful artillery support,

the enemy will surrender. The enemy will not surrender and there will be bitter fighting. The infantry must be prepared to fight and kill, and to continue doing so over a prolonged period.[59]

But Montgomery had no doubt Rommel would be decisively defeated in this killing match; then the pursuit phase could begin. Then 10 Corps, with the New Zealanders included, the *corps de chasse* and a *corps d'elite*, would be unleashed to pursue and destroy the remnants of a defeated Panzerarmee as it sought to escape. This was the third or break-out phase of the battle.

Meanwhile, in the southern part of the line, 13 Corps, commanded by Horrocks and consisting of the 7th Armoured, the 44th Division, and a Free French Brigade, would carry out diversionary attacks in the hope of pinning down one of Rommel's armored divisions in this sector. Montgomery anticipated that the battle would last twelve days.[60] As David Fraser has written, the British Army had not fought a battle like this since 1918. Such a frontal assault would become a battle of attrition "needing perfect preparation, moral force and persistence unto death." While the battle would be costly, it could also be decisive.[61]

While Montgomery's plan, especially the adjustments he made to it in his October 6 Memorandum, have been described as a "bold conception" and "basically sound," there were serious flaws in it.[62] First, expecting 30 Corps to achieve the break-in and 10 Corps to move through the gaps punched in the line in just one night was highly ambitious. Niall Barr has written that Montgomery's plan simply "asked too much of the Eighth Army."[63] The plan also required the infantry and armored divisions to work closely together in all four phases. Yet, apart from 9 Armoured Brigade, which was embedded within the 2nd New Zealand Division, no other armored formation undertook training with the infantry. Some cursory thought had been given to how it might occur but this was totally inadequate. The lack of a common doctrine on how tanks, infantry, and artillery should deal with German anti-tank guns firing behind the protection of their minefields was a major "blank spot in tactics" and a serious omission for which Eighth Army would pay dearly.[64] Then there was the lack of detail in the plan about what was to happen once the dogfight was won and the *corps de chasse* unleashed. Niall Barr writes:

The lack of any developed plan for exploitation and pursuit was highly significant. Montgomery's failure to plan beyond the killing match was to have important consequences at the conclusion of the forthcoming battle.[65]

* * *

There was one element of Montgomery's plan that deserves special mention. For the first time in the North African campaign, the British had
prepared a detailed deception plan that aimed to convince the enemy
that their main effort would be made in the south. Codenamed Operation *Bertram*, the deception plan was elaborate and so thorough that prepared notes recorded that prior to the offensive opening on October 23,
"the Eighth Army practised deception on a scale to be believed to be
unequalled in military history."[66] This bold claim is probably justified
given the extent of the deception measures undertaken. These included
sending false wireless traffic; the building of a 20-mile "dummy" pipeline
with three "dummy" pump houses; the creation of "dummy" supply
dumps; the creation of two false transport parks with approximately
2,000 "vehicles" in each; the open movement of tanks, guns, and artillery heading south, all of which was moved back north by night; and
the creation of a fake railway track made from petrol cans. Meanwhile,
every effort was made to conceal the real build-up for the main attack
in the north. The deception plan also included the diversionary attacks
to be made by 13 Corps on October 23, as well as two "Chinese" attacks
carried out by 9 Australian and 4 Indian Division. The Notes on Operation *Bertram* explain:

> This method was used during the last war and consists of groups of dummy fig-
> ures which are elevated by mechanical means to draw fire. 75 figures were used
> by 9 Australian Division. They were sited in two groups some 300 yards in front
> of the forward defended localities. They were let up in batches from a control
> post about 100 yards away and "accidentally" illuminated. They drew a consider-
> able amount of fire.[67]

That the main direction of the attack and its timings were not detected by Panzerarmee is evidence that a tactical surprise was obtained
by Eighth Army. This was greatly assisted by the DAF denying the enemy aerial observation over the British positions. Between October 18
and 23, not a single German plane succeeded in flying over the British
positions at Alamein.[68] At 1830 hours on October 23, Montgomery's staff
could report "that the enemy showed no signs of expecting to be attacked

that night." The Panzerarmee's evening report to Oberkommando des Heeres (OKH—the High Command of the German Army) informed them that: "Enemy situation unchanged."[69] Eighth Army's senior Intelligence Officer believed that "this was due in great measure to the effectiveness of the deception methods adopted."[70] A report from 9 Australian Division confirmed the effectiveness of the deception plan. Interrogation of prisoners of war captured in the opening attack revealed that "Axis Comd believed up till evening of 24 October (24 hours after the launching of the attack) that the real threat lay in the south."[71] The British official history of deception operations is adamant that "there can be no doubt of the success" of British deception measures prior to Alamein and that a "tactical surprise was complete."[72] Alexander confirmed this in his post-war Despatch. He described the deception operations as being "entirely successful; the main direction of our thrust and the location of our armour were unknown to the enemy at the time the attack began and for some time afterwards." Alexander reported that it was not until the third day of the battle "that he finally concentrated all his resources against our real attack."[73]

There was another successful deception plan that has received almost no attention in histories of the battle. From 1942, Eighth Army's military intelligence section had created several bogus military formations aimed to convince the enemy that Eighth Army was much larger than it really was. In 1942, an additional armored division (15th) and seven bogus infantry divisions had been created. Two of the infantry divisions were from India and one from New Zealand. In addition, a fictitious 25th Corps headquarters had been created.[74] Each bogus formation was supported by fake wireless traffic, forged documentation, empty military camps, and other deception measures. The ruse was stunningly successful. Enemy documents captured after the battle showed that the bogus units were accepted as real. It resulted in Panzerarmee overestimating the strength of its opponent by 40 percent in armor and 45 percent in infantry. The inflated figures "were to remain in German intelligence estimates until the end of the war."[75]

* * *

So, what did the Axis leadership know of the pending attack and how did they prepare to meet it? Rommel was under no illusion about what to expect after Alam Halfa. The initiative had passed to Eighth Army. A senior German staff officer, Generalmajor Alfred Toppe, wrote after the war, "It was clear to Rommel that time was working against him and that as soon as the enemy had brought forward sufficient reinforcements he would launch a powerful counteroffensive."[76] In the battle ahead, the British had several advantages. Rommel wrote prior to El Alamein:

> the British would first have to try for a break through. We had no doubts about the suitability of the British Army for such a task, for its entire training had been based on the lessons learnt in the battles of material of the First World War. . . . In this form of action the full value of the excellent Australian and New Zealand infantry would be realised and the British artillery would have its effect.[77]

But as Rommel noted, at El Alamein those defending a position had "a certain advantage." Those attacking had no choice but to assault prepared defensive positions. Those defending these positions "could dig in and protect itself with mines, while the enemy had to make his attack exposed to the fire of the dug-in defence."[78]

To counter the blow that was coming, Rommel's defenses were prepared in considerable depth. The forward outpost line, the point nearest the enemy, was thinly held but ran to a depth of around 900 meters (1,000 yards). It consisted of mutually supporting strongpoints and its purpose served as an early warning system. The outpost strongpoints "were provided with dogs to give warning of any British approach to the minefields."[79] Behind the outpost line was a gap of up to two kilometers (about one and a quarter miles) before the main defensive position was reached. Each battalion in line occupied a frontage of around 1,500 meters (one mile) and ran to a depth of five kilometers (just over three miles).[80] Only one company in each battalion was deployed to the forward outpost line, the rest occupied the main line of defense. German and Italian battalions were interspersed "so that an Italian battalion always had a German as its neighbour."[81] The panzer divisions were positioned immediately behind the main line so that their guns could cover the front line. They were also ready to move to any threatened sector of the front.

The key to Rommel's defense, though, was his "Devil's Garden." Major General Alfred Toppe explained Rommel's method:

> He therefore did everything possible to improve the German positions, with particular stress on the use of mines, including air bombs which were buried and

prepared for electrical detonation. He even had what he called "mine gardens" lain in the outpost area and had all battalion command posts surrounded by minefields. In distributing the forces in the northern half of the defense line, which he considered the most endangered and which was in the zone of the Italian XXI Corps, he placed Italian battalions and battalions of the 164th Light African Division alternately.[82]

From July 5 to October 20, German and Italian engineers planted almost 500,000 mines in this garden, making for a formidable defense. Most of the mines—more than 360,000 of them—were of British origin, but these would now be used against their former owners. Only 14,509 of the mines were anti-personnel S-mines. S stood for *Springen*. When activated, an initial charge sprang the canister to waist height, where it exploded, sending 360 ball-bearings in all directions.[83] Rommel would have preferred to have had many more of these S-mines. Instead of three percent of the mines being of the anti-personnel type, Rommel had directed that this figure should reach one-third of all mines laid.[84] Despite this good fortune, breaching the German defensive positions at El Alamein was going to be a challenging task. Rommel's problems at Alam Halfa had been caused by some of these very mines in his Devil's Garden and he now had many more of them. There were "at least two belts of mines all along the Axis positions" as well as isolated minefield "boxes" that were designed to channel the attackers into designated killing zones.[85] During the Second World War, no other army to date had used so many mines in its defenses. Rommel placed considerable confidence in his defenses, especially in the effectiveness of the minefields. Niall Barr writes:

> Such deep defences combined with the minefields confronted Eighth Army with a severe challenge. Rommel placed great faith in his "Devil's Gardens" and he believed that any future British offensive would come to grief amongst the dense tangle of wires, outposts and mines.[86]

While the Axis forces knew an assault was coming, knowing when and where it would fall was a different matter. Eighth Army had spent considerable effort on its deception plan but this was only partially successful. On October 21, Colonel Ulrich Liss of the Intelligence section of OKH visited Panzerarmee Afrika. At the conference that followed, Liss "expressed the opinion that the decisive British attack would not start before the beginning of November." But Panzerarmee's own intelligence section, detecting the build-up of medical personnel close to the front line, concluded instead "that an all-out attack by Eighth Army was imminent."[87] The records of the Afrika Korps confirm this. As early as October 1, 1942, 15 Panzer Division's Intelligence Officer had warned that the reinforced Eighth Army "will launch an offensive in mid Oct with the object of forcing a break through our fortified positions and destroying the Axis forces." Further, because the attack could be supported by the Royal Navy and offered the prospect of splitting the Axis forces: "The main weight of the offensive will come between the coast and Ruweisat."[88] It could not be argued then, as the British Official History of deception operations claimed, that Eighth Army obtained a "complete ... tactical surprise" over Panzerarmee.[89]

Rommel was still not well. His commander Albert Kesselring later wrote that after Alam Halfa, Rommel was a changed man. According to Kesselring, Rommel was:

> no longer the bold leader of old; the long period, almost two years, of uninterrupted fighting in the hot climate, with the incessant friction from the co-operation with the Italians, and of the disappointment at the failure of the advance to Cairo, had seriously upset his health and above all his nerves. Rommel needed a rest.[90]

His doctor insisted during this lull period that he return to Germany for a period of rest and recovery. Having made all of the defensive arrangements he could, Rommel handed over command of Panzerarmee Afrika to General Georg Stumme on September 22 and left for Germany. General Stumme is often treated as a non-entity in many accounts of the October battle, especially as he died so early during it. But Stumme had a distinguished career as a panzer commander having commanded divisions and corps in Poland, France, Yugoslavia, Greece, and Russia. For his campaigning in France, Stumme, like Rommel, had been awarded the Knights Cross, which was the highest degree of the Iron Cross.[91] Rommel would not have handed over his command to Stumme if he did not think he was up to the job.

Nor would Rommel have left for Germany if he was not confident of being able to hold off Eighth Army's next attack. In his papers, Rommel wrote of the October Alamein offensive as a "Battle Without Hope." He ended the account of his defensive preparations with one despairing sentence:

> But all our efforts were to prove unavailing against the immensely superior British force—not because of mistakes we had made, but because victory was simply impossible under the terms on which we'd entered the battle.[92]

Niall Barr is correct to claim that Rommel "overlaid a heavy dose of hindsight" when he spoke of having no chance in the battle ahead. As Barr states, senior Axis commanders, including Rommel, "were far from despondent about the coming British offensive."[93] In Berlin on September 31, Rommel received "a hero's welcome" at the Sportpals, where he waved his field marshal's baton presented to him by Hitler. At the Reichchancellery, he had "basked in the Fuhrer's adulatory speech extolling his great desert victories."[94] The mood in Berlin was far from despondent. Generalmajor Eckhardt Christian, a senior staff officer at the Oberkommando der Wehrmacht (OKW—the High Command of the German Armed Forces), recalled a briefing by Rommel at the Führer's Headquarters when Rommel reached Berlin. Rommel "registered uneasiness" about Britain's growing air superiority in the region, "which he termed as the most serious stumbling blocks." He also expressed concern about "the sporadic, usually insufficient, supply shipments." But the main impression Rommel created was one of confidence. Christian remembered:

> He described in detail the strength of the newly occupied position and the plans for improvements. Particularly confident were his remarks concerning the position's defenses which, according to him, had been rendered all the more impregnable by the installation of very dense mine fields. The Field Marshal produced scaled sketches of these so-called "mine orchards" ("Minengarten") which he himself had planned. Continuing his report, Rommel stated that, generally speaking, he was satisfied with the bearing of his troops and of part of the Italian units.[95]

Rommel's report of the situation in North Africa "generally met approval" and OKW undertook to address the problems he raised. The general impression gained was that although the Axis thrust into Cairo had to be postponed, "the situation prevailing at the southern front . . . presented no cause for undue apprehension."[96] At a press conference at the Propaganda Ministry on October 3, Rommel radiated confidence,

Table 5.1. Comparative Strengths October 23, 1942[1]

	Eighth Army	Panzerarmee Afrika
Frontline troops	220,476	110,000 (53,736 Germans)
Tanks	1,020 (170 Grants, 252 Shermans, 216 Crusader II, 78 Crusader III, 119 Stuarts, 194 Valentines)	600 (249 German, of which only 129 were "heavy" tanks)
Armored cars	400	200
Artillery	892	552 (including 26 heavy guns)
Anti-tank guns	1,350 (800 six-pounders, 550 two-pounders)	1,063 (86 were the notorious 88 mm dual-purpose gun)
Mines		500,000
Aircraft	530	350

[1] Figures vary in different accounts of the battle. I have used figures from Walker, 249–250 and Barr, 276.

telling his audience that "they held the door to Egypt in their hands."[97] This was hardly indicative of a battle without hope.

* * *

Eighth Army was not "immensely superior" in force, as Rommel alleged, either. Senior staff officer Generalmajor Alfred Toppe later admitted that during this period "the strengths of both sides were about equal. Neither the Eighth British Army nor the German forces had any appreciable measure of superiority."[98] The comparative strengths on the eve of battle can be seen in table 5.1.

From the figures in table 5.1, in terms of men, armor, and artillery, Eighth Army appeared to have a crushing superiority. It may therefore seem surprising that Panzerarmee managed to stave off defeat for as long as it did. This is especially true when Panzerarmee's fuel shortage was considered. In September, only 20 percent of Panzerarmee's supplies had been lost en route to North Africa. In October, though, this figure had reached "no less than 44 per cent."[99] Rommel's supply lines were being steadily strangled by Allied planes and submarines, which were well-informed about when shipments were being made to him. On the eve of the offensive, Panzerarmee had three consumption units on hand, which gave it enough fuel for just over four days' battle supply.[100] During the battle, Mussolini admitted to the senior Italian commander that the problem of fuel for Panzerarmee "gnawed at his liver, day and night."[101]

But fuel shortages aside, Eighth Army's numerical superiority was not as great as the numbers would suggest. In most areas, Eighth Army had a two-to-one advantage over Panzerarmee. When attacking, a three-to-one advantage is the general rule of thumb used. Walker, the New Zealand official historian, wrote of Eighth Army's two-to-one superiority: "The course of military history shows that such a ratio is not sufficient on its own to ensure victory to the attackers."[102] Eighth Army had often enjoyed this numerical advantage before and had still not been able to defeat Rommel.

Eighth Army's strength in infantry and armor was deceptive. The infantry divisions of 30 Corps had the task of making the breach in the Axis line. There were five divisions but one, the 4th Indian Division, was not ready to take part in a major assault. It had only two brigades and the Corps Commander assessed it as "only capable of holding the line and could only be relied on provided they were very well mined and wired in."[103] It had been planned that 4th Indian Division would carry out a series of raids around Ruweisat Ridge, but these had to be abandoned. Two of the five divisions were below strength and had no replacements available. These were the 1st South African Division and the 2nd New Zealand Division. The New Zealanders would receive no reinforcements in 1942, which meant that their two infantry brigades were well below strength. On the eve of the offensive, Freyberg recorded in his diary:

> men in good form—our trouble is we are short of men now—weapons all right—guns and tanks must do what infantry have done before—it all depends on the gun line and the tanks must go through.[104]

Leese, the Corps Commander, described 2nd New Zealand Division as "a grand Division . . . magnificently commanded by General Freyberg, whose leadership in battle was an inspiration to the whole of the Corps." But Leese recognized that with two understrength brigades and no reinforcement, 2nd New Zealand Division was "incapable of fighting a sustained action."[105] This left only two fully equipped divisions in the Corps who were capable of fighting this type of action. These were the 51st Highland Division and the 9th Australian Division. The 51st Highland Division had been rebuilt after the entire division was captured at St. Valery in 1940. This reconstituted Division had not been in action before. This meant the 9th Australian Division was the only experienced infantry division in 30 Corps capable of slugging it out in a sustained action. Leese was effusive in his praise of this formation. The 9th Australian Division was: "a fine Division, very ably commanded by General Morshead, highly specialised in this type of warfare; intensely confident in itself and full of offensive spirit."[106] Little wonder that, in the battle ahead, the 9th Australian Division played a key role.

Leese's 30 Corps was short of artillery, too. He had 452 field guns and forty-eight medium guns to cover the entire 30 Corps break-in attack.[107] Facing 30 Corps were two well-entrenched enemy divisions. These were the German 164th Light Division and the Italian Trento Division. Between them, these two divisions fielded 250 anti-tank and ninety field guns. But the two divisions were also supported by an additional thirteen heavy, seventy medium, and 160 field guns.[108] Deployed behind the 164th and Trento Divisions were three mixed battle groups from 15 Panzer and the Littorio Divisions, who had their own artillery support embedded. 30 Corps must be regarded as weak in artillery. It did not have a two-to-one superiority in field artillery and was actually outnumbered in terms of heavy and medium guns.

In the southern sector, the British 13 Corps consisted of 7 Armoured Division, the famed "Desert Rats," 44 Division, and a Free French Brigade. It faced the Folgore Parachute and Pavia Divisions and the Ramcke Parachute Brigade. Axis armor consisted of 21 Panzer and the Ariete Division. Ariete was regarded as "the best of the Italian armoured formations."[109]

Eighth Army's superiority in tanks was also deceptive. Only 422 were the US-made Grant and Sherman tanks, which could match the majority of German tanks in terms of armor, mechanical reliability, and firepower.[110] Even then, the M3 Grant had its main 75 mm gun in a sponson attached to the tank's main body at the front right of the hull. Rather than a revolving turret with all-round traverse like the Sherman, the Grant's main weapon had severe limitations. Recently arrived, too, was the Crusader III tank, which at last mounted a decent gun: the six-pounder as opposed to the two-pounder gun of other British tanks. This

new arrival "had been keenly awaited for a long time" and was expected
to be "a big improvement" over previous British tanks. Such high hopes
were soon dashed. The British official history admitted that "before long
the Mark III was being criticized for displaying most of the weaknesses
of the early Crusaders, and like them, for having no capped ammunition."[111] The lack of capped, armor-piercing ammunition for the Crusader
Mark III was a shocking oversight.

* * *

Even with a numerical advantage over Panzerarmee, Eighth Army's
superiority in tanks would "count for very little unless the armoured
brigades could reach the open desert and deploy properly."[112] Few experienced soldiers in Eighth Army expected this to happen. As Leese
recalled, the Dominion troops, that is three of the four attack divisions
in his Corps, had "no faith whatsoever in the British armour."[113]

On the eve of the final battle of El Alamein, Montgomery sent a
personal message to all members of Eighth Army. He informed them
that "We are ready NOW" to destroy Rommel and his army. He assured
his soldiers that they had plenty of first-class equipment and that if they
all fought hard, "there can be only one result—together we will hit the
enemy for 'six' right out of North Africa." The Commonwealth members
of Eighth Army appreciated the cricketing analogy and hoped Montgomery was right. No doubt many joined with Montgomery in praying,
with echoes of Oliver Cromwell, that "the 'Lord mighty in Battle' will
give us victory."[114]

In London that Friday evening after dinner, General Alan Brooke
received a call from the War Office informing him that the attack had
commenced. His diary entry reflected all the hopes, anxiety, and des-
peration the United Kingdom had invested in this battle:

> We are bound to have some desperately anxious moments as to what success
> is to be achieved. There are great possibilities and great dangers! It may be the
> turning point of the war, leading to further success combined with the North
> African attack, or it may mean nothing. If it fails I don't quite know how I shall
> bear it, I have pinned such hopes on these two offensives.[115]

Churchill, too, had much at stake. On the eve of the offensive he wrote
to Alexander that "all our hopes are centred upon the battle you and

Montgomery are going to fight. It may well be the key to the future."
Churchill requested, as with Alam Halfa, that Alexander send him the
word "Zip" when the battle started.[116]

Much closer to the battlefield, writing to his wife from his battle
headquarters, a hole in the ground some 2,000 yards from the start line,
Lieutenant General Leslie Morshead caught the mood and hopes of the
men of Eighth Army. Morshead wrote less than two hours before the
battle began:

> A hard fight is expected, and it will no doubt last a long time. We have no delu-
> sions about that. But we shall win out and I trust put an end to this running
> forward and backward to and from Bengazi. It is the effort to finish the war in
> North Africa, and if successful as we feel it will be, it should have a very mate-
> rial influence on the war.... We have been working very hard on the plans and
> preparation for some weeks. And now the stage is set.[117]

The stage indeed was set for the largest battle yet fought in North Africa.
Whether it would be the turning-point battle everyone hoped it would
depended on how well the Eighth Army fought and how well Montgomery commanded them. On the eve of battle, these were very much
unknown qualities.

NOTES

1. Churchill, *Vol. IV*, 493, 494.
2. Hamilton, *Monty. The Making of a General*, 744.
3. Churchill to Alexander, 11 September 1942, PREM 3/299/1, TNA.
4. Churchill to Alexander, 17 September 1942, quoted in Churchill, *Vol. IV*, 527.
5. Major General Francis de Guingand, quoted in Holmes, *The World at War*, 275–276.
6. Barr, *Pendulum of War*, 256.
7. Churchill to Alexander, 20 September 1942, PREM 3/299/1, TNA.
8. Brooke, diary entry 20 September 1942, in Danchev and Todman, *War Diaries 1939–1945*, 323.
9. Churchill to Alexander, 23 September 1942, PREM 3/299/1, TNA.
10. Brooke, diary entry 23 September 1942, in Danchev and Todman, *War Diaries 1939–1945*, 324.
11. Bungay, *Alamein*, 145.
12. Field Marshall B.L. Montgomery, *El Alamein to the River Sangro*. (London: Arrow Books Ltd., 1960), 34.
13. Hamilton, *Monty. The Making of a General*, 718.
14. Ibid., 727, 728.
15. Barr, *Pendulum of War*, 261.
16. 9 Australian Division, Report on Operations El Alamein 23 Oct-5 Nov 1942, WO 201/2495, TNA.

17. War Diary, 2/43 Australian Infantry Battalion, 23 Sept 1942, 8/3/35, AWM 52, AWM.

18. War Diary, 2/43 Australian Infantry Battalion, 26–30 Sept 1942, 8/3/35, AWM 52, AWM.

19. War Diary, 2/17 Australian Infantry Battalion, Comd's Summary Oct 1942, 8/3/17, AWM 52, AWM.

20. War Diary, 2/24 Australian Infantry Battalion, 18 Oct 1942, 8/3/24, AWM 52, AWM.

21. War Diary, 2/48 Australian Infantry Battalion, 19 Oct 1942, 8/3/36, AWM 52, AWM.

22. War Diary, 2/17 Australian Infantry Battalion, Comd's Summary Oct 1942, 8/3/17, AWM 52, AWM.

23. War Diary, 2/43 Australian Infantry Battalion, 22 Sept 1942, 8/3/35, AWM 52, AWM.

24. War Diary, 2/28 Australian Infantry Battalion, 21 Sept 1942, 8/3/28, AWM 52, AWM.

25. War Diary, 2/28 Australian Infantry Battalion, 29 Sept 1942, 8/3/28, AWM 52, AWM.

26. War Diary, 2/48 Australian Infantry Battalion, 15 Sept 1942, 8/3/36, AWM 52, AWM.

27. Personal Narrative of Action by LT. Ewen Frazer, 1939–45 Army, Liddle Collection.

28. A Very Personal Account of Incidents During the Second World War, 1939–1945, John Laing, 1939–45 Army, Liddle Collection.

29. E.G. Waggett, Contemparary account, 1939–45 Army, Liddle Collection, 21.

30. Geoffrey Giddings, "Oppa's War Years 1939–46," 93/4/1, IWM, 34.

31. Ibid.

32. Walker, *Alam Halfa and Alamein*, 190.

33. Kippenberger, *Infantry Brigadier*, 222.

34. Bernard Freyberg, "The New Zealand Division in Egypt and Libya: Operations 'Lightfoot' and 'Supercharge,'" Part I Narrative and Lessons, Freyberg's Secret After-action Report. Copy in author's possession. (GJH), 2.

35. Ibid.

36. Freyberg to Fraser, cipher message, 3 October 1942, WA II 8/25A, ANZ, 130.

37. Freyberg, letter to Barrowclough, 4 October 1942, WA 8 Part II AA, Miscellaneous 1942, ANZ.

38. Kippenberger, *Infantry Brigadier*, 223

39. Kippenberger, letter to Latham, 24 May 1949, WA II 11/2, ANZ.

40. Barr, *Pendulum of War*, 267.

41. Ibid., 266.

42. B.L. Montgomery, *The Memoirs of Field-Marshal The Viscount Montgomery of Alamein, K.G.* (London: Collins, 1958), 113.

43. Ibid.

44. Barr, *Pendulum of War*, 265.

45. Quoted in Hamilton, *Monty. The Making of a General*, 752.

46. Ibid.

47. Ibid., 753.

48. Ibid., 749.

49. de Guingand, *Operation Victory*, 154.

50. Playfair et al., *Volume IV*, 10.

51. Barr, *Pendulum of War*, 293.

52. Freyberg, "The New Zealand Division in Egypt and Libya," 3.

53. de Guingand, *Operation Victory*, 160.

54. Eighth Army, Personal Message From the Army Commander on the Eve of the Battle of Alamein. This copy is included in Geoffrey Giddings, "Oppa's War Years 1939–46," B, 93/4/1, IWM, 33.

55. War Diary, 9 Australian Division General Staff Branch, 10 Oct 194,1/5/20, AWM 52, AWM.

56. Lightfoot, Conference of all Commanders 9 Australian Division, 10/10/42, Folder 33, 3 DRL 2632, AWM. Also reported in War Diary, 9 Australian Division General Staff Branch, 10 Oct 194,1/5/20, AWM 52, AWM.

57. Montgomery, *El Alamein to the River Sangro*, 35.

58. Barr, *Pendulum of War*, 275.

59. Montgomery's Memorandum, 6 Oct 1942, quoted in Hamilton, *Monty. The Making of a General*, 756.

60. Ibid., 764.

61. Fraser, *And We Shall Shock Them*, 240.

62. Walker, *Alam Halfa and Alamein*, 214, 215.

63. Barr, *Pendulum of War*, 274.

64. Walker, *Alam Halfa and Alamein*, 215.

65. Barr, *Pendulum of War*, 275.

66. Bertram: Notes on Deception Practised by the Eighth Army Prior to Its Offensive of October 1942, WO 204/7977, TNA.

67. Ibid.

68. Hinsley, *British Intelligence in the Second World War: Volume 2*, 435.

69. Playfair et al., *Volume IV*, 31.

70. Bertram: Notes on Deception Practised by the Eighth Army Prior to Its Offensive of October 1942, WO 204/7977, TNA.

71. 9 Australian Division, Report on Operations, WO 201/2826, TNA.

72. Michael Howard, *Strategic Deception in the Second World War*. (London: Pimlico, 1992), 66, 67.

73. Alexander's Despatch, Supplement to *The London Gazette*, 5 February 1948, CAB 106/613, TNA, 853.

74. Howard, *Strategic Deception*, 43.

75. Ibid., 44.

76. Toppe, "Desert Warfare," 45.

77. Liddell Hart, *The Rommel Papers*, 298–299.

78. Ibid., 297.

79. Ibid., 300.

80. Barr, *Pendulum of War*, 270.

81. Liddell Hart, *The Rommel Papers*, 300.

82. Toppe, "Desert Warfare," 45.

83. Bierman and Smith, *Alamein: War without Hate*, 255.

84. Playfair et al., *Volume IV*, 29.

85. Ibid., 27.

86. Barr, *Pendulum of War*, 270.

87. Behrendt, *Rommel's Intelligence*, 197.

88. Captain Kircher, 15 Panzer IO, "Probable Tactics of the British Eighth Army in the Offensive against the Alamein Front," GMDS File 26421/3, WA II 11/23, ANZ.

89. Howard, *Strategic Deception* 66, 67.

90. Field Marshal Albert Kesselring, "The War in the Mediterranean Part I," Being a study written for the US History Division, May 1948, WA II 11/17 German Operations, ANZ.

91. Fraser, *Knight's Cross*, 179.

92. Liddell Hart, *The Rommel Papers,* 300. Chapter XIV, which deals with the October Alamein battle, is titled "Battle Without Hope."

93. Barr, *Pendulum of War*, 268.

94. Hamilton, *The Full Monty*, 640.

95. Eckhardt Christian, "The El Alamein Crisis and its After-effects in the OKW," MS D-172, AHEC, 1–2.

96. Ibid., 2, 3.

97. Bungay, *Alamein*, 158.

98. Toppe, "Desert Warfare," 45.

99. Levine, *The War Against Rommel's Supply Lines*, 29.

100. QT 4077 of 20 Oct 1942, CX/MSS/1562/T23 quoted in Hinsley, *British Intelligence in the Second World War: Volume 2*, 427.

101. Cavallero diary, quoted in Fraser, *Knight's Cross*, 375.

102. Walker, *Alam Halfa and Alamein*, 250.

103. Impressions of the Part of 30 Corps in the "Battle of Egypt," from Papers of Sir Oliver Leese, WA II 11/2, ANZ. The papers from Leese are attached to a letter written by J.L. Scoullar to Kippenberger on 30 September 1953.

104. Freyberg's Diary, 20 October 1942, WA II/45, ANZ.

105. Impressions of the Part of 30 Corps in the "Battle of Egypt," from Papers of Sir Oliver Leese, WA II 11/2, ANZ.

106. Ibid.

107. Hamilton, *Monty. The Making of a General*, 747–748.

108. Barr, *Pendulum of War*, 276.

109. Bierman and Smith, *Alamein: War without Hate*, 255.

110. Playfair et al. *Volume IV*, 8.

111. Ibid.

112. Barr, *Pendulum of War*, 278.

113. Impressions of the Part of 30 Corps in the "Battle of Egypt," from Papers of Sir Oliver Leese, WA II 11/2, ANZ.

114. Montgomery, Eighth Army Personal Message from the Army Commander on the Eve of the Battle of Alamein, in Geoffrey Giddings, "Oppa's War Years 1939–46," 93/4/1, IWM, 34.

115. Brooke, diary entry 23 October 1942, in Danchev and Todman, *War Diaries 1939–1945*, 323.

116. Churchill, signal to Alexander, 20 October 1942, in *Vol. IV*, 528.

117. Morshead, letter to Myrtle, 23 October 1942, Series 1, Item 3, 3 DRL, 2632, AWM.

A twenty-five pounder gun crew training near their camp in Egypt. The twenty-five pounder was the standard field artillery gun of Eighth Army. It was a very effective weapon. Leonard George Thorne Collection, Wairarapa Archive, 15-179/2-3-1.

British I Infantry tanks on the move. These are Matilda tanks: heavily armored but with a weak two-pounder gun. During the Desert Campaign, British tanks were inferior in quality to the German panzers. It was not until the arrival of the Grant and Sherman tanks from the USA that Eighth Army had tanks that could match Panzerarmee Afrika. Leonard George Thorne Collection, Wairarapa Archive, 15-179/2-7-1.

Desert conditions were harsh. Living in these conditions took some adjusting to.
Ernest Maynard Scott Collection, Wairarapa Archive, 07-70/1-10-1.

The weapon most feared by British tank crews—the German 88 mm dual-purpose gun. Its range and hitting power were devastating. Just a few of these guns could halt the advance of an entire armored division. Leonard George Thorne Collection, Wairarapa Archive, 15-179/2-19-2.

A German Mark IV Panzer left burning in the desert after the break out from El Alamein. Leonard George Thorne Collection, Wairarapa Archive, 15-179/2-10-4.

Two medics from Eighth Army examine a damaged Panzer Mark III tank. Defeat in the October–November Alamein battle destroyed most of Rommel's armor, leaving him with just thirty-five tanks with which to conduct his withdrawal. Vivian Ellison Collection, Wairarapa Archive, 08-58/1-1-1.

British tanks and infantry on the move. The October battle of El Alamein enabled Eighth Army to finally push Rommel's Panzerarmee Afrika out of Egypt. Eighth Army's slow, cautious advance allowed the remnants of Rommel's defeated army to escape. Ernest Maynard Scott Collection, Wairarapa Archive, 07-70/1-9-2.

SIX

ATTEMPTING THE BREAK-IN: OCTOBER 23–24

The last battle of El Alamein opened on the evening of October 23 with the largest artillery barrage fired by the British army in the war to date. It did not begin with the "concerted roar" of popular imagination.[1] Instead, at 2030 hours, the first rounds in the offensive were fired by just one of 30 Corps' medium guns. These exploded high in the air and were used to test the meteorological conditions that affected accurate shooting. The information was immediately sent to all of Eighth Army's artillery batteries, who made their last-minute adjustments. Also fired before the main barrage commenced was the odd salvo from a single artillery battery. This was part of Eighth Army's normal nightly routine of harassing fire and no change was made that might alert the enemy that something was afoot. At 2140 hours, five minutes after the leading infantry advanced from their start lines, Eighth Army's artillery barrage opened right on time. The noise from nearly 900 guns was deafening and made the air vibrate. The flames from the muzzle flashes lit up a cloudless black night. The War Diary of the Australian 2/28 Battalion succinctly recorded, "2140 hours. Arty bombardment commences—the hammers of Hell at work."[2]

The barrage made a lasting impression on those who witnessed it. DAF pilot Donald Jack's 80 Squadron was just behind the front line where he saw "the most enormous artillery barrage." Jack described it as "the most gigantic pyrotechnics display you could imagine, the rumbling of those guns really horrifying: thank God we weren't Germans! That went on for a long time."[3] Army Service Corps soldier E.G. Waggett recalled that "we were awakened in the early hours of the morning by a tremendous and continuous roar of guns. The sky was full of flashes and tracers."[4] Waiting for the artillery to open up was "a very tense time," admitted Royal Engineer officer John Laing. When it commenced, Laing was surprised that "there was so much noise." He felt the inner tension drain away as "the deafening din caused a new sort of excitement." The flickering night sky reminded Laing of the aurora borealis.[5] For General Alexander though, while the barrage was an "extraordinary sight" it was also a familiar one for the experienced soldier. It was "reminiscent of the previous world war."[6] General Ritter von Thoma had a similar recollection. Explaining what had happened to another captured German general, von Thoma recalled that that the Eighth Army barrage had lasted "all night long, just as it used to be in the Great War." Von Thoma also had the unpleasant task of informing Rommel upon his return from Germany that "a great many of our anti-tank guns, especially the 5 cms ones, have been put out of action."[7]

For fifteen minutes, the forty-eight medium guns and 424 field guns in 30 Corps pounded the Axis gun positions. The counter-battery fire aimed to destroy the Axis guns and their crews and to create "the utmost disorganisation of the lines of communication, replenishment and reinforcement."[8] At 2155 hours, the barrage paused for five minutes as the assaulting infantry approached their first objectives. Then at 2200 hours, all 900 field and medium guns opened up in direct support of the advancing infantry pounding the enemy positions facing them. The War Diary of the Australian 2/24 Battalion recorded the purpose of each barrage. At 2140 hours, it recorded: "Arty barrage opens. The massed arty of 30 Corps proceeding to pound all known enemy bty positions." Then at 2155 hours, it recorded: "Arty barrage switches from CB [counter-battery] to enemy FDLs [forward defense lines] as a 'creeping barrage' moving at the rate of 100 yards in 3 mins." Not everything went smoothly, though, and the 2/24 Battalion's War Diary recorded a perennial danger for the infantry. It noted that: "Bn experienced some trouble throughout by one our 25 pdr guns dropping short."[9]

Notes produced by the Royal Artillery immediately after the battle showed how far Eighth Army doctrine had come in the space of a few short months. The "chief artillery lesson" to emerge from the battle was "the value of centralised control of artillery and that a really heavy concentration of artillery fire put down on a carefully thought out plan will so neutralise the enemy, that infantry, unsupported by armour, will be able to gain their objectives without undue casualties." The Notes observed that this "lesson" merely "confirms what is already known" but that for too long, "the need for adequate artillery support is so frequently overlooked in training."[10]

The first foot soldiers of 30 Corps to advance from their slit trenches were the engineers and their protection parties. Soldier/historian David Fraser wrote of the British Engineers that "no corps was more constantly in demand, so much master of so many tasks."[11] This was never more true than in this second battle of Alamein. After a whole day of lying concealed in slit trenches close to the start line, the engineers now had vital tasks to perform. First they had to open the prepared pathways through the last British minefield so that the assaulting infantry could assemble on the taped start lines. In total, the engineers of Eighth Army carried 130 miles of white tape and 80,000 hurricane lamps for this task.[12] The hurricane lamps were blacked out except for a small hole that could only be seen by the advancing infantry. Second, they had to assist the infantry through the German "Minengarten" ahead of them. Finally, they had to prepare two cleared corridors through these minefields for the armor of 10 Corps to follow the infantry attack. The New Zealand commander Freyberg was correct when he informed his senior engineer officer on the morning of the attack that "A terrible lot depends on the Sappers." His senior engineer assured him, "I am confident they are well drilled."[13]

All the engineers were certainly well-drilled, although some of the new equipment—the Polish electric mine detector and the "Scorpion" flail tanks—had yet to be tested in battle. The Scorpion was a modified Matilda Infantry tank fitted with a rotating steel drum on its front. Attached to the drum were heavy chain flails that beat the ground ahead of it and thus could clear a path through a minefield. But the Scorpion was still experimental in October 1942 and had serious deficiencies. The drum was spun by a Ford V8 engine mounted in a small armored compartment on the side of the tank. In testing, the Scorpion never missed a mine, but the poorly vented V8 engine soon overheated. In operation, the Scorpion created such a thick dust cloud that its operators had to wear respirators. These teething problems and the low numbers of Scorpions available forced 30 Corps to keep them in reserve to be used for emergencies only. Even the electric mine detectors were in short supply in October 1942 and many sappers had to resort to the old, less reliable method of prodding with bayonets to locate the mines. Working to clear the German minefield facing the 44th Division in 13 Corps, Royal Engineer officer John Laing recalled that his sappers were not troubled by the German artillery firing on them. Instead, "They had enough to contend with locating mines and marking the clear lanes, all the time being on the receiving end of mortar bombs, small arms and machine-gun fire." It was dangerous work, Laing acknowledged. "There were, of course, casualties and we dealt with them as well as we could."[14] At the end of the night, Laing's sappers had successfully breached the German minefield.

The Axis forces were alarmed at how easily parts of the "Minengarten" had been breached. Prisoner of war statements taken during the battle, including one from General Ritter von Thoma, captured on November 4, confirmed that "they thought that no armoured force could get through their extensive minefields."[15] But as German staff officer Alfred Toppe later wrote, "The 'mine gardens' referred to previously did not have the desired effect, because many of the mines had been detonated by the artillery fire or during bombing attacks."[16] Some mines were undoubtedly detonated by bombs and artillery shells. However, the main reason for the "Minengarten" not having the desired effect was the courage and skill of the sappers who cleared pathways through them. Alexander recognized the sappers' contribution in this El Alamein battle and informed Churchill that it was the "incessant mine clearing by engineer battalions often under intense fire, [which] opened the way for . . . the equally hard fighting" that followed.[17] David Fraser, retired general and historian of the British Army in the Second World War, described the mine clearing operations of the sappers as "the key task affecting the speed and success of operations." He wrote that, "Without the successful performance of the Royal Engineers, there would have been no victory of Alamein." The courage and skill of the sappers clearing the mines was "beyond praise."[18]

* * *

The Desert Air Force (DAF) commenced its part in the battle well before the evening of October 23. It had almost 600 serviceable aircraft available to support army operations.[19] The DAF's preliminary air operations commenced on the night of October 18 with bombing attacks against German transport hubs, supply dumps, port facilities, and airfields. This preliminary bombing campaign aimed to destroy vital supply and communication facilities and keep the Axis air force on the defensive. It also aimed to cripple enemy morale by "keeping them awake for three days." Flying up to 700 sorties a day, the DAF "rapidly established effective air control of the battle area." On October 23, the DAF commander, Air Marshal Arthur "Mary" Coningham, informed Montgomery that the DAF now had "complete domination of the air."[20] On the first day of the battle, the DAF flew around 1,000 sorties; by comparison, the German Luftwaffe flew just 107.[21]

At 2200 hours, as the artillery barrage recommenced in direct support of the advancing infantry, the DAF joined in. The first flights were made by some ninety bombers and included flare-dropping Albacores to illuminate enemy locations. Also used were Hurricane fighters especially equipped for night strafing attacks, which targeted the Axis heavy and medium gun positions that were beyond the range of the British artillery. This set the pattern for ground-air cooperation for the duration of the battle. Niall Barr writes, "Finally, the Desert Air Force could put its whole force into the fight."[22]

* * *

The sheer weight of Eighth Army's attack, with the unexpected main effort being made in the north of the Alamein position, stunned the Axis defenders. While their casualties were not heavy and much of their artillery survived the "stonks" and "murders" of their opponents, the initial response of the Axis was "slow and weak."[23] The reason for this was that one essential tool had been effectively damaged by the artillery and air attacks. Most of the telephone cables to forward units had been cut and the DAF was using some of its old bombers to jam Axis wireless traffic. That night, Panzerarmee commander General Georg Stumme knew that the British offensive was underway, but that was the limit of his knowledge. German artillery response was "inefficient" and even on October 24, the Axis armor had not moved forward, "apparently still in doubt as to the point of main attack."[24] Von Thoma's secretly recorded conversation with Crüwell shortly after the battle confirmed that the state of confusion that existed in the first twenty-four hours of the battle. It confirmed that the Panzerarmee had expected Eighth Army's attack to be made further south, where "we would have trapped them easily. But they weren't so obliging." Von Thoma grudgingly admitted that "The swine [Montgomery] had chosen a very good place" to attack and it had caught Panzerarmee Afrika off balance.[25]

When the artillery opened up after their five-minute pause at 2200 hours, it was zero hour for the infantry. Infantry from the eight brigades and four divisions of 30 Corps set off toward their first objectives. The killing time had commenced. This was the largest night attack yet undertaken by the British and it set a pattern for the rest of the war. While the Axis troops often moved into position during the cover of darkness, they seldom chose to fight at night. Generalmajor Alfred Toppe, writing of the German Army's experience in the Second World War, confirmed that "In general the Germans carried out no night attacks." Conversely, from October 1942, "the British carried out their large scale attacks on the German positions at Alamein exclusively at night." Montgomery, Toppe analyzed, "preferred night combat."[26] There was one overriding reason for Montgomery's preference. In terms of tactical ability and combined arms combat, the German military had a definite qualitative edge over its opponents. Only in the use of artillery was this qualitative edge reversed. As David Fraser has written, "the artillery was perhaps the one Arm of the British Army professionally acknowledged by the German enemy as his superior."[27] Night attacks compensated for tactical and doctrinal weaknesses, especially in infantry and armor, while still allowing the artillery to achieve its effects on the enemy. It did not matter to the artillery whether the fighting occurred at night or during the day. It made a world of difference to the infantry, as the darkness offered considerable protection when the inevitable mistakes occurred.

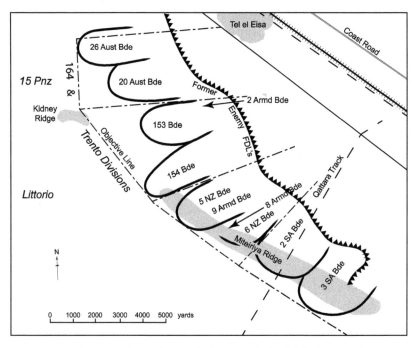

Map 3. 30 Corps' positions at dawn on October 24. The break-in battle was only partially successful and there was much hard fighting ahead.

* * *

Fighting at the northern end of the Alamein position on the Eighth Army's right flank was the infantry of 9 Australian Division. Three battalions were in the front line ready to advance to the first objective. Then, a battalion from each of the two brigades used was scheduled to leapfrog through the newly won position and push on to the final objective some three miles from the initial start line. This was no easy task, as all battalions "faced German infantry and had to pass through heavy belts of mines."[28] On the extreme right flank near the coast, the "Chinese" deception attacks and raids by 2/43 Battalion of 24 Brigade created a diversion that proved costly in casualties. The two platoons that took part in these diversionary raids suffered "about 50 per cent casualties against strong opposition."[29] The dummy figures illuminated during the "Chinese" attack also attracted a lot of enemy fire.

On the right of the divisional sector, as soon as the artillery barrage lifted, the 2/24th Battalion of 26 Brigade charged the enemy posts facing it and easily secured the first objective. It was 2/24 Battalion that was plagued with the one 25-pounder constantly dropping short, probably caused by either human error or a worn gun barrel. But with one exception, all of the battalion's companies reached their objectives "without great opposition." The one exception was D Company, which was "held up for a time until enemy MG post were silenced." Once on the objective, 2/24 Battalion consolidated and laid out a new start line for the next part of the operation. Casualties during the two-hour advance had been light, with four killed and thirty-nine wounded.[30] The leapfrog battalion, the 2/48th, formed up and set off at the appointed time of 0055 hrs on October 24. While 2/48 Battalion met considerable resistance, by 0245 hours the final objective had been captured. The battalion's casualties were similar to those of 2/24: four killed and twenty-five wounded. It had taken seventy prisoners.[31] Once on the final objective, 2/48 Battalion dug in using galvanized iron to provide overhead cover and set out its own portable minefield. Its War Diary recorded that the battalion "made a protective Hawkins double row minefield of 2400 mines around the FDLs . . . and all supporting weapons in posn." Vehicles and Bren gun carriers brought forward stores and ammunition to enable the battalion to be "self supporting and able to hold the ground won for several days even if cut off."[32] It was not going to be an easy task removing 2/48 Battalion. The complete success of the two 26 Brigade battalions secured the right flank of the attack. It was a major contribution to 30 Corps' operations.

To the left of 26 Brigade, 20 Australian Infantry Brigade had a much wider sector allocated to it. It advanced with two battalions forward: 2/17 on the right and 2/15 on the left. Approaching the first objective, 2/17 Battalion came under heavy fire and suffered 80 casualties. Despite these losses, both battalions had taken and secured the first objective by midnight. From here, 2/13 Battalion formed up, ready to continue the advance onto the final objective. This battalion, with a long frontage of 2,200 yards, was to be assisted in its push to the final objective by forty-two Valentine tanks of 40 Royal Tank Regiment (RTR). But at 0055 hours, no tanks had arrived and 2/13 Battalion waited some minutes for them. The lack of armored support and the delay it caused had serious consequences. While the delay in 2/13's advance was only a few minutes, it meant that the battalion had lost the full value of the artillery support from the 25-pounders. After advancing around 1,700 yards, 2/13 Battalion came under heavy fire from both their front and the open left flank. A minefield 1,500 yards deep formed part of the Axis defenses here. Its War Diary assessed the minefield as "creating a serious problem."[33] It was too big an obstacle to be cleared by bayonet or mine detectors, so two Scorpion tanks were brought up. However, their V8 engines soon overheated so that the attempt had to be abandoned. As the casualties mounted, especially amongst its junior officers, 2/13 Battalion's advance was brought to a halt. At 0500 hours, some Valentines from 40 RTR finally reached the beleaguered battalion and the surviving infantry tried to renew the advance. A small advance was made, but the loss of thirteen tanks to mines and the increasing light made it too dangerous for infantry and tanks to remain in the open. The tanks sought shelter where they could and the infantry dug in, still some 1,000 yards short of the final objective. As they were digging, the battalion was bombed by the DAF and suffered another four casualties, including two men being killed. While it did not record the numbers, the battalion's War Diary reported to brigade headquarters that its casualties during the night "have been hy [heavy]" and that "a front line was established in front of enemy minefields."[34]

At dawn on October 24, 9 Australian Division had one battalion in strength on the final objective. But to its left, a greatly weakened battalion was still considerably short of it. The first objective was well secured, though, with three battalions there in good strength who were soon reinforced with the arrival of support weapons and Valentine tanks. The Australian casualties, while "reported as not unduly heavy," were not light and had been particularly heavy in two battalions. During this first night, the Australians captured 137 Germans and 264 Italian prisoners.[35]

* * *

On the Australians' left flank was the 51st (Highland) Division fighting its first action in the desert war. It had a tough task ahead of it: an advance of five miles needed to take and hold a front of almost three miles on the final objective. Its inexperience when compared to the two formations flanking it was obvious. At first, things went well. The gaps in the

British minefield were cleared, the start line laid out, and the first wave of infantry set off on time. Some units had their pipers leading the way playing the stirring tune "Hieland Laddie." But once across the start line, the fog of war descended heavily and the situation became chaotic. For 51 Division, "the advance developed into individual operations by the various assault groups for, with a general breakdown of communications throughout the sector, many of the groups were ignorant of the progress of their neighbours as they fought for the four objective lines."[36]

On the northern part of the sector, 153 Brigade had designated one battalion, the 5th Black Watch, to take the first two objectives. When this was done, another battalion, the 1st Gordons, with Valentine tanks of 50 RTR in support, would push on and take the remaining two objectives. The 5th Black Watch captured the first two objectives without much trouble. But when the two leading companies of 1 Gordons advanced from the second objective, they came under heavy fire, most likely from 30 Corps' artillery dropping short. Lieutenant Ewen Frazer, who was with the Gordons and who would be awarded the DSO for his conduct that night, recalled "a jumble of fleeting incidents." He recalled that the artillery "din was terrific" and that the smoke and dust it caused "reduced visibility to about 50 yards."[37] The two companies pulled back and waited for the fire to subdue, but when they advanced again they had lost their artillery support. Two strong points ahead of them were attacked with a bayonet charge, but the attack was beaten off, leaving the survivors dazed and confused. Some officers and NCOs were able to rally the men and an outflanking maneuver was attempted, which was partially successful. They captured part of the further strongpoint, but the enemy held the rest of it. At dawn, three officers and around sixty men were trapped in this position under constant fire and out of communication with the rest of the battalion.

The rest of 1 Gordons had awaited the arrival of fifteen tanks from 50 RTR. As usual, the tanks arrived late and could not find the infantry. By the time the two arms had married up, all artillery support had ceased and the enemy was alert to the attack. When two of the Valentine tanks were lost on a minefield, the whole force moved back to the second captured objective, where they dug in "fast and furiously." Ewen Frazer recalled a desperate decision made that morning:

> Time was getting on. It was now nearly 0400 hrs and the force was still 1500
> yards at least from the final objective. It was known that the ground was very
> hard and that at least an hours digging was required to get the troops sufficiently
> well into the ground.
>
> It was, therefore, improbable that even if the advance met with relatively
> little opposition, by the time the gap in the minefield was forced and the troops
> got forward onto the objective it would be daylight and the troops very vulner-
> able to a counterattack.[38]

Frazer, the senior surviving officer now commanding the remnants of two companies, dug in on a protected slope surrounded by a minefield. He recalled that, "None of us felt very good taking such casualties to achieve so little, but getting down to a familiar routine helped to relieve the stress."[39]

This was a critical failure when combined with 2/13th Australian Battalion's inability to reach its final objective. The 1st Gordons and 2/13th link up was to provide the corridor for 1 Armoured Division to progress through the minefields and into the battle. This combined failure meant that 1 Armoured Division would not be moving that night or on October 24.

On the left of 153 Brigade's sector, the 5/7th Gordons easily captured their first objective. But when two companies of the battalion set off for their second objective, one became trapped in a dense minefield; the other was forced to take cover well short of it. At dawn on October 24, 153 Brigade was in a precarious state. Its maximum advance was still 2,000 yards short of the final objective, where the remnants of the 1st Gordons were holding an exposed position under fire. The rest of the brigade had gained only their intermediate objective, which they held in isolated pockets. A concerted counterattack would easily remove them. All communications had broken down and most of the officers and NCOs had great difficulty in both navigating at night and plotting their new positions on the map. Brigade and Divisional headquarters had no idea where their units were and which enemy strongpoints still faced them.

The Highland Division's left sector of the attack, which would link with the New Zealanders, was allocated to its 154 Brigade. As this sector was much wider, 154 Brigade had been reinforced with tanks from 50 RTR and additional infantry from the reserve brigade. On the right of this sector, 1 Black Watch set off on time, closely following the artillery barrage and with its pipers to the fore. The first objective was easily taken. Pushing on to the final objective, one company of the battalion fought its way through a dense minefield while under heavy machine gun fire. Despite heavy casualties, this company pushed on, almost reaching the final objective, where it occupied an enemy strongpoint along with the thirty prisoners it had captured. Another company on the right stumbled upon a large German strongpoint that it had to subdue. Elements of this company reached the final objective, but fire from the open right flank forced them to retire back to the captured strongpoint.

In 154 Brigade's center was the 7/10th Argyll and Sutherland Highlanders and the tanks of 50 RTR. The battalion was to advance to the final objective where the tanks were to join it and assist in subduing any opposition. The 7/10th Argyll and Sutherland Highlanders set off on time against little opposition. Casualties soon mounted due to the minefields, booby traps, and mortar and artillery fire. After subduing an enemy strongpoint near the final objective, the battalion, now numbering about 100 men, dug in and awaited the Valentine tanks of 50 RTR. These did not appear until just after 5:00 a.m. and were way to the south and cut off by a dense minefield. With light approaching, no further progress could be made. The lack of support provided by 50 RTR was a telling factor. Knowing what was ahead of them that night, it is hard to understand why 50 RTR had no Scorpion tanks allocated to it, nor why the accompanying sappers "had no detectors in working order."[40] The navigation skills of the tank commanders were also poor. Even at this stage, Eighth Army still had much to learn.

On the far left, 154 Brigade had borrowed two companies of 5 Camerons from the reserve (152) brigade. The Camerons were to capture the first objective from where the 7th Black Watch would push onto the final objective. The two companies of 5 Camerons advanced in concert with the New Zealanders on their left. Despite considerable opposition and heavy artillery fire, the Camerons captured the first objective on time. Closely following them was the infantry from 7 Black Watch, which continued the fight to the final objective. Its casualties were heavy, including all six officers detailed to navigate the battalion along its axis of advance. Despite these setbacks, 7 Black Watch captured the final objective, the northwestern edge of Miteiriya Ridge, known as Point 30, just after 0400 hours. The 7th Black Watch had less than fifty men here and all three officers with them were wounded. Contact was made with 21 New Zealand Battalion on the left, but the right flank was open and exposed. The remnants of two companies of 7 Black Watch now held a forward slope in the midst of a minefield and were exposed to enemy fire. But this was the only portion of the final objective held by 51 Highland Division on the morning of October 24.

The position of 51 Highland Division that morning was tenuous. It is hard to comprehend why an inexperienced division had been allocated such a wide frontage and deep objectives. Contact across their front was patchy at best and no clear picture of it could be obtained for some time. The Highlanders "had encountered more German anti-personnel mines than any other division and casualties had been correspondingly heavy."[41] It was one of only two infantry divisions in Eighth Army to incur more than 600 casualties in the first twenty-four hours of the battle.[42] Several bypassed enemy posts were still active and prevented support weapons and supplies from moving forward. They also thwarted any attempts to clear the minefields. Immediately behind the Highlanders was 1 Armoured Division waiting for the minefields to be cleared and causing considerable congestion. Only on the extreme left was the division on the final objective, but not in any great strength. In fact, it held this portion of Miteiriya Ridge with only one-and-a-half platoons of infantry.[43] Elsewhere, the division was not within 1,000 yards of the final objective and thinly spread across its front. The situation did not look promising.

* * *

On the left flank of 51 Highland Division was another experienced, battle-hardened formation: the 2nd New Zealand Division. The objective the New Zealanders were expected to seize was most of Miteiriya Ridge, the scene of an Australian disaster the previous July and a key feature of the Alamein position. Freyberg believed that this battle, unlike previous ones during the desert campaign, "approximates the battles fought in 1918," and he turned to the techniques developed in that war to plan the New Zealand attack.[44] Of the attacking infantry divisions on the night of October 23, 1942, the 2nd New Zealand Division was the only one to use a quarter of its 104 guns to provide a creeping barrage for the infantry to "lean on" during their advance while the rest of its artillery fired concentrations on known strong points. There is some debate as to how effective the creeping barrage was, although its effect on morale was high. The New Zealand official historian of the divisional artillery wrote that a creeping barrage, when combined with counter-battery concentrations, were the "correct artillery tactics," but that the number of guns was "too few to be fully effective."[45] Lieutenant General Sir Francis Tuker, commander of 4 Indian Division, was blunt in his assessment of the use of artillery at the second Alamein battle. He described the creeping barrage as "wasteful" and believed that the dispersion of the artillery effort prolonged the outcome of the battle.[46]

On the right of the New Zealand sector, 5 Brigade was to advance 7,000 yards while 6 Brigade, on their left, advanced 5,000 yards. This would bring both brigades to their final objective, the Miteiriya Ridge, which they were to hold in equal portions. Once the two brigades were established on the ridge, the support weapons and 9 Armoured Brigade was to move forward to join them, the latter to take up defensive positions in front of the infantry. Freyberg noted that the "Armoured COs were full of confidence and very cheerful—maybe they will be 'sadder and wiser' men but it is good to see them in such fine form."[47] Freyberg, an old warrior, knew the cost of what lay ahead.

Each brigade had decided to take its first objective with only one battalion, and then push through two more battalions onto the final objective of Miteiriya Ridge. The 28th Maori Battalion was allocated to "mop up" any opposition in both brigade areas. This was an important role given what had occurred at Ruweisat Ridge, but one that they felt demeaned their status as proud fighting infantry warriors. A recent history of the battalion records this frustration:

> It is difficult to determine or understand why the Maori were left out of the main attack. Their pre-eminence in attack and their outstanding ability to capture their objective was indisputable. Perhaps their failure to obey orders at Munassib the previous month may have worried Kippenberger.[48]

On the eve of the attack, Brigadier Kippenberger delivered a stirring piece of oratory to 23 Battalion, who were keyed up for action:

> I told them that this was the turn of the war and the greatest moment of their lives: they had the duty and the honour of breaking in, on which everything

> depended; our hats were in the ring and I expected them to do it, whatever the
> cost. Reg [Romans, the Commanding Officer] called the men to their feet and
> they gave three fierce, thunderous cheers. As I went away someone remarked
> that our first objective was as good as taken.[49]

The decision to use the "fiery" Lieutenant Colonel Reg Romans and his most reliable battalion in the initial advance nearly caused disaster. Romans' battalion easily carried the first objective. But resistance had been scanty and, as those counting the paces had become casualties, they were unsure where they were. So, they pushed on. In the words of their adjutant:

> But there was no standing barrage. Reg and I discussed it and we agreed that
> we hadn't seen anything like the fighting that the break-in battalion had every
> right to expect. Reg said "Push on! Push on!" and so we went on to take what we
> thought was our objective.[50]

It was, in fact, Miteiriya Ridge, the brigade's final objective.

Meanwhile, Kippenberger and Brigade HQ had been driven frantic trying to locate or contact 23 Battalion. The brigade's war diary contains repeated references to the battalion's disappearance: "Still NO report from 23 Bn." An entry made as late as 0115 hours on October 24 recorded: "Capt Coop reported he had been right up to barrage and could NOT find 23 Bn. Presumed 23 Bn ahead of the barrage." Word was finally received of the battalion's actions at 0235 hours, when its adjutant reported to Brigade Headquarters.[51] Little wonder that he received "a rather frosty reception" from Kippenberger, and the blunt instruction: "You go back and tell Reg to pull back to his proper, initial objective."[52]

Kippenberger's brigade had easily secured all its objectives, and he wrote proudly back to New Zealand: "Very hard fighting in this attack, but the troops were simply magnificent and my Bde got the whole of its objective on the first night. We lost a lot of good chaps though."[53]

On the left, the two battalions of 6 Brigade had pulled up 500 to 800 yards short of its final objective—the result of faulty map reading rather than enemy resistance. The rest of the ground was taken in another overnight attack on October 26. Its commander, William Gentry, wrote home to his family on October 28: "We have just fought a battle in which the lads did magnificent work in an operation which, whatever the final outcome, will go down in military history as a model of its type."[54]

The 2nd New Zealand Division had been the most successful of all the infantry divisions used on the opening night, thanks to a combination of experience in night fighting in the desert, excellent military leadership, hard realistic training prior to the battle, and the "new" creeping barrage. But Kippenberger was right: losses in both brigades had been heavy. The situation was risky. At dawn the enemy artillery pounded the newly won position. Leese, the 30 Corps commander, informed Montgomery later that morning that, "They [Axis] did a hell of a lot of shooting up this morning" and that Miteiriya Ridge "was full of hate."[55]

* * *

To the south of the New Zealanders on 30 Corps' left flank was the 1st South African Division. Linking with the New Zealanders on its right was the South African 2nd Infantry Brigade. It would use the Natal Mounted Rifles to secure the first objective before pushing the Cape Town Highlanders on the right and the 1/2nd Frontier Force Battalion on the left on to the final objective. The advance was supported by artillery concentrations timed to fall on known enemy defensive positions ahead of each battalion.

The Natal Mounted Rifles easily reached the first objective on time and with sixty-seven Italian prisoners.[56] But enemy strongpoints it failed to clear during its advance delayed the two follow-up battalions. These not only caused heavy casualties but both battalions soon lost their artillery support. As the New Zealanders were now well ahead of the South Africans, several parties of infantry from 6 New Zealand Brigade had to cross the boundary into the South African sector to deal with the enemy posts firing on them. The Cape Town Highlanders eventually reached Miteiriya Ridge at 0500 but, like 25 New Zealand Battalion, it halted on a crest some 800 to 1,000 yards short of the final objective. On 2nd South African Brigade's left flank, the Frontier Force Battalion encountered a heavily defended German position on its way to the ridge. While it captured part of the position, it could not subdue it. Having lost 183 men, of whom forty-two were killed, the battalion dug in at dawn still well short of Miteiriya Ridge.

This defended position also halted the initial advance of 3 South African Brigade. Despite some initial setbacks and hard fighting, the brigade was able to establish two battalions, the Royal Durban Light Infantry and the 1st Battalion of the Imperial Light Horse, on Miteiriya Ridge just after 0500 hours. There they were joined by two squadrons of Valentine tanks of 8th Royal Tank Regiment and an anti-tank gun screen facing into no-man's land. By dawn, 1 South African Division was well established on its final objective except at the vital junction with the New Zealanders on its right flank.

The South Africans and New Zealanders had made a large dent through the dense minefields and captured part of the vital Miteiriya Ridge. At dawn, they were ready with support weapons and some tanks to repel any counterattack. According to Nigel Hamilton, this was "inconceivable to Rommel" and "a magnificent infantry performance."[57]

* * *

This infantry assault by the four divisions of 30 Corps was the largest launched in the desert war. Despite the "Minengarten" and the determined opposition of German and Italian infantry *Lightfoot* had "achieved considerable success."[58] While each division had carried out its attack in its own way, they were fighting to a common doctrine. The hard training had clearly paid off, although not everything had gone according to plan. Only two of the eight brigades involved had captured their final objective. It was, however, a sound start. "By 0800 hours GCT the infantry had advanced about 5 miles and reached initial objectives along Miteiriya Ridge," Eighth Army later reported.[59] But Alexander, in his Despatch, recognized that it was only a partial success. He wrote:

> By 0530 hours 9 Australian Division on the right had secured most of its final objective, nine thousand yards from the start line; the New Zealand Division had also captured its final objective, the western end of the Miteiriya ridge. In the centre, however, the left brigade of the Australian Division and the Highland Division were held up about fifteen hundred yards short of their objective by enemy strongpoints in the middle of what should have been the northern corridor and on the left the South African Division fell short of the Miteiriya ridge by about five hundred yards.[60]

* * *

Other infantry attacks had also occurred on the night of October 23. In the center, 4 Indian Division, under command of 30 Corps, carried out three minor diversionary operations around Ruweisat Ridge, one of which was another "Chinese" attack. Its history described the division's role here as "something more than spectators and something less than participants in the main battle."[61] The raids and a simulated full-scale assault by two battalions on the night of October 23 were noisy and did not "score any obvious success."[62] They did, however, keep the Axis forces guessing and prevented them from moving troops from this sector throughout the battle.[63]

In the south of the Alamein position, 13 Corps also carried out diversionary attacks. Unlike those of 4 Indian Division, those of 13 Corps were "fairly costly."[64] The Corps was holding an extended portion of the El Alamein position from Ruweisat Ridge in the center to the Qattara Depression. The whole sector was overlooked by the large hill known as Himeimat. Its key task was to keep the armor of 21st Panzer Division in the southern part of the Alamein position while preserving its own armor in 7 Armoured Division "as an effective fighting formation."[65] Having a diversionary role meant that 13 Corps was short of artillery, sappers, and armor. As Major General John Harding, then commanding 7 Armoured Division, later stated, "there was a feeling that we . . . were to be the Cinderella of the party."[66] Attempts to breach the minefields were made by the two armored brigades of 7 Armoured Division, which were short of essential equipment. They were also under intense artillery fire. This had not been subdued by counter-battery fire and the enemy gunners were convinced by the deception plan that an attack was likely. The armored brigades managed to clear one minefield, but they faced another one at dawn. This left both brigades trapped at dawn between two minefields and under constant artillery fire. Brigadier "Pip" Roberts went forward to inspect the position on the morning of October 24 and reported:

> The initial impression was of complete chaos; vehicles, tanks and carriers facing in different directions, some still burning, some at curious angles, and enemy shells arriving fairly steadily but not in great quantity.[67]

An attempt by the 1st Free French Brigade to take Himeimat that night failed leaving the whole area overlooked by enemy observation posts. An attempt by 1/7th The Queens's Royal Regiment of 44 Division to capture another enemy strongpoint that night also failed. In making this attempt, 1/7th The Queen's had seventy-six men killed and 104 men wounded. The casualties included the Commanding Officer, who was killed, and the battalion's second-in-command, adjutant, and all the company commanders.[68] "We were stuck," recalled John Harding. "This was the position for the next couple of days."[69] Niall Barr's summation of 13 Corps' efforts on October 23–24 is accurate: "13 Corps operations, in short, had not been attended by success."[70] They had been attended by unnecessarily high casualties.

* * *

The essence of Montgomery's plan was for the heavy armor of Eighth Army, now concentrated in 10 Corps, to move forward and join the infantry on their new positions. This was to be accomplished before dawn on October 24. Once in position, rather than surging forward in another doomed cavalry charge, the armor was to take up defensive positions and shield the infantry during the "dogfight" phase of the battle. Only at one location had this happened on that morning.

For Operation *Lightfoot*, the 9th Armoured Brigade was an integral part of the New Zealand Division. Its leading regiment, the Royal Wiltshire Yeomanry, reached the infantry of 22 New Zealand Battalion just after 0600. They were guided over Miteiriya Ridge, moved well forward of the infantry, and started shooting at the enemy outposts ahead of them. Freyberg's Diary recorded this significant event:

> 0612 [hrs] Our tanks reported coming through on 5 Bde front. They are taking up battle positions forward of FDLs.[71]

One of the Royal Wiltshire squadrons hit a scattered minefield on the ridge and suffered heavy losses: six Shermans and thirteen Grant tanks.[72] At first light, just after 0630 hours, with the German anti-tank guns now firing on them and the danger of more uncleared minefields, the Royal Wilshire Yeomanry returned to 5 New Zealand Infantry Brigade's positions on the reverse slope to take up hull-down defensive positions. The Royal Wiltshire Yeomanry had "the honour of being the first, and only, regiment to break out beyond the infantry's final objective on this first morning of the Alamein battle."[73]

On the left of the New Zealand position, the tanks of the Warwickshire Yeomanry and New Zealand Division Cavalry reached the infantry positions of 6 New Zealand Brigade. They did not try to penetrate the minefields over the ridge but halted in hull-down positions along the entire brigade front. Despite the limited success of 9 Armoured Brigade's move forward, it was a significant development which Freyberg fully recognized. He wrote in his Secret Report of Operation *Lightfoot*:

> The appearance of the Sherman tanks of the 9th Armoured Brigade with their 75 millimetre guns was a great encouragement to the infantry, who, for the first time in the campaign, founds tanks with them in the F.D.Ls.[74]

But the bulk of the armor concentrated to 10 Corps was nowhere near the infantry FDL's. On the right in the north, 1 Armoured Division was stalled behind a mass of congested vehicles and had not even reached the first cleared minefield. To the south, even though there was a cleared pathway right up to Miteiriya Ridge, 10 Armoured Division had sent only one brigade forward to the ridge. When the lead regiment crossed the ridge, a deluge of anti-tank gunfire fell on it, knocking out ten tanks. The brigade retired and dispersed along the ridge waiting for things to improve. Unfortunately, Miteiriya Ridge, now densely packed with around 200 tanks and several battalions of infantry, was "a perfect target and the ridge was heavily shelled throughout the morning."[75] Niall Barr has written that the failure of the armored corps to break through on Miteiriya Ridge on the first day "was in fact predicable." He argues that had the armored brigades pushed on beyond the ridgeline, they would have suffered devastating losses.[76] This is certainly true, but such losses would need to be faced sooner or later. The last thing Montgomery wanted for the morning of October 24 was major traffic congestion along the two cleared corridors and along Miteiriya Ridge. As his biographer wrote, "This was not what Bernard had envisaged for the strongest armoured corps fielded by the Allies in the war so far."[77] Bierman and Smith have written that in comparison with what the infantry had achieved on this opening night, the armored formations in 10 Corps "had put up a dismal performance."[78] Montgomery was soon convinced that "the armour was dragging its feet."[79] He wrote in his diary on October 24:

I began to form the impression at about 1100 hours that there was a lack of "drive" and pep in the action of 10 Corps. I saw Herbert LUMSDEN and impressed on him the urgent need to get his divisions out into the open where they could manoeuvre, and that they must get clear of the minefield area. He left me about 1130 hours to visit his Divisions. So far he has not impressed me by his showing in battle; perhaps he has been out here too long; he has been wounded twice. I can see that he will have to be bolstered up and handled firmly.

Possibly he will be better when the battle gets more mobile. This "sticky" fighting seems beyond him.[80]

Montgomery's opinion of Lumsden and his armored corps was shaped by a conversation he had with Leese just after midday. All morning, the 30 Corps commander had been receiving a barrage of complaints from Freyberg regarding 10 Corps' lack of progress. Repeated entries in Freyberg's diary record his concern:

0745 [hrs] G1 asked LO 9 Armd Bde to confirm message to 10 Armd Div that it is more and more essential that they should get through.

0847 G1 to 30 Corps. Ascertained not in communication with 10 Armd Div. Told BGS they appeared to making slow progress.

0923 G1 spoke to BGS. Position of 10 Armd Div is not clear except they don't appear to be getting on very fast. GOC keeps calling up asking us to please put some energy into 10 Armd Div. Thin skinned stuff cannot cross M. Ridge.

1025 G1 to BGS asking him to press 10 Armd Div to move as above.

As a result of his concerns, Freyberg was informed at 1027 hours that "Oliver [Leese] was on his way here."[81] Leese arrived at 1045 hours to receive a briefing from the New Zealand principal staff officer and met with both Freyberg and 10 Armoured Division commander Major General Alec Gatehouse. He reported the outcome of the meeting to Montgomery just after midday. Leese's side of the conversation was recorded in shorthand by Freyberg's Personal Assistant Major John White. Leese informed Montgomery:

I have seen Bernard [Freyberg] and Gatehouse and I understand Herbert [Lumsden] has talked to you in last hour. There is one bn of 9 Bde over the ridge. On the left infantry are in touch with SAs and an attack is developing. B. is confident that he could get on. The Wilts in front appear to have run on to some mines on his right—rest of bde is behind ridge. He thinks he could go well through provided one of Gatehouse's bdes goes with him. G. says Royals report A/Tk weapons and anything that puts its nose over ridge gets shot up. G's main preoccupation at moment is to get 10 Div into position to receive attack from someone else. . . . I think we damn well do. He keeps on saying he is trained for a static role. I think that is getting above him. I have told Bernard to hold a meeting with G and Briggs. I am placing whole of Corps arty at his disposal and am suggesting that under smoke they try and do something later in day. What did Herbert say Sir? That is happening. . . . Shall I send word that it is your wish provided they think it is feasible that they break out with support of whole of Corps arty. . . . You want to get them into a position so that they can manoeuvre on the far side of M. Ridge. . . . Right I shall do that. I shall find out earliest time Corps arty can be ready.[82]

The failure of Eighth Army's armor to break out beyond the newly won infantry positions was acknowledged by General Alexander to be "a serious delay." It was "essential" to obtaining "the tactical surprise" on the battlefield.[83] It also gave the Panzerarmee a small window of opportunity to recover from the initial assault and prepare their response.

∗   ∗   ∗

While not achieving the armored breakthrough, Operation *Lightfoot* had obtained a tactical surprise, albeit a limited one. As mentioned above, it was some hours after the artillery barrage began at 2140 hours that General Stumme was certain that this was a genuine attack. The War Diary of the Afrika Korps recorded that with the heavy shelling, all its formations were put on alert. "The great weight of shellfire made it seem possible that the enemy were beginning an offensive," its War Diary recorded.[84] While an attack had been anticipated, its weight and direction were unknown. These would not become clear to the Panzerarmee for several hours. As the New Zealand history records, "the *Panzer Army* headquarters [was] almost completely enveloped in the fog of war until well into the following day."[85] Communications with front line units had been badly disrupted, as intended by the Eighth Army barrage. General Stumme was starved of information for most of the night and well into the morning of October 24. Without it, unlike Rommel, he felt powerless to act. It was not until mid-morning that Stumme took action. In the northern sector, he ordered 15 Panzer Division to counterattack and retake any lost ground.

The command situation became even more confused for Panzerarmee later that morning. For a time, it was without a leader. In an effort to find out how serious the breach in the northern minefield was, Stumme set off with his Chief Signal Officer to see for himself. His staff car came under fire from Australian soldiers and the signals officer was killed. The driver panicked and sped off with General Stumme clinging to the vehicle's side. It was too much for an overweight general with high blood pressure. Stumme suffered a fatal heart attack and fell from the car. His body was not recovered until midday on October 25.[86] The Afrika Korps War Diary recorded ominously at 1040 hours of two large gaps in the minefields and that: "No news of the C-in-C, who has gone there to clear up the situation."[87] In Stumme's absence, General Ritter von Thoma, the Afrika Korps commander, took temporary command pending the arrival of Rommel. Von Thoma did not want to launch any large-scale counterattacks until the British renewed their attack at nightfall. That would reveal where their main effort was. The Afrika Korps War Diary recorded that "It was necessary to concentrate on one main task . . . to hold the front, commit reserves early, and establish a strong front line."[88]

Rommel was warned that he might be needed back in North Africa at 1500 hours on October 24. Just after midnight, Hitler called him to say that, "In view of developments at Alamein he found himself obliged to ask me to fly back to Africa and resume my command." Rommel flew out to Africa the next morning and was gloomy at the prospects ahead. He wrote: "I knew there were no more laurels in Africa."[89] He was correct and, on October 26, wrote to his wife, "Situation critical. A lot of work!"[90]

The situation was indeed critical for both sides. The break-in had been only partially successful and nowhere were the armored formations ahead of the infantry. A 9 Australian Division report contained a succinct summary of the "general state of the battle" on October 24:

(a) The attack in the south had failed;

(b) the attack in the north had succeeded in "breaking in" but had not succeeded in its purpose of passing 10 Armd Corps through and out beyond the enemy defences.

(c) Surprise had been gained and 21 Panzer Div was contained in the south, but 10 Armd Corps was unable to take advantage of that situation;

(d) The Axis infantry in the centre had not been pinched out and the attempt had been abandoned.[91]

* * *

The failure to break-in across the whole northern sector placed Operation *Lightfoot* in jeopardy. It gave Panzerarmee "a chance of roping in the

British salient, and bringing such artillery, tank, anti-tank and machine gun fire to bear on the congested, mine-ridden peninsula as to make withdrawal advisable."[92] The battle hung in the balance and Montgomery's "killing match" was about to begin in earnest.

NOTES

1. Walker, *Alam Halfa and Alamein*, 253.

2. War Diary, 2/28 Australian Infantry Battalion, 23 Oct 1942, 8/3/28, AWM 52, AWM.

3. Wing Commander Donald Jack, interview with Wendy Ugolini, November 1996, Liddle Collection.

4. E.G. Waggett, Contemporary account, 1939–45 Army, Liddle Collection, 21.

5. A Very Personal Account of Incidents During the Second World War, 1939–1945, John Laing, 1939–45 Army, Liddle Collection, 69–70.

6. Alexander's Despatch, Supplement to *The London Gazette*, 5 February 1948, CAB 106/613, TNA, 853.

7. Von Thoma, conversation with Crüwell, Most Secret Special Report to CSDIC Middle East No.612 (G), El Alamein Miscellaneous Papers, WO 106/2286, TNA. The Report contains transcripts of secretly recorded conversations of Germans POWs including the two generals.

8. Walker, *Alam Halfa and Alamein*, 254.

9. War Diary, 2/24 Australian Infantry Battalion, 23 Oct 1942, 8/3/24, AWM 52, AWM.

10. RA Notes on the Offensive by Eighth Army from 23 Oct-4 Nov on the El Alamein Position, WO 201/535, TNA, 3. It is interesting to note that this file was closed (restricted) until 1972.

11. Fraser, *And We Shall Shock Them*, 90.

12. Bungay, *Alamein*, 164.

13. Freyberg, conversation with CRE, 23 October 1942, recorded in GOC's Diary, WA 8/5/45, ANZ.

14. A Very Personal Account of Incidents During the Second World War, 1939–1945, John Laing, 1939–45 Army, Liddle Collection, 70.

15. 9 Australian Division, Report on Operations El Alamein 23 Oct-5 Nov 1942, WO 201/2495, TNA.

16. Toppe, "Desert Warfare," 47.

17. Alexander, Most Secret Cypher Telegram for Prime Minister, 9 November 1942, The Advance from El Alamein, Air 8/1087, TNA.

18. Fraser, *And We Shall Shock Them*, 246.

19. Playfair et al., *Volume IV*, 3.

20. "The Battle of El Alamein," Military Reports on the United Nations, 15 Feb 1943, M1.5, WD, El Alamein Miscellaneous Papers, WO 106/2286, TNA.

21. Hinsley, *British Intelligence in the Second World War: Volume 2*, 437.

22. Barr, *Pendulum of War*, 310.

23. Walker, *Alam Halfa and Alamein*, 254.

24. RA Notes on the Offensive by Eighth Army from 23 Oct–4 Nov on the El Alamein Position, WO 201/535, TNA, 2. "The Battle of El Alamein," Military Reports on

the United Nations, 15 Feb 1943, M1.5, WD, El Alamein Miscellaneous Papers, WO 106/2286, TNA.

25. Von Thoma, conversation with Crüwell, Most Secret Special Report to CSDIC Middle East No.612 (G), El Alamein Miscellaneous Papers, WO 106/2286, TNA.

26. Toppe, "Desert Warfare," 82.

27. Fraser, *And We Shall Shock Them*, 360.

28. Johnston and Stanley, *Alamein: The Australian Story*, 163.

29. Walker, *Alam Halfa and Alamein*, 255.

30. War Diary, 2/24 Australian Infantry Battalion, 23 Oct 1942, 8/3/24, AWM 52, AWM.

31. War Diary, 2/48 Australian Infantry Battalion, 23 Oct 1942, 8/3/36, AWM 52, AWM.

32. Ibid.

33. War Diary, 2/13 Australian Infantry Battalion, 23 Oct 1942, 8/3/13, AWM 52, AWM.

34. Ibid.

35. Walker, *Alam Halfa and Alamein*, 257.

36. Ibid., 258.

37. Personal Narrative of Action by LT. Ewen Frazer, 1939–45 Army, Liddle Collection.

38. Ibid.

39. Ibid.

40. Walker, *Alam Halfa and Alamein*, 260.

41. Barr, *Pendulum of War*, 317.

42. Jonathan Fennell, *Combat and Morale in the North African Campaign*. (Cambridge: Cambridge University Press, 2011), 256. The table on page 256 has 51st Highland Division's casualties for the October 23–24 as 627. The other division to exceed 600 was the New Zealanders, with 651 casualties.

43. Barr, *Pendulum of War*, 317.

44. Freyberg, comments on conference regarding "Lightfoot," 21 September 1942, WA II 8/25A, ANZ.

45. W.E. Murphy, *Official History of New Zealand in the Second World War 1939–45. 2nd New Zealand Divisional Artillery*. (Wellington: War History Branch, 1966), 377.

46. Francis Tuker, *Approach to Battle: A Commentary; Eighth Army, November 1941 to May 1943*. (London: Cassell and Co., 1963), 220, 242.

47. Conversation, conference of Brigadiers, 1100 hrs 23 October 1942, recorded in Freyberg's Diary, WA II 8/45, ANZ.

48. Gardiner, *Te Mura O Te Ahi*, 103.

49. Kippenberger, *Infantry Brigadier*, 225.

50. Angus Ross, interview, Dunedin, 17 January, 1995.

51. War Diary 5 NZ Inf Bde, 23–4 October 1942, WA II 1, DA 52/1/34, ANZ.

52. Angus Ross, interview, Dunedin, 17 January, 1995.

53. Kippenberger to Jim Fraser, letter, 31 October 1942, Glue Papers.

54. Brigadier William Gentry to his family, 28 October 1942, in Sally Mathieson, ed., *Bill Gentry's War 1939–45*. (Palmerston North: The Dunmore Press, 1996), 160.

55. Leese to Montgomery, 1205 hours 24 Oct 1942, conversation recorded in in Freyberg's Diary, WA II 8/45, ANZ. "Hate" was a common term used to describe an intense artillery barrage.

56. Walker, *Alam Halfa and Alamein*, 277.

57. Hamilton, *Monty: The Making of a General*, 777.

58. Barr, *Pendulum of War*, 317.

59. "The Battle of El Alamein," Military Reports on the United Nations, 15 Feb 1943, M1.5, WD, El Alamein Miscellaneous Papers, WO 106/2286, TNA.

60. Alexander's Despatch, Supplement to *The London Gazette*, 5 February 1948, CAB 106/613, TNA, 853.

61. Anon, *The Tiger Kills*, 245.

62. Walker, *Alam Halfa and Alamein*, 280.

63. Anon, *The Tiger Kills*, 245.

64. Walker, *Alam Halfa and Alamein*, 281.

65. Recollections of Field Marshal Sir John Harding, quoted in Neillands, *The Desert Rats: 7th Armoured Division*,147.

66. Harding, quoted in Neillands, *The Desert Rats: 7th Armoured Division*, 147.

67. Quoted in Barr, *Pendulum of War*, 320.

68. Walker, *Alam Halfa and Alamein*, 286.

69. John Harding, quoted in Thompson, *Forgotten Voices*, 201.

70. Barr, *Pendulum of War*, 321.

71. GOC's Diary, 24 October 1942, WA 8/5/45 ANZ.

72. Barr, *Pendulum of War*, 323.

73. Walker, *Alam Halfa and Alamein*, 274.

74. Freyberg, "The New Zealand Division in Egypt and Libya," 8.

75. Barr, *Pendulum of War*, 326.

76. Ibid., 325, 326.

77. Hamilton, *Monty: The Making of a General*, 780.

78. Bierman and Smith, *Alamein: War without Hate*, 281.

79. Hamilton, *Monty: The Making of a General*, 780.

80. Quoted in Hamilton, *Monty: The Making of a General*, 780–781.

81. GOC's Diary, 24 October 1942, WA 8/5/45 ANZ.

82. Leese, conversation with Montgomery, recorded in GOC's Diary, 1205 hours, 24 October 1942, WA 8/5/45 ANZ.

83. Alexander's Despatch, Supplement to *The London Gazette*, 5 February 1948, CAB 106/613, TNA, 853.

84. War Diary, DAK, 23 October 1942, GMDS File 2586/1, WA II 11/23 Afrika Korps Records, ANZ.

85. Walker, *Alam Halfa and Alamein*, 289.

86. Liddell Hart, *The Rommel Papers*, 305.

87. War Diary, DAK, 1040 hours, 23 October 1942, GMDS File 2586/1, WA II 11/23 Afrika Korps Records, ANZ.

88. Ibid.

89. Liddell Hart, *The Rommel Papers*, 304.

90. Rommel to Lu, 26 October 1942, in Liddell Hart, *The Rommel Papers*, 308.

91. 9 Australian Division, Report on Operations El Alamein 23 Oct-5 Nov 1942, WO 201/2495, TNA.

92. Hamilton, *Monty: The Making of a General*, 782.

SEVEN

SLUGGING IT OUT

Operation *Lightfoot* on the night of October 23 was only partially successful. Most of the infantry formations in 30 Corps had failed to secure their final objectives. More seriously, the armor of 10 Corps had not come close to striking out beyond the infantry positions and exploiting the enemy's state of confusion in that first twenty-four hours. Montgomery was annoyed at this missed opportunity and always regarded it as "a tragedy."[1] His plan for the "dogfight" phase of the battle depended on the "crumbling" operations beginning on the morning after the break-in when the enemy was vulnerable and off balance. The immediate task for October 24, then, was for the infantry of 30 Corps to try to reach their final objectives while the armor of 10 Corps, with more "ginger" put into their commanders, surged out beyond the infantry, ready to take on the armor of the Afrika Korps.

In 30 Corps sector, the Australians and Highlanders planned to renew their attempts in the late afternoon while to the south, 13 Corps would make another attempt to breach the minefields causing them so many problems. Around Ruweisat Ridge, the 4th Indian Division planned another raid that night.

At 1500 hours on October 24, 51 Highland Division, having incurred nearly 1,000 casualties already, renewed its attack with the aim of clearing a pathway for the 1st Armoured Division. It had taken most of the morning of October 24 for Major General Wimberley to find out where his scattered troops were. His men were exhausted from the battle of the night before and their numbers were seriously depleted. Wimberley was forced to commit a battalion from his reserve, 2 Battalion, the Seaforth Highlanders, to attack and clear two strongpoints holding up further progress. This battalion overran both strongpoints, but at a cost of eighty-five casualties.[2] A force of Valentine tanks in support did not reach the objective and lost seven tanks when it ran onto a minefield. The extended front of 51 Highland Division was too large an objective to be taken by isolated platoons and small companies of men. The attacks made by the remnants of 51 Highland Division on October 24, with the exception of the Seaforth Highlanders, were "small, piecemeal attacks, messy and confused affairs" and "were of limited effectiveness."[3] Operating in the sector was hazardous, as the strong enemy pockets that remained had good observation and could bring fire upon any movement. The Division would not occupy the entire final objective until the night of October 26.

As the Highlanders were making their attacks, to their north two battalions from 20 Australian Brigade advanced toward their final objectives. They had just over 1,000 yards to cover. The advance by 2/17 and 2/13 Battalions was meant to be preceded by another heavy artillery barrage, but earlier patrols had found little opposition to target. Instead, "It was therefore decided to cancel the artillery programme and make the advance silently."[4] It commenced at 0200 hours on the morning of October 25. The final objective was "so nondescript that only the intelligence men, using maps and compasses and counting paces, could tell the company commanders when they had arrived."[5] The 2/17th Battalion reached its objective fifty minutes later "without opposition."[6] However, enemy outposts soon "woke up" to the fact that an Australian Battalion was digging in close by and "made things very uncomfortable with spandau fire." German artillery joined in and the battalion was bombed by an enemy plane. Dawn on October 25 found men who had been without sleep for forty-eight hours ready to face a German counterattack. The Battalion's War Diary described October 25 as "our worst—'Black Sunday' the tps called it." The War Diary explained why:

> We sustained our heaviest casualties and some of the men's nerves cracked under the strain. Superhuman work was continually being done by the offrs and men.[7]

The 2/13th Battalion had a tougher time getting to the objective and encountered pockets of enemy resistance along the way. They reached it at 0235 hours, where the Australians commenced digging in ground so rock hard that the men could not dig deeper than eighteen inches. The worst moment occurred when the tanks of 40 RTR opened fire on the men of 2/13 Battalion while they were digging in. Fortunately, "This was rectified before casualties were inflicted."[8]

The speed with which the objectives were taken meant that the sappers following the advance could clear four tracks up to the objective and cut a lateral track linking them. Australian losses so far had been relatively light. But tragedy occurred at first light, 0700 hours on October 25, when the 7th Rifle Brigade of 1 Armoured Division arrived on the objective heavily bunched. Their vehicles immediately attracted heavy artillery fire and "the carnage was terrible to watch. . . . Soon there were dozens of shattered burning vehicles, and dead and wounded soldiers littering the desert."[9] Despite this setback, and a hard day to follow on October 25, both Australian battalions were firmly on 30 Corps' final objective.

* * *

The main effort for October 24 was to restore some momentum to the armor of 10 Corps by passing them through the infantry positions. This had been the essence of Montgomery's *Lightfoot* plan. Rather than using 10 Corps in the *corps de chasse* role, the armor would instead be used to provide a defensive shield for the infantry and it was expected to help the infantry "crumble" the enemy positions. As Nigel Hamilton explained, "crumbling" to Montgomery "meant attacking the enemy, using concentrated artillery, and assaulting day and night."[10] This had to commence at dawn on D + 1, which was October 24. Montgomery felt that having "eaten the guts" out of the Panzerarmee's forward defenses, Rommel would be forced to counterattack using his armored formations, which was exactly "what we want." If this happened, then "the eventual fate of the Panzer Army is certain—it will not be able to avoid destruction."[11] But this looked unlikely on the morning of October 24, and the "crumbling" operations could not commence as the infantry, which had already incurred 3,000 casualties, focused on its own protection that morning. This was because no armored units of 10 Corps were in front shielding them. They were not even close.

10 Corps was paralyzed by fear of minefields, and the battle was being fought in one vast minefield. It was even more fearful of the dreaded

88 mm gun being used in the anti-tank role. The armored corps commanders from Lumsden down were incapable of driving their men to
achieve the Army Commander's directives. In the north, where the Australians and Highlanders met fierce resistance, instead of joining them in
the fight, 1st Armoured Division "had waited for a safe passage first to be
cleared, like belles waiting to go onstage."[12] In the center, 10 Armoured
Division refused to cross the Miteiriya Ridge despite the example set by
9 Armoured Brigade and the urgings of both Leese and Freyberg.

To get the 10 Corps moving, Leese offered to use all of the artillery
of 30 Corps in support of 10 Corps when it attacked from the New Zealand position on Miteiriya Ridge that afternoon. Montgomery supported
this initiative and the main commanders involved—Leese, Lumsden
and Freyberg—met at the New Zealand Divisional Headquarters that
afternoon. Lumsden was not keen to attack so soon and Freyberg, sens-
ing Lumsden's concern regarding the German anti-tank guns, recommended delaying the attack until nightfall. Montgomery and Leese
reluctantly agreed to this. Montgomery did stress to Lumsden that 1
Armoured Division in the north must move and get through the Highlanders' position by nightfall. It was to accept the possibility of heavy
casualties as the infantry had done. Montgomery's frustration can be
seen in a diary entry on October 24:

> the main lack of offensive eagerness was in the North . . . both 9 Aust Div and 51
> Div were quite clear that 1 Armd Div could have got out without difficulty in the
> morning. Lumsden was not displaying that drive and determination that is so
> necessary when things go wrong; there was a general lack of offensive eagerness
> in 10 Corps.[13]

He also threatened to remove the commanders of 1 Armoured Division if they didn't get moving that afternoon. The emphasis for most of
October 24 was to carry out the armored phase of the original plan but
with additional support provided by the massed artillery of both 30 and
10 Corps.

At 1500 hours, 51 Highland Division carried out another infantry attack that cleared a passage through the minefields for 1 Armoured Division. An hour later, the brigades of 1 Armoured Division moved forward
and by early evening it seemed to be out beyond the forward infantry
units. At 1720 hours, the Division's 2 Armoured Brigade reported that it

was on the feature "Pierson," which had been one of the original *Lightfoot*
objectives. "My application of 'ginger' had worked," a relieved Montgomery recorded in his diary.[14] The entry was premature, as it was later found
that 2 Armoured Brigade was not on Pierson at all, but on the eastern rim
of Kidney Ridge and about 1,000 yards short of where it reported it was.
Kidney Ridge was not a ridge at all, but a contour line on the map in the
shape of a kidney bean. Some accounts of the battle describe it as a low
rise or hillock; others as a shallow depression. As Walker stated in the New
Zealand official history, "to the naked eye," Kidney Ridge "presented no
clearly distinguishable difference from the desert around it."[15] While 2
Armoured Brigade was on the eastern edge of the contour ring, the rest
of Kidney Ridge was occupied by Axis forces, including a number of the
dreaded 88 mm guns. The Brigade was still to the left rear of the foremost
Australian positions and October 24 would be a relatively quiet night for it.

On the left-hand sector, there was less positive news. At 1845 hours,
Lumsden reported that 10 Armoured Division was being held up by
newly laid minefields below the Miteiriya Ridge. More than this, Lumsden reported that the minefield was covered by anti-tank guns and a
force of tanks from 21 Panzer Division, which Montgomery knew at the
time was facing Horrocks 13 Corps in the south. Equally disturbing was
Lumsden's report that he did not know where 24 Armoured Brigade, one
of the two armored formations in 10 Armoured Division, was. However,
Montgomery accepted Lumsden's assurance that 10 Armoured Division
would be out-shielding the New Zealanders by midnight and that the 1st
Armoured Division was in action on the Pierson Line. The first full day
of battle was over and Montgomery was reasonably satisfied. They were
behind schedule, but by dawn on October 25, the armor would be "out"
and the dogfight and crumbling operations could begin in earnest. He
turned in at his usual time just after 2130 hours, little suspecting that he
would have to face a crisis meeting before dawn the next day.

The 10 Armoured Division did try to push out from Miteiriya Ridge,
but the attempts were half-hearted or struck serious misfortune. The
British official history records that "the night's operations were ill-fated
from the start."[16] The 24th Armoured Brigade had considerable trouble
clearing the minefields to its front and it was not until 0345 hours on October 25 that one lane had been cleared. It took even more time to report

this development back to its headquarters. When 8 Armoured Brigade got underway at 2200 hours, it immediately ran into difficulties. As one of its regiments was passing through the narrow cleared laneway, a stick of bombs dropped from some circling Ju 88 bombers caught the regiment in this vulnerable position. Some twenty-five vehicles were set ablaze, illuminating the ridge and providing the Axis forces with some ideal targets. This bombing raid was "the only real success of the Luftwaffe during the early stage of the battle."[17] It forced the two armored regiments of the brigade to seek shelter on their original positions behind the ridge.

Two regiments of an armored brigade did get out beyond Miteiriya Ridge that night. After replenishing and reorganizing, Brigadier John Currie's 9 Armoured Brigade, fighting as part of the New Zealand Division, pushed up the ridge just after midnight. There the brigade came upon a scene of "considerable confusion . . . no one seemed to know what was happening."[18] This was the 8th Armoured Brigade bunched up and illuminated by "a mass of burning vehicles."[19] Brigadier Currie found the gap and led his regiments through it. The Brigade advanced a distance of two miles that night "without damage at all."[20] In doing so, they captured 150 German prisoners including a battalion commander and his staff.[21] The next day, 9 Armoured Brigade "had a battle royal till 3 p.m."[22] The two yeomanry regiments of 9 Armoured Brigade, supported by the New Zealand artillery and infantry, destroyed thirteen tanks, ten guns, and captured hundreds of Axis infantrymen on October 25. This was exactly what Montgomery intended in his "crumbling" operations during the dogfight phase of the battle but it was being carried out by a small fraction of his armored forces. Currie fully intended to advance further on the night of October 25 and was dumbfounded when he received the order to withdraw his tanks back to the Miteiriya Ridge. One of his officers wrote of this fateful decision:

> At 3.30 p.m. we had done well and thought we had the gap and were through. I still think so but the order came to withdraw to the Ridge again.[23]

* * *

Montgomery had gone to bed at his usual early time, satisfied that the armored divisions of 10 Corps were acting according to his plan. Chief of Staff Freddie de Guingand did not share this confidence and stayed up to monitor the situation. Reports from wireless traffic and liaison officers convinced de Guingand that the armored formations had abandoned their attempts to move forward of the infantry positions. Instead, it seemed that the armored corps commanders, with the exception of Currie, "favoured suspending the forward move and pulling back under cover of the ridge."[24] This was contrary to Montgomery's orders. As Freyberg reported to Leese, his Corps Commander, early the next morning, the "Miteiriya Ridge situation is rapidly becoming one of static warfare."[25] The New Zealand official historian wrote of the armored divisions' refusal to follow Montgomery's orders at this time:

> The armour was perpetuating the tradition, established by General Gott (under whom both Lumsden and Gatehouse had served) of giving lip service to the plans but holding to a determination to run the armoured battle its own way.[26]

Montgomery hated having his sleep disturbed and had given strict instructions only to be woken in emergencies. De Guingand felt that he had one now, so at 0300 hours on October 25, he roused Montgomery. De Guingand explained the situation and that he had called the corps commanders in to see Montgomery at 0330 hours that morning. Montgomery made no comment about his disturbed slumber and readily approved de Guingand's actions.

Despite 0330 hours being "not a good time to hold a conference," de Guingand regarded its outcome as the "first stepping stone" to victory.[27] Montgomery was cheerful and asked his corps commanders to report their actions. De Guingand recalled that there was "a certain 'atmosphere' present" that required "careful handling." This was especially true for Lumsden, who was "obviously not very happy about the role his armour had been given."[28] Montgomery again stressed the importance to his plan of the armor being out beyond the infantry positions. Montgomery was surprised when Lumsden asked him to pass this on to Gatehouse personally by telephone which he did. It led Montgomery to conclude that, "The real trouble is that LUMSDEN is frightened of GATEHOUSE and won't give him firm orders."[29] Montgomery stressed to both Gatehouse and Lumsden that the armor must fight its way forward and that he would not permit any departure from his plan. Montgomery also threatened to remove any commander who was not prepared to do their part. Both de Guingand and Leese felt that this early morning conference was one of the battle's key turning points. De Guingand wrote of it:

> I remember the reaction his words had on me. They were a tonic, and we felt not only that these orders would stand, but that there was no possible question that the plan could fail. The firm decision to make no change in the plan at that moment was a brave one, for it meant accepting considerable risks and casualties. Unless it had been made I am firmly convinced that the attack might well have fizzled out, and the full measure of success we achieved might never have been possible. The meeting broke up with no one in any doubt as to what was in the Commander's mind.[30]

The meeting was dramatic and certainly important but it did little to change the mindset or behavior of the armored commanders. That very morning, Lumsden visited Freyberg at the New Zealand Division's headquarters and lectured Freyberg on the use of armor. According to Lumsden:

> Playing with armour is like playing with fire. You have to take your time about it. It is like a duel. If you don't take your time you will get run through the guts. It is not for tanks to take on guns.[31]

But early on the morning of October 25, with some positive reports being received from the armored divisions, Montgomery believed that the immediate crisis had passed. "It is a good thing I was firm with LUMSDEN and GATEHOUSE last night," he recorded in his diary.[32] But at around 1030 hours, the painful truth dawned on Montgomery. He learned that the 1st Armoured Division was not on Pierson nor had 10 Armoured Division advanced beyond Miteiriya Ridge. "The armoured shield" Montgomery believed was in front of his infantry, "did not, in reality, exist."[33] This was the real crisis of the battle and it needed firm action. Montgomery, with "his battle plan unravelling before his eyes," set off for a meeting with his senior commanders at the New Zealand Division's headquarters.[34]

At the meeting, Montgomery asked Freyberg what he thought should happen next. Freyberg, with no faith in any armor not under infantry command, advised Montgomery to put in another large infantry attack. Freyberg said:

> I urged him [Montgomery] to put in another timed bombardment with infantry attacking as before to a depth of about 4000 yards to push him off his guns. . . .

The armour would then have to fight. Thought it was better to face another 500 casualties to each Division and use our guns which is our great asset to whack him.

Freyberg's rationale, which he explained to the officers of the New Zealand Division that afternoon and probably to Montgomery earlier, was based on his recent excursions across the battlefield. Freyberg had come to the view that:

From what I have seen I think the days of armour are rapidly passing. The 88 mm has almost paralysed the armour—they say they have an even chance in the moonlight.[35]

Montgomery rejected Freyberg's suggestion for a second *Lightfoot* style infantry attack as he had no reserve available to launch one. But a seed had been planted. According to Niall Barr, Freyberg's suggestion "eventually grew into Operation Supercharge."[36]

With his original plan in disarray and no fresh infantry assault possible, Montgomery was forced to alter his plan, which he did after this conference. This was "the first major change, indeed turning point, of the battle."[37] The New Zealanders would not conduct crumbling operations to the southwest from Miteiriya Ridge. These would probably be "too costly" for any benefit they achieved.[38] Instead, the 10th Armoured Division would hand over a brigade to the 1st Armoured Division in the north and withdraw from the battlefield. The 1st Armoured Division was then to keep trying to break through the minefields and get onto their original objective. The main crumbling attacks would now be made by the 9th Australian Division and would be directed northwards toward the coast. This was a switch in direction of 180 degrees, but the logic for it was compelling. For a start, it would keep the enemy guessing as to the main weight of the attack. Neither the South African nor the New Zealand Division was capable of fighting a protracted sustained battle of attrition. The New Zealanders had incurred just over 800 casualties since the opening night. This was "about a third of the fighting troops" involved and clearly such wastage could not be sustained.[39] The 51st Highland Division had sustained almost half of Eighth Army's casualties to date and was committed to trying to secure and hold an extensive frontage. It could not be expected to do more. This left the Australians, a tough, battle-hardened formation that had suffered few casualties to date and was still full of fight. They would need to be all this and more as the 9th Australian Division would now do most of the fighting in the battle in the days ahead. Montgomery's change of plan meant that 9th Australian Division "would now face the toughest task of any division at Alamein: to fight northwards through the teeth of Axis resistance."[40] The Australians could also expect to attract the bulk of Axis armor in some vigorous counterattacks. Morshead was ordered to commence their crumbling operations toward the coast that night.

* * *

Another factor that had persuaded Montgomery of the necessity of switching the direction of the attack was the lack of success of 13 Corps' operation in the southern sector of the Alamein position. On the evening of October 24, two battalions of 44 Division, under command of 7 Armoured Division, attempted to break through the second mine barrier, which had prevented the capture of Himeimat on the opening night. When the minefield had been breached, two armored regiments were to "sally out," swing north and clear the front.[41] Two infantry battalions was a totally inadequate force with which to unlock the Axis defenses in the south. Not only were the defenders of the Folgore Division and elements of the Ramcke Brigade fully alert to what was intended, observation posts on Himeimat could bring down fire on anything that moved on the flat below. The two infantry battalions, the 1/5th and 1/6th Queens from 131 Brigade, under cover of an artillery barrage, managed to clear two small gaps through the minefield but suffered heavy casualties. They were soon pinned down by heavy fire only 400 yards beyond the minefield. Heavy fire prevented the battalions' support weapons reaching them and the failure of their wireless sets meant that the infantry could not call for artillery support. Two armored regiments that attempted to advance through the gaps "made perfect targets for the Axis gunners," which had the gaps well covered and engaged the armor at close range.[42] To add to the tragedy, some of the advancing British tanks missed the cleared gaps and ran onto the minefield. At daylight, the attack was called off and the hapless infantry had to remain pinned beyond the minefield, poorly dug in and exposed to enemy fire, for all of October 25. Losses for the night's action were 350 men from the infantry battalions and 26 tanks.[43] These tank losses convinced Harding, 7 Armoured Division's commander and under orders from Montgomery to keep his formation intact, that "[he] could not risk further losses."[44] This attack probably contributed to Rommel's decision to delay the switch of 21 Panzer Division to the north for two more days, but it was an expensive way to do this. This action was the last attempt of 13 Corps to break through the Axis defenses in the south. From October 25, 13 Corps' role was to carry out large-scale raids "to maintain the illusion of a threat" and to provide units and formations to those fighting further north when needed.[45] Harding's 7 Armoured Division was relieved by 44 Division on the night of October 25 and was withdrawn into the Army's reserve.

* * *

There were two areas in which the British forces had established an absolute dominance over the Axis and which by October 25 were making significant contributions to the battle's outcome. Without the air superiority of the DAF, the battle could not have been fought. On October 24, the DAF flew a record 1,000 fighter and bomber sorties, most concentrated in the northern sector.[46] On October 25 the number had fallen to a still impressive 660 sorties with more than 300,000 pounds of bombs being dropped on Luftwaffe landing grounds and Axis positions close to the front. The New Zealand official historian said of this air activity: "the Desert Air Force continued to prove that the air war had already been won."[47] On November 2, Rommel wrote to his wife that, "You can imagine how I feel. Air raid after air raid after air raid!"[48] Reflecting on the battle, he recognized the vital role the DAF had played in it. "The second essential condition for an army to stand in battle," he wrote, "is parity or at least something approaching parity in the air." Without this parity, the enemy "can wage the battle of attrition from the air" and "intensive exploitation by the enemy of his air superiority gives rise to far-reaching tactical limitations for one's own command."[49] Rommel had experienced these "far-reaching tactical limitations" first-hand. It also had, as an Australian after-action report acknowledged, "a marked effect on both our own and the enemy morale."[50]

The other area in which the battle was already won was with Eighth Army's use of artillery. German reports repeatedly referred to the hammering they were receiving from it. An after-action secret report on the use of artillery noted that "Nearly all prisoners captured spoke of the great effect of our artillery fire."[51] Two Australian historians have described this artillery advantage as "clearly the Commonwealth force's greatest asset." They write that, "Abundantly supplied, centrally directed, and available immediately, it gave the infantry a decisive advantage over the enemy."[52] There is little doubt that Eighth Army's artillery dominated the battlefield. As described in the previous chapter, General von Thoma told his fellow captive general that the artillery barrages were reminiscent of the "Great War" and that one of the first things he had to report to Rommel on October 26 was that "a great many" of the Axis anti-tank guns had been destroyed.[53] Rommel later acknowledged that:

> The British artillery once again demonstrated its well-known excellence. A particular feature was its great mobility and tremendous speed of reaction to the needs of the assault troops.[54]

Conversely, while the Axis forces knew the position of Eighth Army's artillery batteries and had superiority in both medium and heavy guns, they "made no use of these in any way to counter our Artillery." The secret after-action report of the Royal Artillery concluded that the Axis artillery in this battle "was most inefficiently handled." It noted too that: "There is no doubt that even before the battle, our artillery had achieved a moral superiority over the enemy's artillery."[55] During the battle, for major actions, "no restriction was placed on ammunition." Throughout the 12-day battle, Eighth Army's 834 25-pounder guns fired more than one million rounds at the enemy. On average, each gun fired 102 rounds per day. The rate of fire of the medium guns was even higher: 133 rounds per gun, per day for the 4.5-inch guns and 157 for the 5.5-inch guns.[56] The effect of this was "to give the Commonwealth infantry a curtain of steel available virtually on call."[57]

When combined with the efforts of the DAF, its effects were even greater. It affected the morale of both armies and was a constant feature throughout the battle. Little wonder that Rommel would write in despair to his wife towards the end of the battle that: "We're simply being

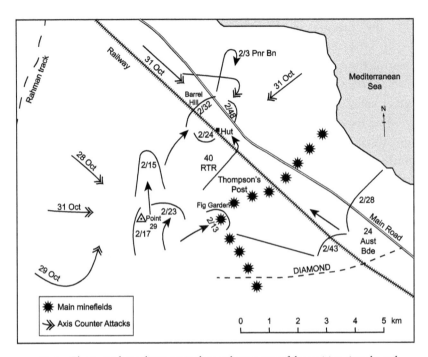

Map 4. The Australians slug it out in the northern sector of the position. Attacks and counter-attacks launched October 28–31.

crushed by the enemy weight."[58] Throughout the days of the battle, it had been the DAF and the Eighth Army artillery that had done a fair proportion of the crushing of the Axis forces.

* * *

The shift of direction of the crumbling operations meant that the bulk of the fighting here would fall on 9 Australian Division. A summary of operations of the division recorded on October 25 that "'Eating the guts' to be continued by 30 Corps (9 Aust Div) attacking northwards to cut off the enemy in the north."[59] These would begin that night with an attack toward the coast by just two Australian battalions.

The main objective was to extend the current front to the north by capturing new ground beyond the current right flank. This included the feature Point 29, a slight rise in the desert terrain offering excellent observation over the Australian positions. Prior to the opening attack on

October 23, "careful consideration" had been given to including Point 29 as an objective given its obvious tactical value. But Morshead felt that his infantry already had enough to do and that Point 29 would have to wait. It was, however, "selected as the first exploitation task."[60] It also included an enemy location known as the Fig Garden, which the Germans called the "Devil's Garden." Two battalions from the 26th Australian Brigade would be used. In the first phase of the attack, 2/48 Battalion would set off just after midnight to capture the area around Point 29. Forty minutes later, the 2/24th Battalion would advance and capture the Fig Garden from the southeast. Both battalions had only a few hours to prepare for their attack, which had to be done while under artillery and mortar fire. Though artillery support for the attack could be provided, it "would have to be done without the assistance of or threat of our own armd [armored] forces."[61] That all preparations were completed on time without a hitch indicated how professional and skillful the Australians had become. For Niall Barr, it was proof that 26 Australian Brigade "was now one of the most experienced and effective formations within Eighth Army."[62]

At dusk on October 25, the Australians had a stroke of luck when a German reconnaissance party was captured. Included among the prisoners were two senior field officers who had not had time to destroy the detailed sketch maps that showed the tracks through their minefields being used. This intelligence coup and the lavish artillery support provided to the attacking infantry were invaluable. However, the Australian infantry still had a hard fight ahead of them.

At midnight on October 25, the two leading companies of 2/48 Battalion crossed their start line and advanced 900 yards to the first objective. With artillery from six field and two medium regiments firing on known enemy positions, the infantry still had "to fight every inch of the way" to reach it.[63] When it had been taken, ten Bren-gun carriers packed with infantry and towing anti-tank guns raced toward Point 29 along the cleared laneways shown in the captured maps. They arrived on the high ground of Point 29 nine minutes later, just as the artillery barrage was lifted onto the next target. "The enemy was greatly surprised. Our men killed with great determination," recorded the Battalion's War Diary.[64] The stunned German defenders put up a brief resistance before

Point 29 was taken. Attempts to extend the position northward, though, met with stiff opposition. Losses in 2/48 Battalion had been heavy and the exhausted battalion was relieved by 2/17 Battalion the next morning. Australian engineers also arrived to strengthen the minefields around the new positions.

The attack by 2/24 Battalion met with less success. The Battalion's infantry strength was already "heavily depleted" before the attack. Only two of the Battalion's four companies could muster more than sixty men.[65] After an advance of 800 yards, the battalion encountered a web of strong enemy positions that had not been previously detected. The delay clearing these meant that the infantry fell behind their artillery support. The first objective was taken and three companies pushed on to reach the final objective. While the Fig Garden was captured, it could not be held against the intense close-range fire being poured into the position. Its War Diary recorded a tense situation: "Casualties were so hy [heavy] however and opposition so strong . . . the CO . . . after reviewing situation decided to withdraw."[66] The battalion withdrew about 1,000 yards and consolidated on the new ground it captured. With more than 100 killed and wounded that night, the battalion's War Diary recorded that it "sustained many casualties."[67]

The Australian attack was a successful limited assault and had advanced its position "some 2000 yards . . . North towards the sea."[68] It had certainly "crumbled" some of the opposition facing them. The attack on the night of October 25 had secured "a valuable area of ground . . . from which crumbling operations could continue."[69] The capture of a key position like Point 29 was also significant. It was bound to provoke serious counterattacks from Panzerarmee, who knew its importance. As the War Diary of the 2/48th Battalion recorded on the morning of October 26:

> The value of Trig 29 as an OP is more than ever realised by us now as it has a range of vision of 4000 to 5000 yds in all directions. The enemy too realises this and it is receiving considerable attention from the enemy arty.[70]

Its capture also drew Rommel's attention to the northern sector as Montgomery intended it should. Rommel was convinced that Montgomery intended to break through not just in the northern sector, "but actually on the very right flank of 8th Army line." This "magnetism of the north" became entrenched in his mind. It was "a conclusion from which he hardly budged during the rest of the battle."[71]

* * *

The Australians were not the only part of 30 Corps in action on October 25–26. Helping to direct Rommel's eyes north were the actions taken by the 51st (Highland) Division, who were still struggling to take their first night's objectives. They had been held up for two days now by three enemy strong points that had so far eluded capture. On the night of October 25, the Highlanders had three battalions in action with the task of reaching its final objective of October 23 across the entire divisional front. In the north, the 1st Gordons were to advance to the Aberdeen/ Kidney Ridge feature. In the center, the 5th Black Watch were ordered to take the strongpoint labeled "Stirling," while to the south, the 7th Argylls took another, codenamed "Nairn." In many ways, the attack by the Highland battalions mirrored that of the Australians. After "Stirling" was pounded by the entire Division's artillery for three hours, the 5th Black Watch attacked to find "Stirling" filled with "dead and dying Germans."[72] "Stirling" was easily taken and the position reinforced by the addition of twenty anti-tank guns and a squadron of 50 RTR. But "Nairn" proved a tougher prospect. As the 7th Argylls approached it, they came under heavy machine gun and mortar fire. The position was eventually taken and the survivors consolidated on the reverse slope of the objective. Losses had been so heavy, though, that the two companies that had assaulted the position had to be combined into a composite force.[73] In the north, only the troublesome Aberdeen/Kidney Ridge feature remained in enemy hands. The 1st Gordons had been forced to attack the feature without artillery support and had committed just a company-and-a-half to the assault. Setting off an hour before the Australian attack started, the Gordons met "unexpected opposition," which brought their advance to a sudden halt.[74] But the 51st (Highland) Division was now in possession of its final objective, the Blue Line, and "just as importantly, the tanks of 2 Armoured Brigade could now take hull-down positions along the entire line of the 'northern ridge.'"[75] It was a small but important gain. Equally significant was the fact that the Highlanders' attempts to capture Aberdeen/Kidney Ridge had also caught Rommel's attention.

* * *

October 26 was a day of frustration for both sides. Rommel launched several counterattacks against the Australians at Point 29, but they were all broken up by the crushing superiority of Eighth Army's artillery. Each group of German or Italian soldiers seeking to assemble for a counterattack attracted attention from at least four artillery regiments. Rommel complained that "Rivers of blood were poured out over miserable strips of land which, in normal times, not even the poorest Arab would have bothered his head about."[76] Such concerns had never bothered Rommel when he was winning. As early as October 24, Lumsden had warned that if the battle became static it "just fizzles out."[77] Two days later, it looked as if this was happening. Freyberg warned his infantry brigadiers that morning the "best chance is to push on in the North." He added:

> We have to be clear that the advance to this present position will not win the War. . . . If the pressure is kept up he is bound to crack.[78]

Two decisions were made on October 26 that were to have a direct bearing on the outcome of the battle. First, at a meeting of his corps commanders at Morshead's headquarters, Montgomery declared a change in policy. Operation *Lightfoot* "had not achieved all that had been hoped of it." The deployment of the armor beyond 30 Corps' bridgehead "had not gone well" and the crumbling operations were well behind schedule.[79] And already Eighth Army had suffered 6,140 casualties. This was so high that "Montgomery saw that he would have to go carefully with his infantry."[80] 30 Corps, which had incurred almost 5,000 of these casualties, needed a short break so that it could rest and reorganize. It was not to carry out major operations for the next few days. Instead, the 9th Australian Division was to renew its attack in the north on the night of October 28, while the rest of 30 Corps prepared for major operations later. It would be regrouped to create a reserve with which to restore the momentum of the offensive. That afternoon, Montgomery conferred with his artillery commander, Kirkman, and was relieved to learn that Eighth Army had enough ammunition on hand to continue the fight for ten days.

That afternoon, Rommel also made a critical decision. It was clear that 13 Corps' operations in the south posed no real threat. To Rommel "it was now obvious that the enemy would make his main effort in the north during the next few days and try for a decision there."[81] Accordingly, Rommel ordered 21 Panzer Division and half his artillery units in the south to move to the northern sector. It was a calculated risk, as Rommel "fully realised that the petrol shortage would not allow it [21 Panzer] to return."[82] Enigma intercepts soon informed Montgomery that 21 Panzer and artillery units were moving north and were instructed to be ready "for a possible counterattack towards the east."[83] That evening, 1 Armoured Division established itself north and south of Kidney Ridge, providing a valuable link with the Australians. It confirmed, in Rommel's mind, that this northern sector was indeed where Eighth Army was making its main effort.

* * *

On the night of October 26, both the New Zealand and South African Divisions carried out minor actions to reach their original final objectives. Despite some "lively" enemy opposition, the final objectives were gained by daylight on October 27.[84] A counterattack launched by the Axis at 0900 hours the same day encountered the tanks of 9 Armoured Brigade forward of the New Zealand infantry. In the brief skirmish that followed, nine enemy tanks were destroyed.[85] There were no further counterattacks on the New Zealanders or South Africans that day, although both divisions were subjected to heavy artillery fire and air attacks throughout the morning. This move to straighten the line and reach the final objectives of October 23 was preparatory to the New Zealanders being withdrawn from their positions on Miteiriya Ridge.

On October 27, around Kidney Ridge, "one of the most gallant actions of the desert war" occurred, which was to have "a great effect on the enemy."[86] Nearly a mile to the northwest of Kidney Ridge, and about the same distance to the southwest, were two localities that became strong centers of enemy resistance. These were known as "Woodcock" and "Snipe." Rommel, having taken over command of Panzerarmee the previous evening, recognized that Kidney Ridge was a vital feature and launched his main counterattack here to drive the British armor from it. The action commenced at first light and continued most of the day. At 1600 hours, Rommel launched an all-out assault using all four of his armored divisions and the 90th Light Division. In addition, "every artillery and anti-aircraft gun we had in the northern sector concentrated a violent fire on the point of the intended attack."[87] The battle was confusing and deadly. One unit of 1 Armoured Division, the 2nd Rifle Brigade (it was actually not a brigade but a battalion of light infantry), was left isolated and exposed on the feature "Snipe," to the southwest of Kidney Ridge, for most of the day. One rifleman recalled that, from the private soldiers' point of view, "the scene was one of utter confusion and mayhem," where every tank and gun barrel in the Panzerarmee "was directed towards them."[88] The 2nd Rifle Brigade held the position until 2100 hours, when its depleted numbers forced it to withdraw. Of the nineteen anti-tank guns it had used during the day, only one was left undamaged. While the 2nd Battalion of the Rifle Brigade lost about one-third of the men who fought on "Snipe" and most of their vehicles and guns, an official investigation credited them with destroying thirty-two tanks and five German self-propelled guns. The action was described by the Rifle Brigades' history as "the most famous of the Regiment's war." The battalion commander, Lieutenant Colonel Victor Turner, was awarded the Victoria Cross for his and the battalion's gallantry on October 27.[89] Axis tank losses around Kidney Ridge on this day amounted to forty-seven.[90] These were devastating losses for Rommel, who recorded that, "we suffered considerable losses and were obliged to withdraw." He also came to an ominous conclusion from this action on October 27:

> It was obvious from now on the British would destroy us bit by bit, since we were virtually unable to move on the battlefield. As yet, Montgomery had only thrown half his striking force into the battle.[91]

Rommel would have been even more alarmed had he known that Montgomery was, on this fateful day, developing a new plan to put more of his strike force into the battle.

* * *

On the evening of October 26, Montgomery had taken the decision that the battle must not be allowed to "fizzle" or end in stalemate. Instead, Eighth Army must "regroup and reposition, with a view to creating fresh reserves for further offensive action."[92] This was a tacit admission that the current battle had stalled and that 30 Corps could not transition

from the break-in to the break-out. In other words, Montgomery's original plan had failed and he needed to try something different. He later
wrote that October 26 and 27 was "the most critical time in the battle."
While the fighting had been intense, "the momentum of our attacks
was diminishing."[93] The essential task now was to create a reserve that
could be used to deliver a knockout blow when the time was right to do
so. To create this reserve on the night of October 27, the 2nd New Zealand Division was withdrawn from Miteiriya Ridge. The New Zealand
artillery regiments, however, moved north into the Australian sector,
where they supported the Australian crumbling operations planned for
the next three days. The attached 9 Armoured Brigade moved with the
infantry into reserve. The New Zealand sector was taken over by 1 South
African Division while 4 Indian Division moved into the position va-
cated by the South Africans. Freyberg described the move as "a general
side-slip" and reported that it "was completed without incident."[94] Also
moved into reserve were the armored formations of 10 Corps less 1 Armoured Division, which would come under command of 30 Corps. The
7th Armoured Division of 13 Corps was warned to be prepared to move
north and 13 Corps was informed that several of its infantry brigades
would also be needed to bolster the reserve force being created. To keep
Rommel's attention riveted to the north and his forces "off balance,"
the Australian crumbling operations were to be not only continued,
but considerably intensified. Niall Barr described these moves as "the
reshuffling of the existing pack of cards," while Stephen Bungay called it
a "change to the bits on his drill."[95] It was a decisive change in plan and
marked, as Barr has written, "Montgomery's firm grasp of the dynamics
of operational command."[96]

   In London, however, Montgomery's regrouping and repositioning
was not taken as an indication of his operational command skills. Indeed, it had the reverse effect on Churchill and Anthony Eden and both
men became convinced that Montgomery was allowing the battle to peter out. Montgomery alluded to this when he wrote that creating his new
reserve "gave to some the impression that I had decided that we could
not break through the enemy and was giving up."[97] Field Marshal Alan
Brooke, later 1st Viscount Alanbrooke, had a very difficult task convincing them otherwise. He recalled:

When I went to see Winston, having been sent for from the COS meeting, I was met by a flow of abuse of Monty. What was <u>my</u> Monty doing now, allowing the battle to peter out (Monty was always <u>my</u> Monty when he was out of favour!). He had done nothing now for the last three days, and now he was withdrawing troops from the front. Why had he told us he would be through in seven days if all he intended to do was to fight a half-hearted battle? Had we not got a single general who could even win one single battle? etc, etc. When he stopped to regain his breath I asked him what had suddenly influenced him to arrive at these conclusions. He said that Anthony Eden had been with him last night and that he was very worried with the course the battle was taking, and that neither Monty nor Alex was gripping the situation and showing a true offensive spirit. The strain of the battle had had its effect on me, the anxiety was growing more and more intense each day and my temper was on edge. I felt very angry with Eden and asked Winston why he consulted his Foreign Secretary when he wanted advice on strategic and tactical matters. He flared up and asked whether he was not entitled to consult whoever he wished! To which I replied he certainly could, provided he did not let those who knew little about military matters upset his equilibrium. He continued by stating that he was dissatisfied with the course of the battle and would hold a COS meeting under his Chairmanship at 12.30 to be attended by some of his colleagues.

At the Chief of Staff meeting, backed by South African statesman General Jan Smuts, Brooke was able to convince the chiefs that Montgomery was simply preparing for the next phase of the battle, which would be another strike at the Panzerarmee. No one present at the meeting was aware that Brooke also had serious doubts of his own about Montgomery's then-unproven generalship. Brooke concluded his notes about this Chief of Staff meeting with a frank admission:

Personally however I was far from being at peace. I had my own doubts and my own anxieties as to the course of events, but these had to be kept entirely to myself. On returning to my office I paced up and down, suffering from a desperate feeling of loneliness. I had, during the morning's discussion, tried to maintain an exterior of complete confidence. It had worked, confidence had been restored. I had then told them what I thought Monty must be doing, and I knew Monty well, but there was still just the possibility that I was wrong and that Monty was beat. The loneliness of those moments of anxiety, when there is no one one can turn to, have to be lived through to realize their intense bitterness.[98]

* * *

From October 28, it was left largely to the Australians in the northern sector to maintain the initiative and to carry the fight to Panzerarmee.

With the exception of the 9th Australian Division in the north, the offensive closed down across the front. This was done to allow Montgomery to concentrate on preparing what he hoped would be the knock-out blow. Accordingly, he issued the Australians with a "brief direction to 'Attack North.'"[99] The 9th Australian Division, now reinforced with additional artillery, had the unenviable task of keeping Rommel's attention focused in the north by continuing their crumbling operations. The second set-piece attack was planned for the night of October 28.

The artillery barrage that opened the Australian attack toward the coast on the night of October 28 was particularly heavy. The German 90th Light Division, on the receiving end of it, recorded in its War Diary that "the northern sector was under a barrage reminiscent of Great War days. The horizon was ablaze with the flashes of enemy guns."[100] Panzerarmee's Battle Report described the barrage as "the heaviest artillery fire which had so far been experienced."[101] Under the protection of the artillery, two infantry battalions from 20 Australian Infantry Brigade set off at 2200 hours in the first phase of the attack. Both battalions had to pass through the congested bottleneck of Point 29, where accurate Axis artillery fire caused casualties. One battalion, the 2/15th, lost both its commanding officer and its adjutant to this shelling. Despite this, the 2/15th Battalion, on the left flank of the attack, pressed on towards its objective some 3,000 yards to the north. It met light opposition and encountered no minefields, reaching the objective with light casualties.[102] After midnight, its support weapons and sappers arrived to lay mines and dig in. The Battalion buried eighty-nine Italians killed in the assault and took a further 130 prisoner.[103]

On the right flank, the 2/13th Battalion, heading for the Fig Garden, had a tougher time. The Battalion was so understrength that its companies, averaging just thirty-five exhausted men, could not cover more than 100 yards of front during the attack. But the infantry made excellent progress and reached the Fig Garden, some 2,500 yards northeast from their start line, just after midnight. The Fig Garden had been heavily mined and booby trapped and 2/13th Battalion lost more men to these than from enemy fire. Mopping up isolated German machine posts also caused casualties. The next day, the Battalion was firmly established in the Fig Garden but the strength of its four rifle companies had dwindled to approximately 100 men. It was being commanded by the senior surviving officer, a captain.[104]

All three battalions from 26 Australian Infantry Brigade were allocated tasks that night. They were depending on 2/23 Battalion, the first in action, reaching and securing its objective of the railway line and the main road from where the other two battalions could exploit. The second phase of the attack commenced at 2340 hours when 2/23 Battalion and tanks from the 46th Royal Tank Regiment moved off. This phase of the attack was an absolute disaster. As the infantry had such a long distance to travel, they were mounted in bren gun carriers and on the Valentine tanks of 46 RTR. But the briefings for the operation had been rushed and none of the tank commanders had gone forward to reconnoiter the gaps in the start line. Inevitably, the tanks of 46 RTR ran onto the Australian minefields, causing complete chaos and alerting the enemy to what was happening. It took more than an hour to reorganize and when the tanks finally set off through the cleared laneways, they were fired on by the Axis anti-tank guns enfilading the gaps. "It was bloody chaos," recalled one Australian infantryman who was there. "You couldn't see for dust and there were dead and wounded everywhere."[105] The Battalion's War Diary recorded an "extremely confused situation" that night.[106] Despite being under fire from three sides, the Battalion's commanding officer, Lieutenant Colonel Bernard Evans, was able to organize one limited counterattack on the most dangerous German strongpoint, which captured the post, 160 prisoners, and six anti-tank guns. That was the limit of 2/23 Battalion's success and it suffered twenty-nine killed in action, 172 wounded, and another six soldiers missing. The battalion dug in on ridges about 900 yards from the start line, having captured 162 prisoners from 125 Panzer Grenadier Regiment.[107] 46 RTR had also suffered heavy casualties, including its commanding officer and all of its squadron leaders. Only seven of its original forty tanks remained battle-worthy, so that "the regiment had almost ceased to exist."[108] Wisely, the third phase of the operation involving 2/24 and 2/48 Battalions was postponed as the dawn approached, "much to the relief of the waiting infantry" who "trudged back to their slit trenches for some sleep."[109]

This attack, although it failed, captured more ground for the Australians, inflicted heavy casualties on the Axis, especially on the German

90 Light Division, and "disrupted and confused the Axis defence."[110] It was this attack on October 28–29 that finally convinced Rommel he was fighting a losing battle. Describing the weight of this attack as "something quite exceptional," Rommel recorded his bleak outlook that night:

> No one can conceive the extent of our anxiety during this period. That night I hardly slept and by 0300 hours [29 October] was pacing up and down turning over in my mind the likely course of the battle, and the decisions I might have to take. It seemed doubtful whether we would be able to stand up much longer to attacks of the weight which the British were now making, and which they were in any case still able to increase. It was obvious to me that I dared not await the decisive breakthrough but would have to pull out to the west before it came.[111]

The next day, he unburdened his deepest fears in a letter to his wife:

> The situation continues very grave. By the time this letter arrives, it will no doubt have been decided whether we can hold on or not. I haven't much hope left.
>
> At night I lie with my eyes wide open, unable to sleep, for the load that is on my shoulders. In the day I'm dead tired.
>
> What will happen if things go wrong here? That is the thought that torments me day and night. I can see no way out if that happens.[112]

His signals to Kesselring in Rome, and soon in the Allies' hands in London and Cairo, described an "extremely critical situation" on October 28. The next day, the situation had not improved. It was communicated as being "grave in the extreme."[113]

On October 29, three counterattacks by tanks and infantry of Battlegroup 200 struck at the Australian infantry on their new positions. All three were driven off by the overwhelming defensive artillery fire protecting the Australians. The Battlegroup suffered heavy losses in these counterattacks. Four successive attacks launched by 90 Light Division against the 2/15th Battalion's position over October 29–30 suffered the same fate.[114] Rommel's forces were being steadily crumbled away, but the Australians were also suffering in the process.

* * *

The last of the Australian crumbling operations occurred on the night of October 30. This was to be a larger operation than the previous two and it required careful planning. It was divided into four phases. In the first phase, the 2/32nd Battalion was to capture the main road and railway that had eluded 26 Infantry Brigade in its previous attack. Its main objective was a small hill just south of the road labeled B11 on maps, but which the soldiers called Barrel Hill because of a navigation beacon on it. The Battalion was to hold a position marked by Barrel Hill near the road and the "Blockhouse" near the railway line. It was to provide a secure base for the other battalions in the subsequent phases of the operation. In the second phase, 2/24 and 2/48 Battalions were to follow this first attack, advance east, and capture the main enemy defenses astride the coast road. The 2/48th Battalion was to advance to the north of the main road while 2/24 advanced in parallel south of it. When 2/48 Battalion reached Ring Contour 25, it was to attack due north and take the feature known as "Cloverleaf" near the coast. At the same time, 2/24 Battalion was to attack due south to take the troublesome feature known as "Thompson's Post." This would complete Phase 3 of the operation. In the final phase, the 2/3rd Pioneer Battalion, fighting now as infantry, was to launch an attack from Barrel Hill toward the coast with the intention of cutting off the entire 125 Panzer Grenadier Regiment. Although 40 RTR was to be in support, the initial attack was to be made without tank support. There would, however, be 360 guns available in support firing on known enemy positions and providing a protective barrage during Phase 1.

It was a "complicated and ambitious" plan, one that asked too much of infantry battalions weakened and worn out from seven days of constant action.[115] Niall Barr has criticized the plan for "expecting too much of the Australian soldiers." With the 2/24th and 2/48th Battalions being required to make advances of nearly 10,000 yards, Barr is certainly correct. Moreover, the plan "hinged on sequential actions of individual battalions rather than their combined effort."[116] Johnston and Stanley concur, noting that an attack down the main road was not only unnecessary given that the breakthrough attack would occur to the south, but that it "was bound to stretch to breaking point the resources of the depleted battalions allotted to it."[117]

The attack began at 2200 hours and it is hardly surprising that events did not go according to plan. The opening barrage was again impressive. Montgomery recorded in his diary that "The attack of 9 Aust Div went in under a terrific artillery fire. My caravan in my Tactical H.Q. shook all night."[118] The 2/32nd Battalion was to lead the attack. It was relatively fresh but 250 men short of its established strength.[119] Congestion on the start line delayed 2/32 Battalion's start so that they lost the effects of the creeping barrage. As a result, 2/32 Battalion had to fight its way forward against an enemy now alert to what was happening. Reasonable progress was made until the battalion reached Barrel Hill. A determined attack captured the position and 175 German prisoners. Soon after its capture, though, the battalion's commanding officer was wounded and the weakened companies could not mop up the strong enemy posts surrounding them. These would cause considerable problems for the follow up battalions in Phase 2. The Blockhouse, a railway hut being used by the Germans as an aid post, was also captured.

The steep railway embankment proved to be a formidable obstacle, too. It was more than twelve feet high and the bulldozer that had been brought forward to cut a gap in it was disabled on a mine. The engineers accompanying 2/32 Battalion finally blew a gap in the embankment, but it took three hours of exhausting digging by fifty men with entrenching tools to clear away the sand and rubble. The gap that had been cut attracted considerable fire. It was, however, used until daylight when it became too dangerous to keep using it.

On the morning of October 31, 2/32 Battalion had two rifle companies north of the railway and covering the road from the slopes of Barrel Hill. Two more were south of the railway and facing west. Support weapons had reached them so that the base was reasonably secure. It was, however, surrounded by enemy positions.

Phase 2 of the operation began less than half an hour later with 2/48 and 2/24 Battalions following the path of 2/32 Battalion. Their progress was delayed by congestion en route and by the numerous enemy posts that had not been mopped up. The 2/48th Battalion found these delays "annoying factors that could have been eliminated if the orders issued by higher authorities had been obeyed by the people concerned."[120] The 2/48th Battalion reached its forming-up point at the railway embankment near the blockhouse but recorded in its War Diary that the position was "far from stabilised and enemy resistance was encountered at almost every step." The Battalion set off at zero hour supported by an artillery barrage that "lacked the accuracy which characterised its previous support." Its War Diary recorded that the men had a stiff fight, as "strong opposition was met and every inch of the way had to be fought for."[121]

The attacking battalions soon lost the support of the artillery barrage—a serious development given their weakened strengths and now facing alerted defenders behind strong defensive positions. Both battalions pushed against increasingly strong opposition.

On the left flank, south of the road, 2/24 Battalion met very determined opposition. It struggled to keep advancing; however, with the help of a platoon from 2/48 Battalion, it managed to reach within 700 yards of the final objective. But with companies greatly reduced in strength, one to just six men, the battalion could not remain in the open. "Intense opposition was encountered . . . Very hy casualties were suffered," recorded its War Diary.[122] Thompson's Post, despite rumors that it had been abandoned by the enemy, "was still strongly held."[123] With daylight approaching, the decision was made to withdraw the remnants of the battalion back to 2/32 Battalion's position south of the railway and dig in facing west.

On the right, north of the road, 2/48 Battalion had an identical experience but managed to capture its first objective. Its losses were heavy and further progress was impossible. The Battalion's War Diary recorded a hard decision reached by its commanding officer. "After careful consideration at 0530 hours the CO decided to move the Bn which now consisted of 41 men, back to a firm base to an area just East of the 2/32 Bn."[124]

With fewer than 400 men and limited artillery support, 2/24 and 2/48 Battalions had cut a swath through the strongest Axis positions about two miles in length and half a mile wide. They had captured more than 250 Germans as well as a "veritable arsenal" of weapons. But the cost had been high, with two "superb battalions . . . all but destroyed" in the process.[125]

Despite the fact that Phase 2 and 3 of the operation had not gone well, Phase 4 continued. The 2/3rd Pioneer Battalion formed up in the congested 2/32 Battalion secure area and set off toward the coast ten minutes behind schedule at 0430 hours, with dawn not far away. The battalion, required to make an advance of 2,900 yards, at first met little opposition. The first objective, 1,500 yards from the start line, was easily captured along with eighty prisoners. Here, C Company dug in while D Company passed through the position ready to advance to the final 1,400 yards to the coast. When D Company set off, a different problem confronted them. The supporting artillery barrage ahead of them was not lifting as it should have. To advance through would have caused many and unnecessary casualties. With daylight approaching, the company dug in 200 yards forward of the first objective and still 1,200 yards from the sea.

Dawn on October 31 found "the situation of the 26 Australian Brigade" to be "somewhat obscure." It was an accurate statement. The situation was not helped by "the pall of dust and smoke" that hung over the battlefield.[126] The 2/3rd Pioneer Battalion was the most vulnerable and had secured a salient that the Australian official historian described as a "brittle wedge."[127] In the morning, the heavy fire of the German defenders, especially from mortars, made it clear the battalion could not remain where it was. It withdrew toward the secure base provided by 2/32 Battalion. One company dug in around Barrel Hill, the other two dug in south of the railway line.

Cluttered around Barrel Hill, the Blockhouse, and the gap in the railway embankment on the morning of October 31 were the remnants of three infantry and one pioneer battalion. Of these, only the 2/32nd Battalion was near the position envisaged in the original plan. It was holding a line running south from Barrel Hill to the railway. In the southern edge of the new position, holding two positions south of the railway line were the remnants of 2/24 Battalion. Its strength had been reduced to one officer and eighty-four men.[128] To the north, 300 yards east of Barrel Hill, with one post north of the railway line, was located what remained of 2/48 Battalion. It was down to just two officers and forty-one men.[129] To the men of 2/32 Battalion, surveying their new location at dawn, the new position resembled a giant saucer. It was called the "Saucer" thereafter.[130]

While this last crumbling operation had failed to attain its objectives, it had maintained pressure on Rommel in the north and certainly held his attention. On the morning of October 31, he mistakenly believed that the Australians, with British armor, had "forced their way through to the coast and cut off the 125th Infantry Regiment." He described the Axis position to his wife that morning as being "very grave again."[131] He gave orders to launch an immediate counterattack using dive bombers and all the artillery they could muster.

The Australian attack on the night of October 30 has been described as the "climax" of their involvement in the battle of El Alamein. This was true in one sense, as the actions that night "were the last and perhaps most desperate Australian attacks of the battle."[132] Yet "climax" implies an ending, and the period following being of less intense activity. For the Australians, this was far from the case. From October 31 until the battle ended, "the Australians would have to defend, in order to hold their gains against everything the Germans could direct against them."[133] The Saucer became the site of some of the most desperate fighting of the battle. For the next three days, Rommel's main effort was committed to ejecting the Australians from the Saucer position. Reporting on the actions of November 1, Morshead informed General Blamey in Australia that:

> One of the most determined attacks ever made against 9 Aust Div was launched at 1215 HRS. It was by inf and tanks against 24 Bde and came from three directions NE, north and NW. The issue was not decided until night and it was not until midnight that it actually ceased.[134]

These counterattacks cost both sides dearly. For the Australians, it "stretched [them] to the limit. Too much had been demanded of them by Montgomery and their own divisional commander."[135]

On October 31, Freyberg had informed the New Zealand Prime Minister that "your Division has stood the test of a most exacting battle and morale of the men is excellent."[136] Such praise was equally applicable to the Australians fighting around the Saucer. Despite the hard conditions and their mounting casualties, their morale, even during the most testing of times, remained "clearly high."[137] For the Germans, believing that Eighth Army was massing in "the northern sector for a decisive attack," these actions absorbed the Axis' precious resources and concentrated their strength here, leaving the rest of their frontline positions vulnerable.[138] It also caused them many "sad losses," as Panzerarmee's strength was being steadily eroded.[139] "We pressed forward slowly, but we had heavy losses," recalled General von Thoma immediately after the battle. When Rommel came forward on the afternoon of November 1, von Thoma recalled that "things were very bad up there and he saw it for himself."[140]

* * *

The American military commander Lieutenant General George S. Patton believed that successful military tactics followed a simple formula. He wrote in his diary on November 2, 1942, that while strategy should be a "steamroller" affair, tactics required more finesse. Patton wrote:

> But in tactics do not steamroller. Attack weakness. Hold them by the nose and kick them in the pants.[141]

The nose/pants analogy was one Patton used many times in his writings.[142] Montgomery, whom Patton would unfortunately repeatedly describe as a "little fart," had succeeded in the first part of Patton's formula.[143] The Australian crumbling operations had fixed Rommel's attention and the cream of his forces in the north. Here Rommel was being held firmly by the nose while Montgomery prepared the knock-out blow. Montgomery now needed to strike where Rommel was weak. It was essential that he dispense a massive kick in the pants with all the force at his disposal.

NOTES

1. Hamilton, *The Full Monty*, 707.
2. Walker, *Alam Halfa and Alamein*, 295.
3. Barr, *Pendulum of War*, 333.
4. 9 Australian Division, Report on Operations El Alamein 23 Oct–5 Nov 1942, WO 201/2495, TNA.
5. Johnston and Stanley, *Alamein: The Australian Story*, 174.
6. War Diary, 2/17 Australian Infantry Battalion, 25 Oct 1942, 8/3/17, AWM 52, AWM.
7. Ibid.
8. War Diary, 2/13 Australian Infantry Battalion, 25 Oct 1942, 8/3/17, AWM 52, AWM.
9. Quoted in Barr, *Pendulum of War*, 334.
10. Hamilton, *The Full Monty*, 677.
11. Ibid.
12. Ibid., 705.
13. Ibid., 710.
14. Ibid., 711.
15. Walker, *Alam Halfa and Alamein*, 326.
16. Playfair et al., *Volume IV*, 45.
17. Barr, *Pendulum of War*, 335.
18. 9th Armoured Brigade War Diary, 25 October 1942, WO 169/4233, TNA.
19. Ibid.

20. Captain C.B. Stoddart, letter to his father, quoted in Hamilton, *The Full Monty*, 718.

21. Barr, *Pendulum of War*, 335.

22. Captain C.B. Stoddart, letter to his father, quoted in Hamilton. *The Full Monty*, 719.

23. Ibid.

24. de Guingand, *Operation Victory*, 199.

25. Freyberg, conversation with Leese, 0915 hours, 25 October 1942, recorded in GOC's Diary, WA 8/5/45, ANZ.

26. Walker, *Alam Halfa and Alamein*, 310.

27. de Guingand, *Operation Victory*, 199.

28. Ibid., 200.

29. Quoted in Hamilton, *The Full Monty*, 716.

30. de Guingand, *Operation Victory*, 200.

31. Lumsden, conversation with Freyberg, 0915 hours, 25 October 1942, recorded in GOC's Diary, WA 8/5/45 ANZ.

32. Quoted in Hamilton, *The Full Monty*, 717.

33. Hamilton, *The Full Monty*, 717.

34. Barr, *Pendulum of War*, 342.

35. Notes of Conference at 1600 hours, 25 October 1942, recorded in GOC's Diary, WA 8/5/45 ANZ.

36. Barr, *Pendulum of War*, 342.

37. Hamilton, *The Full Monty*, 724.

38. Playfair et al., *Volume IV*, 47.

39. Walker, *Alam Halfa and Alamein*, 329.

40. Barr, *Pendulum of War*, 343.

41. Walker, *Alam Halfa and Alamein*, 317.

42. Barr, *Pendulum of War*, 341.

43. Walker, *Alam Halfa and Alamein*, 319.

44. Harding, quoted in Neillands, *The Desert Rats: 7th Armoured Division*, 153.

45. Barr, *Pendulum of War*, 341.

46. Ibid., 328.

47. Walker, *Alam Halfa and Alamein*, 319.

48. Rommel to Dearest Lu, 2 November, 1942, in Liddell Hart, *The Rommel Papers*, 317.

49. Liddell Hart, *The Rommel Papers*, 328.

50. 9 Australian Division, Report on Operations, WO 201/2826, TNA.

51. RA Notes on the Offensive by Eighth Army from 23 Oct-4 Nov on the El Alamein Position, WO 201/535, TNA, 3.

52. Johnston and Stanley, *Alamein: The Australian Story*, 204.

53. Von Thoma, conversation with Crüwell, Most Secret Special Report to CSDIC Middle East No.612 (G), El Alamein Miscellaneous Papers, WO 106/2286, TNA.

54. Liddell Hart, *The Rommel Papers*, 330.

55. RA Notes on the Offensive by Eighth Army from 23 Oct–4 Nov on the El Alamein Position, WO 201/535, TNA, 1, 8.

56. Ibid., 12.

57. Johnston and Stanley, *Alamein: The Australian Story*, 204.

58. Rommel to Dearest Lu, 3 November, 1942, in Liddell Hart, *The Rommel Papers*, 320.

59. Summary of Operations 23 Oct6 Nov 1942, Series 6, Folder 32, Morshead Papers, 3 DRL, 2632, AWM.

60. 9 Australian Division, Report on Operations El Alamein 23 Oct–5 Nov 1942, WO 201/2495, TNA.

61. 26 Australian Infantry Brigade, Report on Operation "Lightfoot," AWM 54 527/6/9, AWM.

62. Barr, *Pendulum of War*, 345.

63. Quoted in Barr, *Pendulum of War*, 346.

64. War Diary, 2/48 Australian Infantry Battalion, 25 Oct 1942, 8/3/36, AWM 52, AWM.

65. Johnston and Stanley, *Alamein: The Australian Story*, 183.

66. War Diary, 2/24 Australian Infantry Battalion, 26 Oct 1942, 8/3/24, AWM 52, AWM.

67. Ibid.

68. Alexander, Most Secret Cypher Telegram for Prime Minister, 9 November 1942, The Advance from El Alamein, Air 8/1087, TNA.

69. Walker, *Alam Halfa and Alamein*, 324.

70. War Diary, 2/48 Australian Infantry Battalion, 26 Oct 1942, 8/3/36, AWM 52, AWM.

71. Ronald Lewin, *The Life and Death of the Afrika Korps*. (London: Corgi Books. 1979), 214.

72. Quoted in Barr, *Pendulum of War*, 344.

73. Barr, *Pendulum of War*, 344.

74. Walker, *Alam Halfa and Alamein*, 324.

75. Barr, *Pendulum of War*, 345.

76. Liddell Hart, *The Rommel Papers*, 306.

77. Lumsden, conversation recorded on 24 October 1942, recorded in GOC's Diary, WA 8/5/45 ANZ.

78. Freyberg, conversation with Kippenberger and Gentry, 26 October 1942, recorded in GOC's Diary, WA 8/5/45 ANZ.

79. Playfair et al., *Volume IV*, 51.

80. Ibid., 52.

81. Liddell Hart, *The Rommel Papers*, 308.

82. Ibid.

83. CX/MSS/1590/T18, 26 October 1942, HW 1/1015, German Records, TNA.

84. Walker, *Alam Halfa and Alamein*, 338.

85. War Diary 6 NZ Inf Bde, 23-4 October 1942, WA II 1, DA 58/1/25, ANZ.

86. Walker, *Alam Halfa and Alamein*, 341.

87. Liddell Hart, *The Rommel Papers*, 308.

88. Albert Martin, quoted in Holland, *Together We Stand*, 381.

89. Playfair et al., *Volume IV*, 53.

90. Walker, *Alam Halfa and Alamein*, 345.

91. Liddell Hart, *The Rommel Papers*, 308.

92. Montgomery, Alamein Diary, quoted in Hamilton, *The Full Monty*, 732.

93. Montgomery, *El Alamein to the River Sangro*, 52.

94. Freyberg, "The New Zealand Division in Egypt and Libya," 11.

95. Barr, *Pendulum of War*, 352. Bungay, *Alamein*, 177.

96. Barr, *Pendulum of War*, 352.

97. Montgomery, *El Alamein to the River Sangro*, 52.

98. Danchev and Todman, *War Diaries 1939-1945*, 335-336.

99. 9 Australian Division, Report on Operations El Alamein 23 Oct–5 Nov 1942, WO 201/2495, TNA.

100. War Diary, 90th Light Division, 28 October 1942, GMDS File 2586/1, WA II 11/23 Afrika Korps Records, ANZ.

101. Playfair et al., *Volume IV*, 58.

102. War Diary, 2/15 Australian Infantry Battalion, 29 Oct 1942, 8/3/15, AWM 52, AWM.

103. Johnston and Stanley, *Alamein: The Australian Story*, 197.

104. War Diary, 2/13 Australian Infantry Battalion, 29 Oct 1942, 8/3/13, AWM 52, AWM.

105. Warrant Officer Ken Joyce, quoted in Johnston and Stanley, *Alamein: The Australian Story*, 200.

106. War Diary, 2/23 Australian Infantry Battalion, 28 Oct 1942, 8/3/23, AWM 52, AWM.

107. War Diary, 2/23 Australian Infantry Battalion, 29 Oct 1942, 8/3/23, AWM 52, AWM.

108. Barr, *Pendulum of War*, 368.

109. Ibid.

110. Ibid.

111. Liddell Hart, *The Rommel Papers*, 311, 312.

112. Rommel to Dearest Lu, 29 October 1942, quoted in Liddell Hart, *The Rommel Papers*, 312.

113. QT s 4592 and 4603 of 28 October, CX/MSS/1549/15 and CX/MSS/C62, and QT 4682 of 29 October 1942, CX/MSS/1599?t23, quoted in Hinsley, *British Intelligence in the Second World War: Volume 2*, 441.

114. War Diary, 2/15 Australian Infantry Battalion, 29 Oct 1942, 8/3/13, AWM 52, AWM.

115. Johnston and Stanley, *Alamein: The Australian Story*, 210.

116. Barr, *Pendulum of War*, 372.

117. Johnston and Stanley, *Alamein: The Australian Story*, 210.

118. Quoted in Hamilton, *The Full Monty*, 750.

119. War Diary, 2/32 Australian Infantry Battalion, 30 Oct 1942, 8/3/32, AWM 52, AWM.

120. War Diary, 2/48 Australian Infantry Battalion, 30 Oct 1942, 8/3/36, AWM 52, AWM.

121. Ibid.

122. War Diary, 2/24 Australian Infantry Battalion, 31 Oct 1942, 8/3/24, AWM 52, AWM.

123. Ibid.

124. War Diary, 2/48 Australian Infantry Battalion, 30-31 Oct 1942, 8/3/36, AWM 52, AWM.

125. Johnston and Stanley, *Alamein: The Australian Story*, 222.

126. 9 Australian Division, Report on Operations, WO 201/2826, TNA.

127. Maughan, *Tobruk and El Alamein*, 719.

128. 9 Division Report, 527/6/9 AWM 54, AWM.

129. War Diary, 2/48 Australian Infantry Battalion, 30-31 Oct 1942, 8/3/36, AWM 52, AWM.

130. Maughan, *Tobruk and El Alamein*, 711.

131. Rommel to Dearest Lu, 31 October, 1942, in Liddell Hart, *The Rommel Papers*, 315.

132. Johnston and Stanley, *Alamein: The Australian Story*, 226.

133. Ibid.

134. Morshead, Message to Blamey, 2340 Hrs, 2 November 1942, 9 Australian Division General Staff Branch, July-Nov 1942, Personal reports from Morshead to Blamey, 1/5/20, AWM 52, AWM.

135. Barr, *Pendulum of War*, 381.

136. Freyberg, message to Prime Minister Fraser, 31 October 1942, GOC's Papers "Lightfoot" and "Supercharge," WA II 8/25A, ANZ.

137. Johnston and Stanley, *Alamein: The Australian Story*, 226.

138. Liddell Hart, *The Rommel Papers*, 316.

139. Rommel to Dearest Lu, 1 November 1942, Liddell Hart, *The Rommel Papers*, 316.

140. Von Thoma, conversation with Crüwell, Most Secret Special Report to CSDIC Middle East No.612 (G), El Alamein Miscellaneous Papers, WO 106/2286, TNA.

141. George Patton, diary entry 2 November 1942, quoted in George S. Patton. Jr, *War as I Knew It*. (New York: Bantam Books, 1981), 5.

142. See Patton, *War as I Knew It*, 330, 380.

143. David Irving, *The War Between the Generals*. (London: Penguin Books, 1982), 43.

EIGHT

OPERATION *SUPERCHARGE*: THE BREAKTHROUGH

When it became clear to Montgomery that Operation *Lightfoot* had failed to achieve a breakthrough, he set to work on a new plan. Montgomery had been impressed with both Freyberg's logic and his fighting spirit at the meeting held at the New Zealand Division's Headquarters on Sunday, October 25. At this meeting Freyberg had:

> urged him [Montgomery] to put in another timed bombardment with infantry attacking as before to a depth of about 4000 yards to push him [Rommel] off his guns. They could have had the tanks following behind. We would have been clear of his minefields—the first attack very nearly achieved that. The armour would then have had to fight. Thought it was better to face another 500 casualties to each Division and use our gun which is our great asset to whack him.[1]

This became the essence of Montgomery's plan for the breakout he called Operation *Supercharge*. He spent the morning of October 30 drafting his directive for this breakthrough attack before handing it over to his staff to work on the details. With characteristic immodesty, Montgomery wrote of its importance in his Memoirs: "This was the master plan and only the master could write it."[2]

The plan for Operation *Supercharge* was "in many respects a repetition of *Lightfoot*," albeit on a much smaller scale.[3] It relied on a concentrated timed artillery barrage with infantry brigades assaulting in the darkness to capture objectives some 4,000 yards from their start line. Following immediately behind would be the tanks of 9 Armoured Brigade, but again part of an infantry division commanded by Freyberg. They were to pave the way for support weapons to reach the infantry and for the heavy tanks of a complete armored division to follow. The

9th Armoured Brigade, with its 105 tanks, was to advance a further 2,000 yards beyond the final infantry objectives to the high ground marked by the Rahman track. This would create the initial hole from which an entire armored division could surge out beyond the newly won objectives, head due west, and destroy the enemy armored forces in the tank clash that was sure to follow. The new plan was succinctly summarized in Freyberg's War Diary. It also expressed Freyberg's doubt that the armored division would follow it:

> Attack to be 4000 yds front to depth of 4000 yds. Australians attacking tomorrow night. We do ours night afterwards. 12 Fd Regts in support and Armd Div as well as our own Armd Bde. 151 and Scottish Bde to attack—own Div behind and one Div of armour. "I" tanks to be on one side and armour on the other. Intention is to get right out beyond his defences and launch the armour who come up centre route. Armoured battle followed by NZ Div in buses to exploit. General: We can ask for what we want . . . It will be a slogging match.
>
> GOC said he would take his Tac HQ forward and lead the armour through himself if necessary.[4]

The location of the new assault was just south of the Australians fighting on the coastal sector and slightly north of Kidney Ridge. Montgomery had wanted to do the attack "as Far North as possible" but was persuaded by de Guingand and others to adopt an axis of advance further south. De Guingand wrote, owing to the Australian's crumbling operations: "The further north we went, the more Germans, mines and prepared defences we would meet."[5]

Montgomery's plan envisaged the infantry being used as a "self-replenishing battering ram" to force open a breach in the enemy's position.[6] The infantry would, however, have the protection of the Army's effective artillery and could dig in once the objectives had been captured. The formation with the most difficult tasks and therefore most at risk was the 9 Armoured Brigade. As the first armored formation in action, it would need to provide protection for the infantry while taking on the Panzerarmee's guns and tanks. It was a critical and dangerous assignment, which Montgomery clearly recognized. Freyberg recorded in both his War Diary and his secret after-action report, "The Army Commander was quite prepared to accept heavy losses in the 9th Armoured Brigade in order to get 1st Armoured Division through."[7] Accepting that 9 Armoured

Brigade would take heavy casualties, Montgomery was confident of success. He wrote in his planning directive:

> This operation if successful will result in the complete disintegration of the enemy and will lead to his final destruction.
> It will therefore be successful.... SUPERCHARGE will win for us the victory.

Montgomery warned in his directive that "determined leadership will be vital; complete faith in the plan, and its success, will be vital; there must be no doubters; risks must be accepted freely; there must be no 'bellyaching.'"[8] Not all commanders heeded Montgomery's warning.

* * *

Montgomery entrusted command of Operation *Supercharge* to the person he regarded as his best battlefield commander: Lieutenant General Bernard Freyberg. On October 28, Montgomery recorded in his diary: "Easily my best fighting Divisional commander is FREYBERG, and then MORSHEAD."[9] Four days later, Montgomery wrote to General Brooke and assessed all of his senior subordinate commanders. Montgomery wrote that Freyberg was:

> superb, and is the best fighting Div Comd commander I have ever known. He has no great brain power and could never command a Corps. But he leads his Division into battle going himself in front in a Honey tank.[10]

Niall Barr has written that it was "particularly apt" that Freyberg was chosen to organize and command this new breakthrough attempt. This was because it was Freyberg who had "originally suggested the idea of a further infantry attack."[11]

Morshead's Australians were fully engaged, pinning the bulk of Panzerarmee to the coastal sector. It was time for Freyberg and the 2nd New Zealand Division to be put back into the battle. But the weak New Zealand Division needed to be reinforced with infantry, armor, and artillery from elsewhere. The Corps commander, Lieutenant General Oliver Leese, wrote on Montgomery's intent in using Freyberg and the New Zealanders: "The Army Commander decided to make use of General Freyberg's magnetic personality and to employ the New Zealand Division as the background for the new attempt to break through."[12]

There was good reason to keep the New Zealanders in the "background" for Operation *Supercharge*. They were far too weak in infantry to mount another full-scale assault against the Axis line. When Freyberg had first suggested the idea on October 25, his two infantry brigadiers were aghast at the prospect and forcibly voiced their objections. Freyberg's Diary recorded their protest:

> Kippenberger: Another infantry attack means 5,000 yds at least—very hard to do. Must be regarded as serious as we can't pin his positions as before. It is not a soft spot opposite us.
>
> Gentry: Have we not to consider very carefully this further attack. Bns after similar casualties in another attack will be little more than coys. If we take them in again and lose 50% it would take a very long time to build up.
>
> Kippenberger: The 5,000 reinforcements on the water are not the men to fill the gaps. I have had 11 Officers killed and they are all old hands. We have only 1,200 bayonets left.
>
> Gentry: They are the survivors of god knows how many battles.[13]

At this time, Freyberg overruled his brigadiers, believing that "it was better to face another 500 casualties to each Division and use our guns, which is our great asset, to whack him. . . . If the pressure is kept up he is bound to crack."[14] But when the pressure on the Panzerarmee eased with no new infantry attack possible in the short term, Freyberg had to accept that his brigadiers were right. On October 27, he wrote to Leese, informing him of the cost of using the New Zealanders in another infantry assault. Freyberg's diary records:

> GOC wrote letter to Corps Comd re our casualties to infantry carrying the rifle and the Bren and pointing out that any further attacks would finish the 2 NZ Div as a striking force while as it was it remained a powerful force for a mobile role.[15]

Freyberg's letter explained that since the battle commenced, the New Zealanders had suffered nearly 900 casualties with a further 800 men evacuated sick with jaundice. Its fighting strength as a result had been reduced to just 1,400 infantrymen.[16] The New Zealanders were withdrawn from the line the following night.

Montgomery needed Freyberg to command Operation *Supercharge* and the expertise of the New Zealand Division staff to coordinate and direct it. His solution was to boost the New Zealanders with additional British formations. Montgomery recorded in his diary on October 28 that, "To keep the NZ Div up to strength and to enable it to operate offensively British Inf Bdes in turn will be put into it."[17] While this was "an elegant and effective solution," it was also somewhat ironic.[18] As earlier chapters have shown, detaching brigades from their parent formation and sending them to fight alone or embedded in other organizations was anathema to both the Australians and New Zealanders. They had protested loudly about it in 1940–41 and then refused to allow these detachments from July 1942. But for Operation *Supercharge* in November 1942, it was the obvious solution and one offering the best prospects of success. And Montgomery had no intention of either fighting the detached formations as independent "Brigade Groups" or allowing the practice to became a standard operating procedure in his army. The temporary arrangement was an admission that Eighth Army was running short of infantry soldiers. General Alexander wrote that it was "an historical illusion" that Eighth Army had overwhelming strength during the battle. The battle, as anticipated, had been one of "gruelling attrition" and by October 29, "Eighth Army had reserve strength enough for only one last big push."[19] It was critical to get it right and this required some flexibility in arranging the assets that could do the job.

For Operation *Supercharge*, the New Zealanders again had under its command the 9th Armoured Brigade. This armored formation was to spearhead the breakthrough and so had "the highest priority for tank replacements."[20] Also joining the 9th Armoured Brigade under Freyberg's command in the 2nd New Zealand Division were two British infantry brigades and an additional armored brigade to provide direct infantry support. The two British infantry brigades and 9th Armoured Brigade would do most of the fighting in the battle ahead. Detached from 50 Division of 13 Corps was 151 Brigade consisting of three battalions of Durham Light Infantry, while the 152th Brigade was detached from Wimberley's 51 Highland Division. One New Zealand Brigade, the 6th, was to play a limited static role in the attack but one battalion, the 28th (Maori) Battalion, which had been sparingly used to date, would be actively involved. Freyberg's enhanced 2nd New Zealand Division was a powerful armored and infantry force ideally suited for the break-in role. It would need to be as Freyberg correctly anticipated that the battle ahead was going to be "a very tough slogging match."[21] Freyberg's Order of Battle (ORBAT) was impressive, though, and he outlined it to his government in his secret after-action report. It was:

Our order of battle for this attack, as quoted in the operation order, was as follow:

23rd Armd. Bde.	**9th Armd. Bde.**
40th RTR	3rd H.[Hussars]
50th RTR	R. Wilts. Yeo.
8th RTR	Warwick. Yeo.
121st Fd. Regt. (16 self-	14th Foresters
propelled 25-pounders)	31st N.Z. A.Tk. Bty.
168th Lt. A.A. Bty.	**2nd N.Z. Div. Cav.**
295th Fd. Park. Sqn.	
N.Z.A.	**N.Z.E.**
4th N.Z. Fd. Regt.	6th N.Z. Fd. Coy.
5th N.Z. Fd. Regt.	7th N.Z. Fd. Coy.
6th N.Z. Fd. Regt.	8th N.Z. Fd. Coy.
H.Q. 7th N.Z. A.Tk. Regt.	5th N.Z. Fd. Coy. Pk. Coy
14th N.Z. Lt. A.A. Regt.	One Fd. Coy., R.E. (51st
	(Highland) Div.)
5th N.Z. Inf. Bde. Gp.	**6th N.Z. Inf. Bde. Gp.**
21st N.Z. Bn.	24th N.Z. Bn.
22nd N.Z. Bn.	25th N.Z. Bn.
23rd N.Z. Bn.	26th N.Z. Bn.
28th N.Z. (Maori) Bn.	33rd N.Z. A.Tk. Bty.
32nd N.Z. A.Tk. Bty.	One Coy. 27th N.Z. (M.G.) Bn.
One Coy. 27th N.Z. (M.G.) Bn.	
151st Inf. Bde.	**152nd Inf. Bde.**
6th D.L.I.	2nd Seaforths
8th D.L.I.	5th Seaforths
9th D.L.I.	5th Camerons
34th N.Z. A.Tk. Bty.	One M.G. Coy (from 51st
One A.Tk. Bty (provided by	(Highland) Div.)
30th Corps)	One A.Tk. Bty (from 51st
Two Coys. 27th N.Z. (M.G.) Bn.	(Highland) Div.)
	2nd N.Z. Div. Sigs.[1]

[1] Freyberg, "The New Zealand Division in Egypt and Libya: Operations 'Lightfoot' and 'Supercharge,'" Part I Narrative and Lessons, 14-15, Freyberg's Secret After-action Report. Copy in author's possession.

Artillery support would again provide the crucial edge to the attack. There was plenty of it, too. In addition to the New Zealanders' own field artillery, that of 51st (Highland) Division, 1st Armoured Division, 10th Armoured Division, and one regiment of 9th Australian Division was placed under command of the New Zealand C.R.A. Two regiments of medium artillery were also added.[22] This made a total of 296 field guns and forty-eight medium guns.[23] Such a concentration of firepower enabled the New Zealand C.R.A. Brigadier Steve Weir to develop a comprehensive fire plan, one that could fully utilize the benefits of a creeping barrage. With the guns and ammunition at his disposal, "the creeping barrage came into its own" and has been described by Niall Barr as "Weir's masterpiece."[24] When the attack commenced in the early hours of November 2, every gun of 30 Corps opened fire. In the space of four and a half hours, with "flashes like lightning" and the sound "merging into one tremendous rumble," the gunners of 30 Corps "sent off 150,000 rounds along a 4000 yard front."[25] Those observing the barrage on November 2 "commented on the accuracy of the fire," too.[26]

Air support for Operation *Supercharge* was also impressive. On the night of November 1, sixty-eight Wellington bombers flew over the Axis positions and bombed them for a period of seven hours.[27] That night, the bombers dropped a total of 184 tons of bombs and managed to hit Afrika Korps' headquarters. Not only was von Thoma, the Afrika Korps' commander, injured in this bombing, but all telephone lines were destroyed and the DAF was effectively jamming all signals communication. These measures "badly disrupted the enemy's communication system for some hours."[28] Allied air activity during this Alamein battle peaked during the two-day period of Operation *Supercharge* on November 2 and 3. Average daily sorties numbered 977, with the top figure of 1,044 being achieved on November 3.[29]

With this substantial artillery and air support, Operation *Supercharge* had every prospect of success. Indeed, it would have been foolish to attempt this breakout battle without it. But success was not guaranteed, as the infantry and armored formations needed to play their parts. As Freyberg informed a visiting British officer:

> We have no illusions—it will be a tough battle but we shall be fighting him with the maximum amount of our artillery and all our tanks. If we are beaten, it will be our own fault.[30]

Operation *Supercharge* required careful planning and preparation and experienced staff officers to tie it all together in one coordinated effort. This was why Freyberg and the New Zealanders were chosen to carry it out. Montgomery knew that Freyberg had the skills and the team "who can make a difficult operation work."[31] But even Freyberg's team could not do the impossible, especially when using formations that had not been under their command before. There was just so much to do. The artillery, infantry, armor, engineers, signallers, and all supporting arms had to be incorporated into the plan and each unit had to know their part in the plan and what was expected of them. The recent July experience of the New Zealanders and others have driven home the point that attacks risked failure if they were not properly planned and coordinated. There was so much at stake in this attack, as "the cost of a mistake this time would be [another] defeat."[32] On October 30, Alexander signaled Churchill that another large-scale attack with infantry and tanks was about to be launched. He advised Churchill, "If this is successful it will have far-reaching results."[33] If it failed, the results would also be far-reaching but catastrophic.

At noon on October 28, Freyberg was allocated the task of preparing the attack. It was not until the following day, though, that it was confirmed that *Supercharge* would be made south of the Australian positions and within forty-eight hours.[34] While work on the plan for Operation *Supercharge* "was commenced at once," it was clear that "time was short."[35] It was, in fact, too short and on the evening of October 30, Freyberg requested that the attack be delayed for twenty-four hours. He later admitted that it had been "impossible to prepare for this most vital operation in forty-eight hours."[36] Montgomery reluctantly agreed to this postponement primarily because he accepted Freyberg's judgment. It went against his natural instincts, as Montgomery knew from Ultra intercepts that Rommel's forces "have [been] reduced ... to such a state that a hard blow *now* will complete his overthrow." On November 1, Rommel's tank force was estimated at 140 German and 130 Italian effective tanks. In reality, it was considerably less. The Afrika Korps had a total of 102 tanks; the Italians were down to just sixty-five.[37] Montgomery also admitted that the delay "gives an advantage to the enemy" and that "there were doubts in high places about SUPERCHARGE and whisperings about what would happen if it failed."[38] The delay certainly made things more difficult for the Australians who, after their last attack on October 31–November 1, had to absorb the wrath of almost the entire Panzerarmee for another twenty-four hours. But as Freyberg acknowledged, despite these disadvantages, delaying the attack until the early hours of November 2 was "unavoidable." He explained that "it eased the strain and made the staging of the battle less hurried."[39] Even then, the opening of *Supercharge* did not go smoothly.

* * *

Just after 0100 hours on the morning of November 2, Operation *Supercharge* was launched. In the initial assault, two British infantry brigades, supported by 350 guns and a brigade of "I" tanks, were to strike out due west and punch a 4,000-yard hole in the Panzerarmee's defenses. Montgomery recorded in his diary on November 2, 1942:

> 0100 Attack went in under a creeping barrage on a front of 4000 yds fired by over 300 25-pdrs. It was probably the first creeping barrage ever used in EGYPT. The attack was a complete success.[40]

Montgomery was wrong on two counts. The New Zealanders had fired a creeping barrage during Operation *Lightfoot*, but more significantly, the attack on the morning of November 2 was far from being the "complete success" Montgomery claimed it was.

While the artillery support was lavish for a two-brigade infantry attack, some who witnessed it experienced a sense of disappointment. The War Diary of the New Zealand Division recorded:

> 0105 hours artillery barrage opens. The opening was not considered as impressive as 23/24 October.[41]

Freyberg's diary recorded a "tremendous barrage" that made the ground shudder and "flashes like lightening" [sic] illuminating the landscape near the guns. But he did note that, "Opening not considered as impressive as 23/24 October."[42] With only one-third of the guns that had been fired on the opening night of *Lightfoot* and with a much slower rate of fire—just two rounds per gun per minute—it was to be expected that the barrage that opened *Supercharge* appeared weak and "slow."[43] But it was both accurate and effective. Dropping 150,000 rounds along a 4,000-yard front in the space of just over four hours was bound to have the desired effect on the enemy.

Of more concern was the "poor communications between the two attached brigades and the New Zealand headquarters," which meant that their attacks "did not start as auspiciously as they might."[44] The New Zealand Division's War Diary recorded a serious problem that its staff and liaison officers worked frantically to resolve. It logged in the closing hours of November 1: "Some confusion was experienced on the Start Line but by Z hour all was straitened and both 151 and 152 bdes crossed on time."[45]

Both infantry brigades did set off right on time and behind the protection of the creeping barrage. On the right, close to the Australians, were the infantry battalions of 151 Brigade. As this was the brigade most likely to meet stiff opposition, the 28 (Maori) Battalion was moved into the front to provide protection to this vulnerable right flank. On the left, to the south, were the Scottish battalions of 152 Brigade. Each brigade had the Valentine tanks of a Royal Tank Regiment in support. Holding the start line and providing a "firm base" for the attack was 6 New Zealand Brigade.[46] The Scots on the left advanced to the "skirl of pipes," a sound that was echoed by the hunting horn blown by a company commander in the 9th Durham Light Infantry.[47] A lieutenant in 9 Durhams recalled that with the Māoris screaming on the right, combined with the bagpipes and hunting horn, there was "a continuous wall of sound." But the noise "kept our minds off other things."[48]

* * *

The two brigades that crossed the start line in the early hours of November 2 experienced mixed fortunes. Freyberg commented on this contrast in his secret after-action report: "The attack provided an interesting comparison, as on the left everything went like clockwork while on the right resistance was stronger and the situation remained obscure for hours."[49] Each brigade covered a frontage of 2,000 yards and advanced with two battalions leading. On the left flank of the advance, the Scottish battalions of 152 Brigade had a much easier task than 151 Brigade further north. The 5th Seaforths on the right captured their first objective against "very little opposition."[50] They then managed to bypass some dug-in tanks to

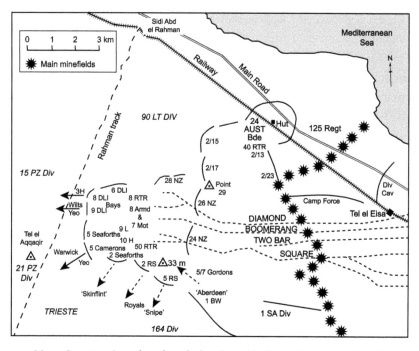

Map 5. Operation *Supercharge* launched on the night of November 2, 1942. The 9th Armoured Brigade followed the infantry assault and charged the Axis gun line at dawn. The Brigade suffered catastrophic losses.

reach their final objective just after 0400 hours. Their casualties had been "extremely light."[51] On the left flank, the 5th Camerons encountered more dug-in tanks than the Seaforths, but by keeping close to the creeping barrage they gained their final objective just after 0400 hours. Though somewhat disorganized when they reached it, 5th Camerons had incurred just twelve casualties.[52] In the rear, 2 Seaforths, allocated the mopping-up role, advanced with all four of its infantry companies in line and covering the whole brigade sector. They found that the enemy had abandoned their defensive positions, even the dug-in tanks that had been bypassed. The battalion collected more than thirty prisoners. On reaching the final objective, the 2 Seaforths swung left and dug in forming a front just to the rear and facing south. Behind the infantry battalions, New Zealand sappers soon cleared passages through the minefields so that the Valentine tanks and support weapons reached the final objective early on November 2. The Valentine tanks of 50 RTR did suffer losses to mines, some anti-tank fire, and breakdown. From a starting strength of thirty-eight tanks, 50 RTR could muster just twenty-four "runners" at first light on November 2.[53] At 0218 hours on November 2, the New Zealand Division received the welcome news from 152 Brigade that "Everything appears to be going according to plan." At 0417 hours, it was confirmed that "both battalions have reached objective" and later that morning that "enemy tanks are melting away."[54] Freyberg was elated, later recording that:

> The attack had gone like a drill, both objectives being taken according to schedule. It was a very fine performance.[55]

To the north, though, 151 Brigade had a much tougher time and its assault definitely did not go to plan. This brigade had been the first formation to move, setting off from Tel el Eisa just after 1900 hours on November 1. The brigade had considerable support, including a field company of New Zealand engineers and the forty-four Valentine tanks of 8 RTR. Things did not go well from the start. On the extreme right 28 (Maori) Battalion set out to capture an intermediate objective that would provide the link with 9 Australian Division in the north. All four companies struck heavy opposition and suffered casualties. While the objectives were taken, the battalion was not holding them in strength, nor had they linked with the Australians on their right or the 8th Durham Light Infantry on the left. The Maori Battalion had taken 162 German and 189 Italian prisoners, but had suffered more than 100 casualties, including their commanding officer and his second-in-command. This was from "an already depleted battalion."[56] Major Charles Bennett, who took over command of the battalion that night, described the action of November 1–2 as "the most spirited attack that I . . . had taken part in." He decided that the companies needed to stay put that morning, recalling that "We were like a little finger poked out into the enemy positions and likely to be nipped off with ease."[57] Throughout November 2, the Māori held their exposed positions "constantly under fire and without communications to the rear, even by runner."[58]

On the left of 28 (Maori) Battalion, the 8th Durham Light Infantry also hit several enemy strongpoints and suffered casualties. By 0230 hours, the leading companies reached their first objective but were too

weak and disorganized to continue. The following company, still relatively intact, was ordered to push on, which it did. It managed to reach
the final objective against little opposition just after 0400 hours. There
it was isolated and relatively unprotected, although some of the Valentine tanks and two troops of New Zealand anti-tank guns joined them
before first light. Contact was later established with the other Durham
battalions, but "the battalion was low in strength and not well sited for
defence."[59] On the left of 151 Brigade's sector, 9 Durhams easily captured
the first objective. Advancing to the final objective behind the creeping
barrage, 9 Durhams encountered many enemy strongpoints and dug-in
tanks. But the artillery had done its work and the Axis defenders were
thoroughly demoralized. By 0400 hours, 9 Durhams had joined its sister
battalion on the final objective, where it was soon joined by anti-tank
and machine gunners in support. The third Durham battalion, 6 DLI,
left the start line after its two sister battalions were 500 yards ahead. At
first, things went well thanks to the work of the Māori infantry. No direct
opposition was encountered in the first 1,000 yards. Once beyond the
Māori objective, though, it faced heavy opposition that prevented this
battalion from capturing all of the final objective. In fact, a dangerous
gap existed between 6 DLI and 28 Maori Battalion that left the New
Zealanders exposed to fire from three directions. However, 151 Brigade
had occupied most of its final objective, although in some places it was
"very thin on the ground." Its casualties had been heavy: fifty killed,
211 wounded, and eighty-seven missing.[60] That morning, though, once
the armored regiments and commander of 151 Brigade, Brigadier J.E.S.
Percy, realized that the New Zealand Engineers had done their job in
breaching the minefields, three squadrons of Valentine tanks from 8
RTR reached the forward troops at daylight. There were, however, now
only twelve effective runners in each squadron.

All morning, Freyberg and the headquarters of the New Zealand
Division had been frantic about lack of information regarding 151 Brigade's progress. All that had been learned was that there was considerable opposition and Brigadier Percy complained that the New Zealand
sappers had failed his brigade. Freyberg later noted with some satisfaction, "It was not until 0400 hours that it was confirmed that the gaps had
been made exactly as arranged, and that tanks and supporting arms were

passing through satisfactorily."[61] At one stage, with information about 151 Brigade's progress so sparse, Headquarters New Zealand Division requested its own 6 Brigade holding the forward defense line "to assist in clearing up the obscure posn on 151 Bde front."[62] Just before 0600 hours, though, the situation was no longer obscure. Freyberg informed Corps Headquarters that "151 Brigade reported they were on their final objective and that the Northern gap was through."[63] It was time to unleash the Shermans, Grants, and Crusaders of 9th Armoured Brigade.

* * *

The responsibility for "the key action of the whole operation" rested upon 9 Armoured Brigade.[64] The infantry brigades had torn open the Axis front line and penetrated it to a depth of 4,000 yards. The task of 9 Armoured Brigade now was to extend that gap by a further 2,000 yards to reach the last Axis anti-tank gun line along the Rahman track. Once this had been done, 9 Armoured Brigade was expected to draw out the enemy's armor and absorb the first blows until 1 Armoured Division arrived to finish them off. This meant that 9 Armoured Brigade had the unenviable task of taking on both the Panzerarmee anti-tank guns and then its armor. As outlined above, Montgomery was prepared for the inevitable heavy casualties all commanders expected 9 Armoured Brigade to incur.

The brigade formed up near the Alamein station with 132 tanks allocated across the three regiments. Just after 1900 hours, as darkness fell, it advanced in battle order to fight the action that would determine the outcome of the battle. During the twenty-five-mile approach march, visibility was poor and progress slow. In the lead, on the right or northern flank, was 3 Hussars. They actually made reasonable progress and, after stopping to refuel at midnight, reached the infantry start line just after midnight. Progress from here was slow and some casualties were incurred from enemy artillery fire. Six of the Hussars' tanks were damaged or broke down, but by 0515 hours, the Hussars had reached the new forward line being assisted to reach it by 9 Durhams. Immediately behind came the tanks and vehicles of the Royal Wiltshire Yeomanry. As this regiment was to be in the center of the new advance, attached to the Wiltshire Yeomanry was the brigade tactical headquarters and the headquarters of the Divisional Cavalry and support group. The

Wiltshire Yeomanry refueled at 0145 hours, but their advance was held up by scattered mines, which required a Scorpion flail tank to clear a path. However, the Wiltshires reached the forward infantry shortly after the Hussars and formed up ready to attack. The third regiment of the brigade, the Warwickshire Yeomanry, following a different track, reached the forward infantry positions at 0545 hours.

Owing to the damage caused by artillery and mines, especially to the soft-skinned vehicles and the delay in getting forward on time, Brigadier Currie requested a half-hour delay before the attack commenced. A "disappointingly large number" of tanks had failed to reach the start line so that 9 Armoured Brigade had just "94 fit to go into action."[65] While this delay meant extending the artillery barrage by an extra thirty minutes, Freyberg approved the request. It was a decision Freyberg later regretted, writing in his secret report that "the advance of the armour was too slow." The half-hour delay "was a great pity" because with another hour of darkness, "9th Armoured Brigade might have got through [the gap] before first light."[66] At 0610 hours, the New Zealand Division Headquarters informed Freyberg that "Currie . . . ready to go forward when the barrage starts" and that the situation "appears to be reasonably good." Freyberg, at his battle headquarters on the frontline, agreed. "It looks good here too," he replied. Five minutes later, Freyberg's diary recorded "Barrage for 9 Armd Bde advance opens."[67] The tanks of 9 Armoured Brigade surged forward behind it.

On the right, 3 Hussars, now down to only twenty-three tanks, set off on a much narrower front than intended. To their left, the Royal Wilshire Yeomanry, with thirty-three tanks, set off at the same time. Both regiments advanced at the rate of 100 yards every three minutes to keep to the protection of the creeping barrage. At first things went reasonably well, the anti-tank guns encountered being rushed and destroyed. The Royal Wiltshires even managed to penetrate beyond the Rahman track. But as the light improved, anti-tank fire intensified and enemy tanks joined in the fight. Both regiments suffered heavy losses but they fought on. The Royal Wiltshires destroyed another fourteen anti-tank guns and six tanks but they were "almost wiped out" in the process.[68] In a later examination of the battlefield, here both regiments were credited with destroying some thirty-five anti-tank guns. They had made "a dent, if not a complete breach, in the enemy's gun line that only needed immediate exploitation."[69]

Over a mile to the south, the third regiment of 9 Armoured Brigade, the Warwickshire Yeomanry, fought an almost independent battle that morning. It was much further south than it should have been, probably as the result of faulty map reading. It advanced from the forward line being held by the infantry of 152 Brigade with thirty-eight "runners" of the forty-four it had started with. Just beyond the start line, the Warwicks struck a concentration of anti-tank guns and some enemy tanks. The Warwicks were "especially unlucky" that morning, as the regiment had created a salient and was being engaged from three sides.[70] Many of these guns were shot up, but the regiment also suffered heavy casualties. The surviving Warwick tanks were forced to withdraw behind their own hastily constructed gun line, which consisted of just two six-pounder guns.

At dawn on November 2, the situation for 9 Armoured Brigade was precarious. While Currie and his tank crews were determined to keep the gap they had created open, Currie witnessed his brigade being steadily destroyed. It was fighting "a grim and gallant battle right in the enemy gun line."[71] At first light on November 2, the brigade was down to just seven heavy tanks in 3 Hussars, nine in the Wiltshires, and seven in the Warwicks.[72] To make things worse, reports were received from Eighth Army wireless intercepts that the Afrika Korps were preparing a counterattack from the north. Just before 0800 hours, enemy tanks were observed assembling to the west of the Wiltshires. Freyberg's diary recorded that: "Enemy tanks were coming in and our tanks of 9 Armd were in action with these."[73] While 9 Armoured Brigade did not reach their final objectives and had suffered heavy casualties, according to Freyberg "the action was a success as the enemy gun line was smashed." He believed that "it may well prove to have been the deciding factor in breaking the German line, though advantage was not taken of the breach until later."[74]

At first light, Brigadier Currie looked out on a scene of total devastation and the remnants of what had once been his armored brigade. Brigadier Lucas Phillips described the scene:

> As far as the eye could see lay the terrible record—tank after tank burning or wrecked, the smoke of their burning mingled with the cold mist, the crimson

shafts from the eastern sky tincturing all objects with the hue of blood. Only
here and there could he see a tank still defiantly shooting it out with the more
distant guns and the tanks of the Afrika Korps. He was very angry, very bitter. In
fulfilment of his orders, he was ready to sacrifice all if Fisher's brigade had been
there to crash through whatever ragged breaches he had torn in the enemy's wall
of guns.[75]

Currie had lost seventy-five of his ninety-four tanks and 230 of his 400
men.[76] These were grave losses. The Australian official historian asserted,
"If the British armour owed any battle debts to the New Zealand infantry, 9th Armoured Brigade paid them dearly and liberally that morning
in heroism and in blood."[77] It was a point Montgomery publicly repeated
fifty years later.[78]

Currie had indeed sacrificed most of his brigade in extending the gap
to the Panzerarmee's gun line. If 9 Armoured Brigade's three regiments
had not punched a hole through the Axis positions, "they certainly left
a crack that was ripe for exploitation."[79] They had knocked out forty
enemy tanks.[80] Equally important, a subsequent inspection showed that
9 Brigade had also knocked out thirty-five anti-tank guns, which "paid
large dividends in the later stages of the battle."[81] But the brigade needed
urgent reinforcement. Several times that morning, Brigadier Currie radioed Freyberg urging that 1 Armoured Division join in the fight. Currie's
urging was in vain. In a repeat of the October 23–24 action, 1 Armoured
Division was again very slow to join the battle. An entry in the New
Zealand Division's War Diary at 0735 hours recorded:

> Posn reported to Corps Comd: 9 Armd Bde is out where it should be. There is
> one 88 mm behind them which is being dealt with. He considers he has broken
> through. The Bde has suffered casualties and is therefore very thin on the
> ground. He says the 1 Armd Div are moving very slowly. There is an opportunity
> there and we suggest 1 Armd Div should be pushed out as far as it can be. Corps
> Comd replies "I will definitely."[82]

Three minutes later Freyberg urged Leese to apply "more ginger" to 1
Armoured Brigade. Seven minutes later he was more blunt, asking the
New Zealand headquarters to: "Tell Oliver [Leese] to tell them [1Armd
Bde] to get a bloody move on."[83] In total, Freyberg and the New Zealanders made five separate requests that morning to the Corps commander Leese to have 1 Armoured Division join 9 Armoured Brigade
in the battle.

In fact, the first regiment of 1st Armoured Division had reached 9 Armoured Brigade just after 0700 hours. This was the 9th Lancers of Brigadier Bertie Fischer's 2nd Armoured Brigade. Currie informed the Lancers' commanding officer, Colonel Gerald Grosvenor, that he needed to move through the gap they had cut "bloody quick." Grosvenor looked around at the scene of devastation and destruction in front of him, including several burning British tanks, and replied, "I have never seen anything, sir, that looks less like a gap."[84] Grosvenor refused to move his tanks forward, a decision that was supported by both his brigadier and the commander of 1st Armoured Division, Major General Raymond Briggs. Instead, 2nd Armoured took up defensive positions along the new front line. Currie was furious and he and several senior commanders, including Freyberg and Leese, believed that an opportunity to break through that morning had been lost. Oliver Leese wrote to his wife on the following day:

> Our break through attack on Sunday was magnificent. The Infantry did 4000 yds behind a barrage & my armour [123 tanks of 9th Armoured Brigade, attached to the New Zealand Division] followed it up with another 2000 yds in the dash. It was not so difficult as our first night. The Armour then again failed to get out.[85]

At 1000 hours, an angry and frustrated Freyberg reported to his headquarters that:

> The posn on the front was NOT very satisfactory. Additional armour had NOT moved up, and what was there was NOT moving fwd.[86]

After the war, Leese was even more critical of the armor's failure to push through the gap created by the infantry and 9 Armoured Brigade. The infantry part of Operation *Supercharge* "exceeded all expectations," he wrote. With all objectives taken, "a definite opportunity for the armour to break out" had been created. But it was not to be. The armored formations were "again late and as before remained on our own infantry Forward Defence Lines."[87]

* * *

The location of Operation *Supercharge* caught Rommel by surprise. While his front had not broken, he knew the situation was desperate and that his tank losses had been "severe." He knew, too, what had prevented the British Eighth Army from breaking through: "It was only by the desperate fire of all available artillery and anti-aircraft guns, regardless of the ammunition shortage, that a further British penetration was prevented."[88] Rommel took the immediate decision to commit his armor on the morning of November 2 "to pinch out the enemy wedge." The 21st Panzer Division would counterattack north of the wedge and 15th Panzer from its south. The "gravity of the situation in the north" forced Rommel to commit another armored division, the Italian Ariete Division, early in the afternoon. As he recorded of this counterattack: "Violent tank fighting followed."[89] This was exactly what Montgomery had planned for. At last he had his clash of armor on ground of his choosing.

Signals intercepts confirmed that the Axis armor was on its way. Freyberg's diary recorded at 0935 hours:

> Message in from 30 Corps that 21 Panzer Div is expected to counter-attack West South West from 868302. It was also said that 15 Panzer Div would counter-attack about the inter-bde boundary. Situation of various batteries was also reported. Passed this to NZA.[90]

Not only had the artillery readied itself to meet the counterattack but, along the new front, 2 and 8 Armoured Brigades also prepared to meet the Afrika Korps attack. At noon, the remaining twenty-four tanks of 9 Armoured Brigade were grouped to form a composite regiment and placed on the right flank of 2 Armoured Brigade just where the weight of 21 Panzer's attack would fall. For the rest of the morning and into the afternoon of November 2, "there was the fiercest and most prolonged tank engagement of the whole battle."[91] An early report described the action: "All day the battle raged. One hundred and seventy-six enemy tanks were reported counterattacking furiously from the north and southwest."[92] Losses were heavy on both sides, but the Afrika Korps suffered most of them. In the first encounter of the day, 2 Armoured Brigade knocked out twenty-five enemy tanks, of which eighteen continued to burn for most of the day.[93] Two Stuka raids that the Luftwaffe attempted were driven off before they even reached the battlefield and the DAF pounded the Afrika Korps during the day. The War Diary of the 90th Light Division recorded a critical moment in the battle:

> During the morning the fighting reached its climax. Smoke and dust covered
> the battlefield, and visibility became so bad that the general picture was of one
> immense cloud of smoke and dust. Tanks engaged in single combat; in these few
> hours the battle of Alamein was decided.[94]

Sometimes called the battle of Tel el Aqqaqir, this great tank encounter
was the climax of the battle. General von Thoma later described the
battle as "Tank against tank." For him it was "the biggest tank battle I
have ever experienced."[95] During the battle, the Afrika Korps and one
Italian armored division were exposed to the fire of hull-down Grants
and Shermans, the superiority of the British artillery, and the bombs
of the DAF and "took a mortal pounding."[96] In total, "77 German and
40 Italian tanks had been put out of action" that day.[97] It had been "an
unequal battle from every point of view." Not only did the British have
air supremacy and more tanks, but Afrika Korps was forced to attack in
daylight across open ground. The result was that Afrika Korps "suffer[ed]
the kind of losses which they had so often in the past inflicted upon their
opponents."[98]

General Freyberg, whose reading of the battle was as good as any
other, felt that by the end of November 2, "it was clear that the enemy
was cracking." He warned his brigadiers to be ready for the exploitation
phase, believing that the enemy would soon withdraw. "I felt certain that
the war on our front was over," he wrote.[99] Rommel, whose experience
matched Freyberg's, had reached a similar conclusion. But while the Afrika Korps was "virtually destroyed during the day of intense fighting,"
1st Armoured Division had still not been able to penetrate beyond the
Rahman track.[100] Some British commanders despaired that they could
ever get beyond the Axis gun line. As the Australian official historian recorded, even on November 2: "The Eighth Army was not hitting Rommel
for six, nor even penetrating his outfield to the boundary."[101] Operation
Supercharge was similar to *Lightfoot* in that it had made a sizable advance,
but had still not achieved the desired breakthrough.

In the end, this did not matter. That evening, with "only 35 serviceable
tanks left" and with an "absolutely desperate" supply situation, Rommel
gave the order to break off the attack and withdraw.[102] The Afrika Korps'
War Diary recorded of the decision: "The situation compels Panzer Army

to withdraw slowly by bounds to a new line. Afrika Korps will withdraw on a wide front."[103] That "new line" would be at Fuka, some sixty miles away. After ten days of fighting, Eighth Army had won the battle.

* * *

The battle spluttered on for two more days. On the evening of November 2 at 1950 hours, Rommel sent a message to OKW hinting at the need to withdraw, but not actually stating that he had already given the order to do so. It was "his famous admission of defeat."[104] Rommel's message read:

> Despite today's defensive success, the army's strength is exhausted after ten days of tough combat against immensely superior British ground and air forces. The army will therefore no longer be capable of impeding the strong enemy tank formations expected to repeat their breakthrough attempt tonight or tomorrow. For want of motor transport it will not be possible for the six Italian and two German nonmotorized divisions to withdraw in good order. A large part of these units will probably be overrun by the enemy's mechanized formations. But even our mechanized troops are engaged in such heavy fighting that only part will be able to disengage from the enemy. . . . In this situation the gradual destruction of the army must therefore be assumed to be inevitable despite the heroic resistance and exemplary spirit of the troops. Sgd. Rommel, Field Marshal.[105]

The message has been accurately described as "a clever piece of expectation management."[106] In the early hours of November 3, Rommel's follow-up report to OKW retrospectively announced that he had given the order to withdraw commencing at 2200 hours on the night of November 2.[107] Both messages were intercepted and decoded by Bletchley Park in England and in Brooke and Montgomery's hands by noon the next day. On the night of November 2, those German and Italian troops not locked in combat at the front began hastily retreating westward.

The Panzerarmee, however, did not withdraw from the Alamein position on November 3. The entry in the Afrika Korps War Diary for November 3 confirmed a change in intent. It recorded that, "Now that the situation had altered, and a mobile defensive policy was about to be instituted on the Alamein front, this withdrawal was stopped."[108] There had been no change in policy, nor had the situation altered in Rommel's favor. Instead, Hitler had responded poorly to Rommel's "expectation management." In fact, David Irving has written that Rommel's signal about the withdrawal of Panzerarmee from Alamein "poleaxed Hitler." After venting his anger and frustration at General Walter Warlimont for not immediately passing on Rommel's signal, Hitler dictated an immediate message to be radioed to Rommel. It would become "one of the most famous signals of the war."[109]

Around midday on November 3, Rommel returned to his headquarters after inspecting the situation along the coast road. He had narrowly missed being killed by "a carpet of bombs laid by 18 British aircraft," only avoiding the bombs by "some frantic driving."[110] At 1330 hours, an order arrived from Adolf Hitler. While it praised the leadership of Rommel and the courage of his soldiers, it was emphatic that there would be no withdrawal from the Alamein position. The Führer told Rommel:

> In the situation in which you find yourself there can be other thought than to stand fast, yield not a yard of ground and throw every gun and every man into the battle.... Your enemy, despite his superiority, must also be at the end of his strength. It would not be the first time in history that a strong will has triumphed over the bigger battalions. As to your troops, you can show them no other road than that to victory or death.[111]

Rommel was infuriated and puzzled by this order. He admitted that he was "completely stunned" by it. More than this, it filled him with indecision: "For the first time during the African campaign I did not know what to do."[112] He later described November 3, 1942, as "a memorable day in history." One of Rommel's biographers has written that Hitler's signal on November 3 "marked a turning in Rommel's life and views."[113] It certainly had a profound effect on him. This was because "not only did it become finally clear on that day that the fortunes of war had deserted us, but from that day on the Panzer Army's freedom of decision was continually curtailed by the interference of higher authority in its conduct of operations."[114] This interference "came as a considerable shock" to Rommel, but he did his best to comply with the order.[115] He ordered movement to the west to be halted and made some attempts to strengthen his defenses. He also reported back to Hitler that while he would comply with the order, it meant soon losing the entire army and with it their position in North Africa. To emphasize how serious the situation was, Rommel sent his personal assistant Leutnant Alfred-Ingemar Berndt to report directly to Hitler that if his "stand fast" order was upheld, "the final destruction of the German-Italian Army would be a matter of days only."[116]

Reversing the withdrawal once it had commenced proved to be extremely difficult. Rommel read Hitler's "stand fast" order to von Thoma, commander of the Afrika Korps, and informed him that the withdrawal was canceled. "We have no other choice," he told von Thoma. "We must make a stand, and if there's no other way out, we must be prepared to die." Von Thoma agreed and assured Rommel that he would not withdraw without orders to do so. But there was a huge problem. Von Thoma informed Rommel that:

> the position is that we do not have a continuous front, the Italians have all pushed off . . . Still more bad news has arrived. Tanks have broken through at various points. The situation is now critical, Sir.[117]

Rommel agreed with von Thoma that he could withdraw to the first bound as planned, some fifteen kilometers (nine miles) east of El Daba, but from here "this line is to be held to the last man."[118]

According to Rommel, Hitler's order "had a powerful effect on the troops." They would obey it and "sacrifice themselves to the last man." But "an overwhelming bitterness welled up in us." This was because they all knew "that even the greatest effort could no longer change the course of the battle."[119] A superb army was being destroyed because of rash decisions made thousands of miles away.

The New Zealand official history described November 3, 1942, as "a curious day in the Battle of Alamein." This was because "confusion, indecision and caution were more prominent than action."[120] Alexander reported to Churchill that on November 3, "progress was slow owing to mines and anti-tank gun screens."[121] On the evening of November 2, three battalions of the 7th Motor Brigade tried to secure objectives across the Rahman track prior to the armor of 1st Armoured Division moving across the track the next morning. Only one battalion, the 2nd King's Royal Rifle Corps (2 KRRC), secured any new ground but it did not get to the Rahman track. At first light on the morning of November 3, 2 KRRC, in its exposed forward position, was attacked by the tanks of the Italian Littorio Division. With its six-pounder guns in support, it was able to hold off the attack and during the morning it destroyed seven M13 tanks in the firefight.

The anti-tank gun screen across the Rahman track was still effective, so no advance of the armor of 1st Armoured Division took place that morning. Instead, 8th Armoured Brigade moved south of Tel el Aqqaqir toward a newly captured feature known as "Skinflint." Both armored brigades of the division engaged in long-range shooting that day and claimed to have knocked out another twenty-two tanks and twenty-three guns during it.[122] It was a frustrating day for the British commanders. They could sense that Rommel's front was broken, but they still could not penetrate the Panzerarmee's anti-tank gun lines.

This was also the day that the air effort of the DAF reached its peak in the North African campaign. Around the small hill of the Tel el Aqqaqir feature, the DAF bombed anything that moved. Tel el Aqqaqir was a slight elevation where 15 Panzer Division had taken up strong defensive positions. Its height offered superb observation over this part of the battlefield and protection for gun emplacements. It was "ideal for placing artillery" and it was here that that "the vast majority of Rommel's remaining 88 mms were situated."[123] But the hill was a prominent feature, which made it an ideal target for aerial bombing. Tel el Aqqaqir "rapidly became the crucial ground under contest."[124] During "the busiest and . . . probably the most successful day of the battle," the DAF flew 1,094 sorties and dropped 199 tons of bombs. Its losses, though, were "heavy, with 16 planes being lost and a further 11 damaged."[125]

A series of hastily mounted infantry attacks on the afternoon of November 3 produced negligible results. One carried out by 5/7th Gordons of 51 Highland Division, supported by Valentine tanks of 8 RTR, in the evening of November 3 was disastrous primarily because artillery support had been canceled for fear of hitting the armor of 1st Armoured Division. The tanks were in fact nowhere near where the attack was made. The Gordons managed to capture a position near the Rahman track south of Tel el Aqqaqir, but suffered ninety-four casualties. Nine Valentine tanks had been destroyed and a further eleven damaged from the thirty-two that had taken part.[126] Niall Barr is critical of these improvised attacks, writing that they "proved yet again that Eighth Army found it difficult to conduct effective small-scale operations." These attacks of November 2–3, according to Barr, "had borne a striking similarity to many of the hastily organised and poorly prepared operations mounted in July."[127]

There is no denying, though, that these actions had an acute impact on Panzerarmee and Rommel felt the loss of every single tank and gun.

More promising, though, was the foray by two armored car squadrons of the Royals and by some South African armored cars that managed to slip behind the Axis positions and reach the El Daba area. Here they shot up soft-skin vehicles and caused considerable alarm.[128] It was these vehicles that von Thoma reported to Rommel as the tanks that had broken through their positions.[129] General Freyberg wrote that the operations on November 3 amounted to obtaining some "further elbow room." Traveling across the front in the afternoon, Freyberg noticed "a great change. Everything seemed to point to a general enemy withdrawal."[130] Freyberg was correct but there was one final infantry effort to come.

* * *

Even as the battered tanks of 8 RTR returned "covered with the dead bodies of my Highlanders," Major General Wimberley was ordered to make another two infantry attacks that night.[131] But his 51st Highland Division, like other formations in Eighth Army, had run out of infantry. To make what would be the last infantry assault at Alamein, Wimberley was given the 5th Indian Brigade for the task. This brigade was still "relatively fresh" and it was to try to capture part of the Rahman track immediately south of the 5/7th Gordons that night.[132] It was to advance on a narrow front southwest of Tel el Aqqaqir for a distance of two miles. This would be followed by a two-battalion assault by 51 (Highland) Division on the Tel el Aqqaqir feature.

In support of 5 Indian Brigade's attack were the surviving Valentine tanks of 50 and 46 RTR and a massive amount of artillery. This artillery support included the field guns of 1 Armoured, 51 Highland, and the New Zealand Divisions, as well as two medium regiments. This was a total of 360 guns similar to what had been used to commence Operation *Supercharge* two nights before. In total, these guns fired 37,000 rounds that night.[133] The New Zealand CRA, Brigadier "Steve" Weir, coordinated the artillery fire plan. His task was made much harder by the combination of the short time period to prepare the plan and the fact that 5 Indian Brigade had never before advanced behind a creeping barrage.

There was considerable confusion at the start of the attack. It was so muddled that zero hour was delayed by an hour. However, some artillery batteries did not get word of the postponement and opened fire at the arranged time. At 0230 hours, the attack went ahead and commenced with a full artillery barrage. However, only one complete battalion, 1/4 Essex and two companies from 4/6 Rajputana Rifles, which was meant to be the reserve battalion, advanced behind it. In spite of the confused start and the weak attacking force, "the operation went with complete success."[134] There was little opposition encountered as the artillery had been so effective that the Indian brigade encountered mostly dead or demoralized defenders and little resistance. The Essex battalion was on their objective at first light with more than 100 prisoners. The Rajputs had similar success and that morning the tanks of 50/46 RTR joined the infantry on their objectives without losing any tanks. While the Indian infantry earned "high praise at the time" for this attack, there is little doubt that its success was primarily due to the overwhelming artillery support it had been allocated.[135]

The final infantry operation of the battle was made by the 7/10 Argyll and Sutherland Highlanders. This battalion was allocated the task of capturing the Tel el Aqqaqir feature. Advancing at 0515 hours on a narrow 600-yard front, under a barrage provided by seven regiments of field artillery, the advance was unopposed. However, eight men were killed and twenty-three wounded from artillery rounds dropping short. Clearly the gunners were fatigued and some of their gun barrels worn out.[136] At 0710 hours when the barrage ceased, the Argyll and Sutherland Highlanders "found themselves in complete and unopposed occupation of the Tel el Aqqaqir feature."[137] Only two German prisoners were captured and it was clear that the enemy had abandoned the position in considerable haste. These two infantry attacks had finally opened up gaps in the Axis frontline, which Eighth Army's armor could exploit.

In the north, on the morning of November 4, the Australian infantry probed the enemy lines. The patrols found the troublesome Thompson's Post and other Axis positions abandoned. Instead, the enemy were now holding a line around a mile west of the Australian positions.[138] The "dogfight" phase of the battle was over.

At 0830 hours on the morning of November 4, the 7th Armoured Division was through the gap. It had moved north on October 31, "ready to exploit the breakthrough he [Montgomery] shortly expected to achieve in the northern sector."[139] It had taken longer than expected but the breakthrough had been made. "We got out into the open, a tremendous feeling," recalled John Harding.[140] The 11th Hussars in the lead, with 22 Armoured Brigade of 7 Armoured Division following, drove beyond Tel el Aqqaqir for five miles before it encountered any opposition. This happened in the early afternoon, when 22 Armoured Brigade encountered the tanks of the Italian Ariete Division. Although their tanks were seriously outmatched, the Italians fought desperately for several hours. In this last fight, the Ariete were joined by the remnants of the Littorio and Trieste Divisions. The action lasted all afternoon and ended at dusk when "all three Italian divisions were destroyed."[141] Rommel received a report from the senior field officer present that his Axis partners had "fought with exemplary courage." He described their annihilation as "a very gallant action" and admitted that "we had probably always demanded more than they, with their poor armament, had been capable of performing."[142] The Italian 20 Corps had certainly proved capable and courageous that afternoon. These often-maligned Italian formations had sacrificed themselves in this last armored encounter at Alamein. In doing so they gave the Afrika Korps the chance to escape a similar fate.

* * *

Rommel had a terrible dilemma. His defenses at Alamein had been "crumbled." His front was broken and the powerful armor of Eighth Army was about to be unleashed. Yet his Führer had forbidden him to withdraw, instead urging Rommel and Panzerarmee to "yield not a yard of ground" and travel the single road to "victory or death." In November 1942, victory was out of the question and Rommel did not relish needlessly sacrificing himself or his army. On the morning of November 3, Rommel's commanding officer, Field Marshal Albert Kesselring, arrived at Panzerarmee's headquarters. There Rommel vented his frustrations about Hitler's "crazy order" and admitted that "some angry words passed between us."[143] According to Rommel's son Manfred, Kesselring sympathized with Rommel and restored his freedom of action. Manfred Rommel noted that:

> Kesselring did, in fact, discuss with my father the possibility of circumventing Hitler's order. Kesselring gave it as his view that Rommel, as the man on the spot, should do what he thought was right.[144]

On the afternoon of November 4, 1942, there was only one prudent course of action left to Rommel. As he recorded of his decision:

> So now it had come, the thing we had done everything in our power to avoid—our front broken and the fully motorised enemy streaming into our rear. Superior orders could no longer count. We had to save what there was to be saved. After a preliminary talk with Colonel Bayerlein, who had now assumed command of the Afrika Korps again, I issued orders for the retreat to be started immediately.[145]

Von Thoma was correct when he informed Crüwell that it was "a very important decision" and that the delay making it made the withdrawal that night "extremely difficult."[146] Rommel did send an immediate signal to Hitler explaining that to prevent the loss of North Africa, he needed to resort to "mobile warfare" and that he would contest with the enemy "every foot of ground" from a new defensive position running from Fuka to the south. Rommel sought retrospective approval for his decision.[147] Afrika Korps received Rommel's order at 1450 hours that day. It recorded that at dusk it was to "withdraw to the area south of Fuka."[148] Having taken the decision to abandon the Alamein position, Rommel must have been relieved to receive two signals the next morning, one from Adolf Hitler, the other from Kesselring. While they were "far too late," they did authorize his withdrawal to the Fuka position.[149]

* * *

On November 4, with Rommel's signals to Hitler being intercepted and translated by Bletchley Park almost as fast as he was sending them, General Alan Brooke allowed himself a measure of satisfaction. He recorded in his diary that "The Middle East news has the makings of the vast victory I have been praying and hoping for." If Montgomery had failed to defeat Rommel in this third battle of Alamein, "I should have had little else to suggest beyond my relief by someone with fresh and new ideas!" But the news was promising and Brooke ended his entry on November 4 saying, "It is very encouraging at last to begin to see results from a year's hard labour."[150] While the botched pursuit of the defeated Afrika Korps did not result in the "vast victory" many hoped for, it was a decisive victory nonetheless.

Six days later, at the Lord Mayor's luncheon banquet in London on November 10, a jubilant Winston Churchill was in fine form. He said in his speech that he never promised anything to the British people but blood, sweat, tears, and toil. Then he described a novel development in the war. Churchill explained to the audience:

> Now, however, we have a new experience. We have victory. A remarkable and definite victory.... Rommel's army has been defeated. It has been routed. It has been largely destroyed as a fighting force.[151]

It had been no easy victory. After twelve days and thirteen nights of hard fighting with the heavy casualties this entailed, Rommel's Panzerarmee was broken and had been forced to withdraw from the battle. It was not yet destroyed as a fighting force, though. Despite this, the democracies had won their first offensive battle against a German-led army in the Second World War.[152] This October–November Alamein battle was a considerable achievement and indisputably one of the war's great turning points. Why this was so is explained in the concluding section of this book.

An officer in the 7th Battalion of the Argyll and Sutherland Highlanders recalled a moving event at the end of the battle. Lieutenant John Campbell remembered:

> When it was all over, and the Germans had withdrawn, the pipe major went up on the skyline and played "Flowers of the Forest." Everybody wept.[153]

NOTES

1. Notes of Conference at 1600 hrs, 25 October 1942, recorded in GOC's Diary, WA 8/5/45, ANZ.
2. Montgomery, *Memoirs*, 133.
3. Playfair et al., *Volume IV*, 64.
4. New Plan summed up in conversation with G1, 29 October 1942, recorded in GOC's Diary, WA 8/5/45, ANZ.
5. de Guingand, *Operation Victory*, 206.
6. Hamilton, *The Full Monty*, 741.

7. Freyberg, "The New Zealand Division in Egypt and Libya," 11. Also Conference, 0800 hrs 1 Nov 1942, recorded in GOC's Diary, WA 8/5/45, ANZ.

8. Operation SUPERCHARGE, Eighth Army Plan, quoted in Montgomery, *Memoirs*, 135.

9. Montgomery, Alamein Diary, quoted in Hamilton, *The Full Monty*, 741.

10. Montgomery, letter to General Sir Alan Brooke, 1 Nov 1942, quoted in Hamilton, *The Full Monty*, 755.

11. Barr, *Pendulum of War*, 364.

12. Impressions of the Part of 30 Corps in the "Battle of Egypt", from Papers of Sir Oliver Leese, WA II 11/2, ANZ.

13. Freyberg Diary, 26 October 1942, WA II 8/45, ANZ.

14. Freyberg Diary, 25 and 26 October 1942, WA II 8/45, ANZ.

15. Freyberg Diary, 27 October 1942, WA II 8/45, ANZ.

16. Freyberg, letter to Leese, 27 October 1942, WA II 8/25, ANZ.

17. Montgomery, Alamein Diary, quoted in Hamilton, *The Full Monty*, 741.

18. Barr, *Pendulum of War*, 365.

19. North, *The Alexander Memoirs*, 27.

20. Barr, *Pendulum of War*, 365.

21. Freyberg Diary, 1 November 1942, WA II 8/45, ANZ.

22. Freyberg, "The New Zealand Division in Egypt and Libya," 15.

23. Walker, *Alam Halfa and Alamein*, 386.

24. Barr, *Pendulum of War*, 383.

25. Freyberg Diary, 0105 hrs 2 November 1942, WA II 8/45, ANZ.

26. RA Notes on the Offensive by Eighth Army from 23 Oct–4 Nov on the El Alamein Position, WO 201/535, TNA, 3.

27. Christopher Shores and Giovanni Massimello, with Russell Guest, Frank Olynyk, & Winifred Bock. *A History of the Mediterranean Air War 1940–1945 Volume Two: North African Desert February 1942-March 1943*. (London: Grub Street, 2012), 685.

28. Walker, *Alam Halfa and Alamein*, 383.

29. "The Battle of El Alamein," Military Report on the United Nations, 15 Feb 1943, El Alamein Miscellaneous Papers, WO 106/2286, TNA.

30. Freyberg Diary, 30 October 1942, WA II 8/45, ANZ.

31. Pugsley, *A Bloody Road Home*, 356.

32. Barr, *Pendulum of War*, 365.

33. Alexander to Churchill, signal, 30 October 1942, in Churchill, *Vol. IV*, 535.

34. Freyberg Diary, 29 October 1942, WA II 8/45, ANZ.

35. Freyberg, "The New Zealand Division in Egypt and Libya," 12.

36. Ibid.

37. Hinsley, *British Intelligence in the Second World War: Volume 2*, 445–446.

38. Montgomery, Alamein Diary, 28 and 31 October 1942, quoted in Hamilton, *The Full Monty*, 754.

39. Freyberg, "The New Zealand Division in Egypt and Libya," 13.

40. Montgomery, Alamein Diary, 28 and 31 October 1942, quoted in Hamilton, *The Full Monty*, 756.

41. Headquarters 2 NZ Div G Staff War Diary, 2 November 1942, DA 21.1/1/35, ANZ.

42. Freyberg Diary, 0105 hours, 2 November 1942, WA II 8/45, ANZ.

43. RA Notes on the Offensive by Eighth Army from 23 Oct–4 Nov on the El Alamein Position, WO 201/535, TNA, 3.

44. Walker, *Alam Halfa and Alamein*, 383.

45. Headquarters 2 NZ Div G Staff War Diary, 1 November 1942, DA 21.1/1/35, ANZ.

46. Headquarters 2 NZ Div G Staff War Diary, 2 November 1942, DA 21.1/1/35, ANZ.

47. Barr, *Pendulum of War*, 384.

48. "Scotty" White, quoted in Thompson, *Forgotten Voices*, 218.

49. Freyberg, "The New Zealand Division in Egypt and Libya," 15.

50. Walker, *Alam Halfa and Alamein*, 390.

51. Ibid.

52. Ibid.

53. Ibid., 391.

54. Headquarters 2 NZ Div G Staff War Diary, 2 November 1942, DA 21.1/1/35, ANZ.

55. Freyberg, "The New Zealand Division in Egypt and Libya," 16.

56. J.F. Cody, *Official History of New Zealand in the Second World War 1939–45: 28 (Maori) Battalion.* (Wellington: Historical Publications Branch, Department of Internal Affairs, 1956), 241.

57. Quoted in Cody, *28 (Maori) Battalion*, 240.

58. Walker, *Alam Halfa and Alamein*, 388.

59. Ibid.

60. Ibid., 389.

61. Freyberg, "The New Zealand Division in Egypt and Libya," 16.

62. Headquarters 2 NZ Div G Staff War Diary, 2 November 1942, DA 21.1/1/35, ANZ.

63. Freyberg, "The New Zealand Division in Egypt and Libya," 16.

64. Walker, *Alam Halfa and Alamein*, 391.

65. Playfair et al., *Volume IV*, 66.

66. Freyberg, "The New Zealand Division in Egypt and Libya," 16.

67. Freyberg Diary, 0610 hours 2 November 1942, WA II 8/45, ANZ.

68. Barr, *Pendulum of War*, 388.

69. Walker, *Alam Halfa and Alamein*, 395.

70. Barr, *Pendulum of War*, 388.

71. Freyberg, "The New Zealand Division in Egypt and Libya," 17.

72. Walker, *Alam Halfa and Alamein*, 396.

73. Freyberg Diary, 0743 hours 2 November 1942, WA II 8/45, ANZ.

74. Freyberg, "The New Zealand Division in Egypt and Libya," 17.

75. Quoted in Hamilton, *The Full Monty*, 760.

76. Hamilton, *The Full Monty*, 760.

77. Maughan, *Tobruk and Alamein*, 731.

78. Montgomery, in the *Sunday Star Times*, 22 October 1967, quoted in Bierman and Smith, *Alamein: War without Hate*, 326.

79. Bierman and Smith, *Alamein: War without Hate*, 327.

80. Robin Neillands, *Eighth Army: From the Western Desert to the Alps, 1939–1945.* (London: John Murray Publishers, 2004), 187.

81. Ronald Lewin, *Rommel as Military Commander.* (New York: Ballantine Books, 1968), 228.

82. Headquarters 2 NZ Div G Staff War Diary, 0735 hours 2 November 1942, DA 21.1/1/35, ANZ.

83. Freyberg Diary, 0738 and 0740 hours 2 November 1942, WA II 8/45, ANZ.

84. Quoted in Hamilton, *The Full Monty*, 761.

85. Leese to Lady Margaret Leese, 3 November 1942, quoted in Hamilton, *The Full Monty*, 757. Hamilton has inflated the number of tanks in 9 Armoured Brigade. The Brigade commenced Operation *Supercharge* with 105 tanks.

86. Headquarters 2 NZ Div G Staff War Diary, 0735 hours 2 November 1942, DA 21.1/1/35, ANZ.

87. Impressions of the Part of 30 Corps in the "Battle of Egypt," from Papers of Sir Oliver Leese, WA II 11/2, ANZ.

88. Liddell Hart, *The Rommel Papers*, 318.

89. Ibid.

90. Freyberg Diary, 0935 hours 2 November 1942, WA II 8/45, ANZ.

91. Hinsley, *British Intelligence in the Second World War: Volume 2*, 447.

92. "The Battle of El Alamein," Military Report on the United Nations, 15 February 1943, El Alamein Miscellaneous Papers, WO 106/2286, TNA.

93. Freyberg, "The New Zealand Division in Egypt and Libya," 17.

94. 90th Light Division War Diary, 2 November 1942, WA II 11/23, ANZ.

95. Von Thoma, conversation with Crüwell, Most Secret Special Report to CSDIC Middle East No.612 (G), El Alamein Miscellaneous Papers, WO 106/2286, TNA.

96. Hamilton, *The Full Monty*, 762.

97. Maughan, *Tobruk and Alamein*, 732.

98. Pitt, *The Crucible of War*, 406.

99. Freyberg, "The New Zealand Division in Egypt and Libya," 18.

100. Barr, *Pendulum of War*, 391.

101. Maughan, *Tobruk and Alamein*, 732.

102. Liddell Hart, *The Rommel Papers*, 318, 319.

103. Afrika Korps War Diary, 2 November 1942, WA II 11/23 Afrika Korps Records, ANZ.

104. Hamilton, *The Full Monty*, 762.

105. David Irving, *The Trail of the Fox*. (New York: Avon Books, 1978), 273–274.

106. Bungay, *Alamein*, 184.

107. Hamilton, *The Full Monty*, 763.

108. Afrika Korps War Diary, 2 November 1942, WA II 11/23 Afrika Korps Records, ANZ.

109. Irving, *The Trail of the Fox*, 274–275.

110. Liddell Hart, *The Rommel Papers*, 321.

111. Ibid., 321. The full text of Hitler's order is in the footnote on this page.

112. Ibid.

113. Fraser, *Knight's Cross*, 381.

114. Liddell Hart, *The Rommel Papers*, 320.

115. Ibid., 322.

116. Ibid.

117. Von Thoma, conversation with Crüwell, Most Secret Special Report to CSDIC Middle East No.612 (G), El Alamein Miscellaneous Papers, WO 106/2286, TNA.

118. Afrika Korps message 1745 hours, 3 November 1942, quoted in Walker, *Alam Halfa and Alamein*, 425.

119. Liddell Hart, *The Rommel Papers*, 322.

120. Walker, *Alam Halfa and Alamein*, 411.

121. Alexander, Most Secret Cypher Telegram for Prime Minister, 9 November 1942, The Advance from El Alamein, Air 8/1087, TNA.

122. Barr, *Pendulum of War*, 394.

123. Holland, *Together We Stand*, 392.

124. "The Battle of El Alamein," Military Report on the United Nations, 15 Feb 1943, El Alamein Miscellaneous Papers, WO 106/2286, TNA.

125. Playfair et al., *Volume IV*, 74.

126. Ibid., 75.

127. Barr, *Pendulum of War*, 396.

128. "The Battle of El Alamein," Military Report on the United nations, 15 Feb 1943, El Alamein Miscellaneous Papers, WO 106/2286, TNA.

129. Von Thoma, conversation with Crüwell, Most Secret Special Report to CSDIC Middle East No.612 (G), El Alamein Miscellaneous Papers, WO 106/2286, TNA.

130. Freyberg, "The New Zealand Division in Egypt and Libya," 18.

131. Barr, *Pendulum of War*, 396.

132. Ibid., 397.

133. Walker, *Alam Halfa and Alamein*, 419.

134. Ibid.

135. Ibid., 419–420.

136. Barr, *Pendulum of War*, 399.

137. Walker, *Alam Halfa and Alamein*, 420.

138. Maughan, *Tobruk and Alamein*, 739.

139. Harding's recollection of Montgomery's orders, 31 October 1942, quoted in Neillands, *The Desert Rats*, 160.

140. John Harding, quoted in Thompson, *Forgotten Voices*, 237.

141. Barr, *Pendulum of War*, 401.

142. Liddell Hart, *The Rommel Papers*, 325.

143. Ibid., 323–324.

144. Ibid., 324.

145. Ibid., 325.

146. Von Thoma, conversation with Crüwell, Most Secret Special Report to CSDIC Middle East No.612 (G), El Alamein Miscellaneous Papers, WO 106/2286, TNA.

147. Text of Signal from Rommel to Hitler admitting defeat at Alamein, Appendix I, in Behrendt, *Rommel's Intelligence*, 198.

148. Afrika Korps War Diary, 4 November 1942, WA II 11/23 Afrika Korps Records, ANZ.

149. Liddell Hart, *The Rommel Papers*, 326.

150. Danchev and Todman, *War Diaries 1939–1945*, 338.

151. Quoted in Bungay, *Alamein*, 199.

152. Hamilton. *The Full Monty*, 769.

153. John Campbell, quoted in Thompson, *Forgotten Voices*, 238.

NINE

REFLECTIONS AND REPUTATIONS

On November 4, the time had come for Eighth Army to pursue a crippled and defeated Axis force. Montgomery was well aware that Rommel's army was now gravely damaged and in retreat. He launched two armored divisions, the 1st and the 10th, and the New Zealand Division, with an attached armored brigade, in pursuit. The Panzerarmee's withdrawal presented Montgomery with a priceless opportunity because, according to many German sources, it was poorly conducted. Afrika Korps' War Diary reported:

> Officers of all ranks had lost their heads and were making hasty and ill considered decisions, with the result that confidence had been lost, and in some places panic had broken out. Some vehicles were set on fire on or beside the road, and guns were abandoned or destroyed because there were no tractors for them. A large number of vehicles had left their units and were streaming back without orders.

The Diary also recorded with some surprise, "No contact with the enemy all day."[1]

The War Diary of the 90th Light Division chronicled similar conditions, admitting that there was "very little discipline during the withdrawal." It also claimed German transport and supply units were "fleeing in wild panic." As a result, its withdrawal from Alamein was "very difficult."[2]

The pursuit phase of the Alamein battle has been strongly criticized by many writers who believe that Montgomery acted with undue caution. The British official history made a perceptive observation that, "Whether they could have captured or destroyed more of the *Panzerarmee* than they did will be argued as long as military history is read."[3] This has certainly happened. Alexander McKee accurately stated, "There was no pursuit, merely a follow up."[4] Correlli Barnett has been one of Montgomery's harshest critics, believing that Montgomery "signally fail[ed] to take advantage of this astonishing flow of precisely accurate intelligence, which removed all guesswork from generalship" and that his failure to destroy Panzerarmee at Alamein "calls in question Montgomery's generalship at this stage of his career."[5] Johnston and Stanley wrote, "The pursuit was poorly planned and confused, a fact Montgomery never acknowledged."[6] As early as the evening of November 3, Freyberg had warned Lieutenant General Herbert Lumsden, 10 Corps commander, that Rommel "will slip away if they are not careful."[7] The cautious pursuit, including by Freyberg, ensured that this happened.

There was one overriding factor, however, that explains and perhaps excuses Montgomery's caution. This was the state of his armored corps, his prized *corps de chasse*. So far in the Alamein battle, 10 Corps had failed in every task it had been allocated, had demonstrated excessive caution, and an inability to follow even the simplest directives. His trust in his armored commanders, especially in 10 Corps commander Lumsden, was "at an all time low."[8] As it was, this Corps that would be used during the pursuit, it was only natural that Montgomery wanted to keep it on as tight a leash as possible to ensure that it did in fact accomplish even the most limited of tasks assigned to it. John Harding, commanding 7 Armoured Division during the pursuit and "in favour of pressing on all-out, hard as I could go," thought at the time that Montgomery was being "overcautious" in restraining his armored formations. Harding later changed his mind. "Montgomery was very conscious of the fact that we had already been twice up and twice back and he was determined not to be pushed back for a third time," Harding said. A third defeat could have prolonged the war in North Africa. "Looking back on it all, I think he was right to be cautious," was Harding's conclusion.[9]

And, as John Keegan has pointed out in his history of the Second World War, with the exception of the Soviets' Operation *Bagration*, the Allies were never able to encircle and destroy retreating German armies.[10] Montgomery cannot be judged too harshly for not achieving something other British or American commanders were also unable to do when given the opportunity.

Montgomery initially planned to use the New Zealand Division, augmented by an armored brigade, as the main pursuit force. He directed them to the Fuka escarpment some 45 miles to the west. As the New Zealanders set off for Fuka, the British armor of 10 Corps made a series of shorter wheels to the coast of some 10 to 15 miles. But there was a considerable delay before the New Zealanders could get moving. Freyberg recorded about the lull, "The congestion of vehicles in the forward area would have done credit to Piccadilly. Fortunately the RAF ruled the skies."[11] Montgomery's fears about his armored formations soon proved justified as the armor "swanned" about the desert out of coordinated control in several fruitless encircling movements. Nor did the New Zealand Division, which de Guingand described as Montgomery's "mobile shock troops," demonstrate much dash or daring.[12] Freyberg was especially concerned not to let his division get mauled by the Afrika Korps for the fourth time. He still erroneously estimated Rommel to have a powerful armored force under command. To his subordinate commanders, Freyberg had stated that "the policy is not to fight but to position our force to bottle him."[13] Freyberg, the commander of the three left hooks carried out by the New Zealand Division, was in no doubt as to the purpose of a left hook and tended to view it as a substitute for heavy fighting—a way of achieving a victory with minimal casualties. The New Zealanders made three attempts to entrap Panzerarmee using the wide encircling "left hook." All three failed. Kippenberger informed the New Zealand official historian:

> You have one or two tricky questions to deal with in this volume, particularly the conduct of the three "Left Hooks" which seem to me to have been clumsily and rather timidly executed. I thought so at the time and am inclined to the same opinion still.[14]

Ironically, both Montgomery's and Freyberg's caution, though understandable, was to prove more costly in the long run. As Rommel pointed out, if Montgomery had abandoned his restraint after Alamein, it "would have cost him far fewer losses in the long run than his methodical insistence on overwhelming superiority in each tactical action, which he could only obtain at the cost of his speed."[15] The failure to prevent Panzerarmee from withdrawing, especially after the Alamein battle, meant much hard fighting ahead with the North African campaign dragging on for another six months.

* * *

There were many reasons for the defeat of the Axis forces at Alamein, not the least important being their weakness in logistics and firepower. Rommel devoted nine pages of his papers analyzing "the decisive battle of the African campaign," which he had lost. He did this primarily to counter accusations from the armchair strategists that the Axis troops and their commanders had performed poorly at Alamein. Rommel wrote that these accusations came from those whose military careers were "notable for a consistent absence from the front."[16] Rommel attributed his defeat at Alamein primarily to his weak logistics, especially in weapons, fuel, and ammunition and to British air supremacy. The "extreme concentrations" of Eighth Army's artillery fire and "locally limited attacks" by infantry with an "extremely high state of training" was also important.[17] He was especially impressed with the British infantry's ability to attack at night, writing that "Night attacks continued to be a particular speciality of the British."[18] Rommel finished his analysis by stating that the bravery of all German and many Italian troops "was admirable." Alamein had been a struggle and a defeat but it was still "a glorious page in the annals of the German and Italian peoples." But in the end, the enemy was just too strong and their own material resources too small. In this imbalance "lay destruction."[19]

Other German accounts placed considerable stress on their material weakness at Alamein when compared to the resources available to Eighth Army and the DAF. They seldom gave credit to the performance of Eighth Army's commanders or soldiers. The War Diary of 15 Panzer Division was especially critical:

> The English did not win the battle of Alamein by superior leadership or dash. On the contrary, after their original plan of attack failed they worked their way systematically forward, always probing ahead with the greatest care choosing limited objectives. Often, particularly after our withdrawal from the Alamein line, the enemy failed to perceive or take advantage of good opportunities to destroy German troops.

The main reasons given for the British victory were Eighth Army's overwhelming artillery firepower and the DAF's air superiority. The War Diary did admit, though, that Eighth Army's infantry were stronger and rested and that this infantry was "superior to the Germans, and still more to the Italians, in night fighting." But Panzerarmee, it stated, had been crushed by the sheer weight of numbers brought against it.[20] As explained in Chapter 5, Eighth Army's successful deception plans had convinced Panzerarmee and German military intelligence that its opponents were more than 40 percent stronger than they actually were.[21]

The secretly recorded conversation of a German infantry officer captured on the night of October 29 was particularly revealing about the state of Panzerarmee's logistics. The lieutenant from 2 Battalion, 125 Infantry Regiment told his cell mate, an officer from submarine U-559:

> We've been in FRANCE, in the BALKANS, and in CRETE. Throughout the whole of the French campaign my Company only had thirty-five killed and seventy-five wounded. This time there was no way out for us, it was either death or capture. I was right in the front line, about fifty metres behind my platoons. When the infantry came along there was practically nothing more I could do with our 7.65 guns. As for our M.P.'s [Machine Pistols: the German Schmeisser submachine gun], none of them would fire because of the magazine. We've had them since 1940. All the springs were bad and we couldn't get replacements. You can fire one round and that's all. Our lack of supplies in AFRICA is appalling.[22]

German intelligence officer Hans-Otto Behrendt believed that Ultra intelligence "played a major part" in the defeat of the last German-Italian offensive at Alam Halfa and had played "a crucial part in the sinking of Rommel's oil tankers and supply convoys." For the final October battle, though, "The decisive factor now was quite simply the sheer British superiority in tanks, artillery and aircraft for which no amount of tactical skill and self-sacrifice could compensate."[23]

Certainly, Eighth Army had superior logistics and firepower, tanks that could match the Germans, and the DAF dominated the skies above the battlefield. But it was the way these assets were used that made the critical difference. The Eighth Army's artillery was concentrated and its firepower coordinated with infantry and armor in a master fireplan. In the twelve days of the battle, Eighth Army's artillery fired more than one million rounds of twenty-five-pounder ammunition and throughout the battle "some artillery action was occurring all the time, and heavy action for most of the time."[24] The DAF made extraordinary efforts to support the troops on the ground and was most effective at disrupting enemy concentrations and their communications. During the October battle, the DAF flew 10,405 sorties and their American allies flew 1,181. This compares with just 1,550 German and 1,570 Italian sorties.[25] It made a telling difference and the effect on morale on both sides was critical.

An American study compiled in 1947, written by the German officer Generalmajor Hans-Henning von Holtzendorff, was adamant that Eighth Army's success at Alamein was primarily through its use of tanks. Von Holtzendorff wrote, "El Alamein was decided by the numerically far superior Panzer forces of the British, which were not dispersed as before, but were now concentrated and to some extent were equipped with American material."[26] All of these elements made vital contributions to Eighth Army's victory.

In infantry, though, Eighth Army's margin was not so pronounced as many historians have claimed, and the October Alamein battle was primarily an infantry battle. While it was a considerable advantage having a materiel superiority over the enemy, it still needed skill, courage, and determination to effectively apply what you had. One thing Eighth Army did in this October battle was to keep the fight going for over a week, which ultimately wore down the Panzerarmee. This was an old-fashioned battle of attrition, but it produced a decisive outcome. The 9 Division's Report on Operations believed that this was the most crucial "lesson" of the battle. It began this section of the Report with the heading <u>Maintenance of Pressure</u>. Under this heading it perceived:

> So often in military history, the battle has gone to the side which had the will or the strength to hang on just long enough to outlast the opponent. By maintaining offensive pressure, the enemy is forced to use his reserves and if this pressure can be maintained until these reserves are used up and he has insufficient resources to meet the new threat, defeat follows.
>
> In this battle, by maintaining pressure by a series of attacks to the north and to the west, the Axis reserves were drawn in and steadily worn down until on 4 November—11 days after it had been planned to occur—penetration was effected.[27]

This pressure was maintained throughout the battle by the numerous sorties of the DAF, the interdiction of Rommel's supply line by the Royal

Navy, and the cooperation of all arms of Eighth Army. An Air Ministry Report recorded that the Alamein battle "demonstrated untold value of good cooperation between all arms and services."[28] It was an old lesson to learn, but this cooperation between arms and services was a critical development. It signified, as Alexander McKee noted, a crucial shift. He wrote of the battle: "At long last the British were learning how to make war—which is not the same thing as fighting."[29]

There was little doubt, though, that the primary responsibility for breaking the Alamein position had been with the infantry divisions backed by heavy artillery and air support. Freyberg's report on the El Alamein operations concluded that the "value of well-trained infantry, capable of attacking by night with the bayonet against any form of defence, was fully proved."[30] Jonathan Fennell was correct in his assessment that the infantry units of Eighth Army were "Montgomery's main offensive force." Fennell also observed that in winning this last Alamein battle, "many of the frontline battalions of Eighth Army suffered over 50 per cent casualties."[31] Being the Army commander's main offensive weapon came with a heavy cost.

It has been argued that Alamein could not have been won without the contributions of the two elite infantry divisions in Eighth Army identified earlier by Rommel—9 Australian Division operating in the north, and two brigades of New Zealand infantry plus supporting units in the center, and later in the pursuit.[32] That the New Zealanders played a vital role was uncharacteristically recognized by Montgomery:

> The Battle of Egypt was won by the good fighting qualities of the soldiers of the Empire. Of all these soldiers none were finer than the fighting men from New Zealand.... Possibly I myself am the only one who really knows the extent to which the action of the New Zealand Division contributed towards the victory.[33]

Montgomery sent the Australian commander a similar message of praise on November 2, just as Operation *Supercharge* was underway. Montgomery wrote to Morshead that, "Your men are absolutely splendid and the part they have played in this battle is beyond all praise."[34] General Alexander was also effusive in his praise of the 9th Australian Division when he addressed them at a parade on the Gaza airstrip on December 22. He pointed out that "The battle of Alamein has made history, and you are in the proud position of having taken a major part in that great victory."

Alexander concluded his address by telling the Australians that "one thought I shall cherish above all others—under my command fought the 9th Australian Division."[35] Churchill too acknowledged in his history of the war that it was the "ceaseless, bitter fighting" that the Australians had endured at Alamein that "had swung the whole battle in our favour."[36] Twenty-five years after the battle, Montgomery wrote that "it would not be right to single out any for special praise" when all had performed well. But then Montgomery did exactly that, stating, "I must say this—we would not have won the battle in ten days without that magnificent 9th Australian Division."[37]

It was heady stuff and it was entirely appropriate that the Australians and New Zealanders received high praise for their efforts in the October battle. No historian could ever dispute their key roles. But Montgomery was correct when he gave credit to the fighting qualities of the soldiers of the Empire, although he perhaps should have mentioned the Empire airmen as well. Throughout the battle Eighth Army had "complete protection from serious air attack and, at the same time, had the benefit of such close co-operation and continuous air support as never before."[38] There were, of course, other formations and corps that contributed significantly to the outcome of the battle. All German accounts comment on the weight and effectiveness of Eighth Army's artillery. No infantry division made more attacks nor suffered heavier casualties than 51st Highland Division. And while the armored divisions may not have performed as well as Montgomery and the infantry commanders wanted, no formation did more to win the battle than the 9th Armoured Brigade. The New Zealand official history was correct when it stated that "Finally, tribute for the victory should be bestowed on all those Allied troops who had a share in the fighting and behind the lines."[39]

* * *

It was surprising that General Alexander, in his Despatch published in 1948, was somewhat dismissive of the casualties incurred in this third battle. Alexander claimed that Eighth Army's losses at El Alamein "were not unduly severe" and later that: "Our casualties were a negligible factor as far as the pursuit was concerned."[40] But Alexander was comparing Alamein to the attritional battles of the First World War. As he pointed out in his Memoirs, there was "one rather big difference." At Alamein, casualties averaged just over 1,000 a day. On the first day of the Somme they had numbered "some 60,000."[41]

As with any battle of attrition, the cost of success was high. Eighth Army suffered 2,350 men killed in action; 8,950 wounded; and 2,260 men missing—a total of 13,560. In addition, 500 tanks and 111 guns were put of action and the DAF lost ninety-seven aircraft during the battle. These are not negligible figures and prove, as the British official history stated, "the battle was anything but a walk-over."[42] Panzerarmee losses were high too. An estimated 1,149 German and 971 Italians were killed in action, with a further 3,886 Germans and 933 Italians wounded.[43] A more precise figure was recorded for the number of Axis prisoners taken during the battle. By November 11, it had reached 30,000.[44]

The breakdown of Eighth Army's losses indicates its multinational character. Of the total casualties incurred in the October battle, the percentages suffered by various nationalities were: UK troops 58 percent, Australians 22 percent, New Zealanders 10, South Africans 6, Indians 1, Allies (Free French, Greeks) 3.[45] Two Australian historians have made much of these figures. They write that:

> The Australian Division, although representing just under a tenth of the Eighth Army's strength, had suffered more than one in five of its casualties. Further reports revealed the scale of the Australian contribution to the battle. Thirteen per cent of the 9th Division's men had been killed or wounded, which is exactly double the British percentage and three times that of the other Dominion formations.[46]

No one could ever question the contribution of the Australians to the final outcome of the battle and their heavy casualties are just one indication of the hard fighting they endured. But using casualty figures as a yardstick of contribution is misleading. It needs to be remembered that the UK casualties were not evenly spread across all its formations and some UK formations, such as the 51st Highland Division and 9 Armoured Brigade, suffered heavier percentage casualties than the Australians. In fact, 51st Highland Division, with 2,827 killed, wounded, and missing, suffered the highest number of casualties during the battle. The bulk of this Division's casualties were in its nine infantry battalions, which collectively had a casualty rate of around 40 percent.[47] The 2nd

New Zealand Division losses had also been heavy, given that it was well understrength before the battle began. More than 1,700 New Zealanders became casualties during this second battle of El Alamein. More than a third of these casualties, some 651, had occurred in the first twenty-four hours of the battle, the highest number suffered amongst the five infantry divisions used on the opening night.[48] Among the 7,350 graves of Allied servicemen in the Alamein cemetery are those of 1,049 known and fifty-six unknown New Zealanders. After the October battle, the New Zealand Division was now below strength by 3,600 men, a deficiency felt especially keenly in the infantry, the artillery, and the engineer corps. It had commenced the long campaign in June with nearly 20,000 men. In November 1942, its strength had almost reached 13,000 again.[49] Niall Barr was correct in his assessment of the human cost of the last Alamein battle. He wrote that, "Eighth Army had finally crushed the Panzerarmee but the human cost to both sides had been grievous."[50]

In his later years, Montgomery was acutely aware of this human cost and felt it deeply. In 1967, on the 25th anniversary of the battle, Montgomery went to Egypt on what would be his last overseas trip. With a former staff officer, he visited the Commonwealth War Graves Cemetery on the ridge near Alamein station, which has a clear view of most of the battlefield. Montgomery had been there on October 24, 1954, when the cemetery was officially opened, but this visit in 1967 was a more poignant and restrained affair. After spending considerable time before the headstones of two brothers killed on successive days, Montgomery quickly left the cemetery. That evening, walking beside the Mediterranean, Montgomery was silent and subdued. He confessed to his concerned companion, "I've been thinking of all those dead."[51] That forlorn feeling, no doubt tinged with a sense of guilt, often returned. In the last month of his life, Montgomery awoke after a troubled night. He told his friend, Sir Denis Hamilton, the reason for his disturbed sleep:

> I couldn't sleep last night—I had great difficulty. I can't have very long to go now. I've got to go to meet God—and explain all those men I killed at Alamein.[52]

*   *   *

At Alamein, Montgomery demonstrated considerable skill fighting "with the army he has rather than the one he wants it to be."[53] When

Lightfoot failed to achieve the break-in and the battle's momentum was waning, Montgomery, "resilient but resolute, did not hesitate to change his plan."[54] The new plan, *Supercharge*, while not entirely successful, did enough to break the will of his skillful opponent. Throughout the battle, despite many anxious moments, Montgomery radiated "confidence and determination amid all the stress and urgency."[55] It was an impressive performance. But despite achieving a decisive victory, Montgomery never received the accolades, plaudits, or adulation that his defeated opponent did. As Nigel Hamilton, Montgomery's sympathetic biographer, noted with some concern:

> Author after author would play down or denigrate Monty's leadership. Not only did Auchinleck acolytes feel duty-bound to do so, but non-military historians waded in, too.[56]

The first book to be thoroughly critical of Montgomery's performance as a military commander was Correlli Barnett's *The Desert Generals*. It first appeared in 1960 and "caused a scandal when published." It has since been reprinted four times; the last revised edition appeared in 2007, nearly fifty years after its initial publication. Barnett's book was followed by many others all "intent on chipping away some of the polished marble of Monty's reputation."[57]

Conversely, Rommel's standing as a skilled, daring battlefield commander, maybe even a brilliant one, has endured, especially among British and American historians. David Fraser, for example, described Rommel as "a master of manoeuvre on the battlefield and a leader of purest quality." He "stands in the company" of other military greats such as Napoleon Bonaparte and Robert E. Lee.[58] Ronald Lewin, not quite as praising, ranked him with Jeb Stuart, Attila, Prince Rupert, and George Patton. For Lewin, who had been an artillery officer in Eighth Army, Rommel's place "as one of the last great cavalry captains ... cannot be denied."[59] For Martin Blumenson, Rommel's reputation has only grown since the war. Rommel was "a master of modern warfare" and undoubtedly a military genius; one of the "great captains who epitomized generalship on the field of battle."[60] In a similar vein, Antulio J. Echevarria II wrote:

> Indeed, the decades since the end of the Second World War have seen historians and other writers both add to and clear away substantial portions of the Rommel

myth. What remains, however, seems enough to qualify Rommel as one of history's great, if controversial, captains—perhaps even a military genius. He did, after all, defeat a number of able British commanders before the run was broken by Montgomery at El Alamein.[61]

Rommel's reputation was not always so high, especially among those he commanded. Reflecting on what had gone wrong in this last battle, the Afrika Korps commander, Wilhelm Ritter von Thoma, felt that Rommel deserved much of the blame. He agreed with Ludwig Crüwell that Rommel "never worried about anything apart from his own fixed ideas." But Rommel had other poor qualities that had contributed to his defeat. He was cocky and overconfident. Von Thoma described the incident that revealed this serious character flaw:

> BURCKHARDT interpreted when that NEW ZEALAND General [Brigadier George Clifton] was taken prisoner—I've forgotten his name. Field Marshal ROMMEL said: "Tell the General that the war will be over in six weeks and I shall have occupied CAIRO and ALEXANDRIA." BURCKHARDT told me himself that it would have been most painful for him to have to say such a thing to this General who was standing there so pensively and had had the misfortune to be taken prisoner in the front line, which is no disgrace. So he simply said: "You'll find you are mistaken, Sir." I mean later on, if he ever comes to write of his experiences, what will he say about our appreciation of the situation and our over-confidence? Our tanks were nothing but scrap-iron. It wasn't a Panzer Division, it was just miserable odds-and-ends. To ALEXANDRIA, to CAIRO!

There was more, too. According to von Thoma, Rommel's battle tactics "were those of an infantryman. . . . He took no interest . . . in all the rest, that is personnel or supplies, which are the decisive factors for the whole theatre of war." Rommel's reliance on the dense "Minengarten" for protection, especially when they could not be covered by fire, "was fundamentally incorrect."[62] It was a damning indictment of the man who had recently been von Thoma's commander, but it was by no means a lone criticism of Rommel. Writing soon after the war, Generalmajor von Holtzendorff felt that Rommel's forward command and aggression made him an excellent Kampfgruppen [combat team] commander but "seriously impaired his efficiency as an Army commander." And, according to Holtzendorff, Rommel never understood how armor should be used:

> His attitude toward the Panzer arm and its employment suffered from the lack of knowledge of its technical capabilities. This attitude and his constant rejection

of material and fully justified objections on the part of the Panzer commanders repeatedly caused heavy losses in material (especially Panzers), which then jeopardized the very idea of the mission.[63]

These criticisms, if valid—and von Thoma was certainly in a position to know what he was talking about—hardly justify the Rommel "myth" or the notion that he was one of history's "Great Captains" or a military genius. The reality is that Rommel as a military commander was not as exceptional as some of his biographers have described him, nor was Montgomery the disaster he has often been portrayed to be.

* * *

On October 23, 2012, a date that marked a significant commemoration of the Alamein battles, the United Kingdom's *Daily Mail* ran a story by Guy Walters with a provocative headline. It read: *Was Monty's finest hour just a pointless bloodbath? Historians claim El Alamein—which began 70 years ago today—sacrificed thousands for the sake of propaganda.* The headline, which probably caused distress to some veterans of the battle, was misleading. In his article, Walters claimed that "detractors" of the battle's significance "maintain that it was a pointless battle in a pointless campaign, fought for political reasons to boost morale throughout the Empire, and not from any strategic necessity." Once again, Montgomery's generalship was denigrated. He was described as a "hugely over-rated and unimaginative commander" who "should never have been raised to the status of national hero." Walters' headline is misleading in that his article, while not naming any of the "detractors," actually dismisses their arguments. He concludes:

> El Alamein may not have been an elegant victory, and Montgomery may have been a ponderous general who was happy to steal much of the credit from the RAF, but it was a battle that gave the British what it most badly needed—confidence with which to go on and win the war.[64]

Correlli Barnett had certainly dismissed the October Alamein battle as pointless. With Operation *Torch*, the Allied landings in French North Africa, due to commence in early November, for Barnett this raised "the really interesting question . . . why this bitter battle . . . was fought at all." Barnett was emphatic that the "famous Second Battle of Alamein must therefore, in my view, go down in history as an unnecessary battle."[65] The hindsight in Barnett's judgement is clearly evident. As David Fraser, with the wisdom of experience, has astutely observed: "In war no man can say how an untried alternative course of action would have gone, since in war nothing is certain until it is over."[66]

Some senior military commanders were also dismissive of the October Alamein battle. The US Chief of Staff George Marshall was one. Marshall was never impressed with the British campaign in North Africa or with Montgomery's generalship. In some off-the-record comments made in 1949, his interviewers noted:

> He [Marshall] explained that our opinion of the British at that time was not very high in that the President thought the 8th Army at El Alamein would lose again in the desert. FDR said to have them attack at night. The General discussed what was wrong with British command in Africa at some length. He said that the British in the Middle East [8th Army] had committed about every mistake in the book. It was no model campaign. The pursuit of Rommel across the desert was slow. The British even laid a minefield in front of them which benefited the Germans more than it did the British. Here Marshall formed an opinion that Montgomery left something to be desired as a field commander. The experience with Montgomery in northwest Europe confirmed Marshall's opinion about that.[67]

Even the Chief of the German High Command, Field Marshal Wilhelm Keitel, was dismissive of Alamein and the North African campaign. Shortly before his execution at Nuremberg, Keitel reflected on Rommel's career. During his interrogation, Keitel had expressed "unlimited admiration of Rommel's military achievements and courage." While Rommel's efforts in North Africa had resulted in some "unexpected victories," this talented commander's skills had been wasted there. Keitel wrote, "One cannot help wondering what this daring and highly-favoured tank commander would have achieved had he been fighting with his units in the one theatre of war where Germany's fate was to be determined."[68] Clearly, Keitel's delusions continued to the end of his life. Rommel and the units he commanded in North Africa would have made no difference at all to the outcome of Germany's defeat on the Eastern Front.

The October or second battle of El Alamein was an important tactical victory for Montgomery and Eighth Army. As Stephen Bungay concluded, "However one looks at it, in the third round of fighting at El

Alamein Rommel was decisively defeated."[69] It was "the climax to two years of to-and-fro struggle in the Western Desert."[70] And there was a strategic effect to the battle as well, which transformed it into one of the turning points of the war. A senior German staff officer at their Supreme Command, the Oberkommando der Wehrmacht (OKW), recalled after the war that this battle was indeed "the turning point at which the initiative passed from German into Allied Hands." Generalmajor Eckhardt Christian admitted that the OKW "doubtlessly underestimated Africa's strategic importance" and that by November 1942, "The realization of the enemy's strength and our own weakness came too late to avert disaster. The enemy now had the initiative and retained it."[71] Alexander also wrote of the strategic effect of the battle. There were several reasons why the battle had to be fought:

> In the general context of our war strategy in 1942, the battle of Alamein was fought to gain a decisive victory over the Axis forces in the Western Desert, to hearten the Russians, to uplift our allies, to depress our enemies, to raise morale at home and abroad, and to influence those who were sitting on the fence. The battle at Alamein was very carefully timed to achieve these objects—it was not a question of gaining a victory in isolation.

And as Alexander pointed out, both his knowledge of military history and his battlefield experience "convince me that a war is not won by sitting on the defensive."[72]

Winston Churchill certainly saw the battle as a key turning point. For him, the October–November Alamein battle was "the turning of 'the Hinge of Fate.'" He explained why in two sentences that have become the most quoted (and misquoted) assessment of the battle's importance. Churchill wrote that:

> It may almost be said, [This first part is often omitted] "Before Alamein we never had a victory. After Alamein we never had a defeat."[73]

Little wonder then that on Sunday, November 15, 1942, to mark the victory, the church bells rang all over the United Kingdom. It was the first time in three years that Britons had heard their church bells ring. The BBC made a point of recording the bells of Coventry Cathedral for their Overseas Service. "Did you hear them in Occupied Europe?" a gleeful radio commentator asked. "Did you hear them in Germany?"[74]

The transformation was far more than a tactical and strategic shift. This was alluded to in Guy Walters' conclusion quoted above. The October–November battle marked a major change in how the British Empire thought and felt about its warfighting capabilities. It was a critical transformation. For British soldier and historian David Fraser, the victory at El Alamein in November 1942 "was the best moment experienced by the British Army since another November day long ago in 1918." It meant that "the tide had finally and irrevocably turned."[75] When writing about the British defeat in June 1942 during the Gazala battle, which lead to the "deplorable" loss of Tobruk, Fraser made a profound observation that has often been overlooked by military historians. Fraser perceived that "battles are won and lost in the minds of men, and this one had been lost."[76] To date, the British armies had experienced few victories and many, costly defeats. There were doubts in the minds of men and women at the highest and lowest levels whether the British could ever defeat an army that included German panzer and motorized formations. That doubt was infectious and had spread to Britain's allies. The October Alamein battle, inelegant as all Allied victories in this war were, provided convincing and much-needed proof that a British army could achieve a victory over German forces.

After the battle, the Australian commander, Lieutenant General Leslie Morshead, wrote a revealing letter to a friend. In it, Morshead highlighted why Eighth Army had won the battle. He also recorded a significant mind-shift in the Australian soldiers:

> It was a very hard and long battle, twelve days and nights of continuous and really bloody fighting, and it was not until the last day that the issue was decided. A big battle is very much like a tug-of-war between two very heavy and evenly matched teams, and the one which can maintain the pressure and put forward that last ounce that wins. . . . I shall always remember going round the line during the battle and a real digger saying to me "Yes Sir it's tough all right . . . but we've at last got these bloody Germans by the knackers."[77]

The feeling towards the end of the Alamein battle was that the Germans were on the ropes and losing the battle. The British Eighth Army, after a hard fight, did at last have "these bloody Germans by the knackers." While this sentiment wasn't expressed in quite so colorful vernacular, it certainly became infectious. The Alamein battle "was crucial to the morale of the free world." The news of Rommel's defeat at Alamein electrified that free world. Nigel Hamilton wrote that "the sense of a change in the fortunes of democracy was palpable."[78] It signified, as many noted at the time and after, a crucial shift. The spell was broken and the Germans could be beaten. As the New Zealand official historian wrote, the battle of Alamein deserves its place in military history "because it was the first victory of any magnitude won by the British forces against a German command since the Second World War began."[79] That victory transformed the British forces. Instead of doubt, bewilderment, confusion, and a feeling of inferiority, there was now the strong belief that your side could fight hard and win. It at last had all the tools to do the job. The long string of defeats, what Churchill called the "galling links in a chain of misfortune and frustration," was finally over.[80] The British army, with its allies, had turned a corner and it was to experience a string of victories, albeit marked with some setbacks. It had taken a very long time for the Hinge to turn.

NOTES

1. Afrika Korps War Diary, 6 November 1942, WA II 11/23, GMDS File 2586/1, Afrika Korps Records, ANZ.

2. 90th Light War Diary, 11 November 1942, WA II 11/19, GMDS File 288761, Records of 90th Light and 164 Light Division, ANZ.

3. Playfair, et al., *Volume IV*, 79.

4. Alexander McKee, *El Alamein, Ultra and the Three Battles.* (London: Souvenir Press, 1991), 176.

5. Barnett, *The Desert Generals*, 310, 312.

6. Johnston and Stanley, *Alamein: The Australian Story*, 259.

7. Freyberg, conversation with Corps Commander 2130 hrs 3 November 1942, Freyberg's War Diary, WA II 8/45, ANZ.

8. Barr, *Pendulum of War*, 403.

9. John Harding, quoted in Holmes, *The World at War*, 277.

10. John Keegan, *The Second World War.* (London: Arrow Books, 1990), 407.

11. Freyberg's War Diary, 3 November 1942, WA II 8/45, ANZ.

12. de Guingand, *Operation Victory*, 467.

13. Freyberg's War Diary, 6 November 1942, WA II 8/45, ANZ.

14. Kippenberger to J.L. Scoullar, author chosen for official history of the "Left Hooks," 7 June 1955, WA II 11/2, ANZ.

15. Liddell Hart, *The Rommel Papers*, 360–361.

16. Ibid., 327.

17. Ibid., 328–329.

18. Ibid., 331.

19. Ibid., 332–334.

20. 15 Panzer War Diary, Preliminary Remarks, WA II 11/23, GMDS File 24902, Afrika Korps Records, ANZ.

21. Howard, *Strategic Deception in the Second World War*, 44.

22. M 42 3403 (Lieut 2 Bn, 125 Inf Regt), conversation with N 42 801 (Lieut U-559), Most Secret Special Report to CSDIC Middle East No.612 (G), El Alamein Miscellaneous Papers, WO 106/2286, TNA.

23. Behrendt, *Rommel's Intelligence*, 190–191.

24. Maughan, *Tobruk and Alamein*, 743.

25. Fennell, "Air Power and Morale," 11, 12.

26. Generalmajor Hans-Henning Holtzendorff, "Reasons for Rommel's Success in Afrika 1941–42," FMS D739, DO 24, AHEC, 32.

27. 9 Australian Division, Report on Operations El Alamein 23 Oct–5 Nov 1942, WO 201/2495, TNA, 45.

28. The Advance from El Alamein, Air 8/1087, TNA, 5.

29. McKee, *El Alamein, Ultra and the Three Battles*, 112.

30. Freyberg, "The New Zealand Division in Egypt and Libya," 2, Freyberg's Secret After-Action Report, 27, copy in author's possession (GJH).

31. Fennell, "Steel my soldiers' hearts," 31.

32. Pugsley, *A Bloody Road Home*, 358. Harper, *Kippenberger*, 193. Johnston and Stanley, *Alamein: The Australian Story*, 266.

33. Montgomery, Foreword to Freyberg's Secret Report, December 1942.

34. Montgomery, message to Morshead, 2 November 1942, Series 2, Item 2/8, Morshead Papers, 3 DRL, 2632, AWM.

35. Quoted in Johnston and Stanley, *Alamein: The Australian Story*, 268.

36. Churchill, *Vol. IV*, 536.

37. Montgomery, quoted in Neillands, *Eighth Army*, 200.

38. Playfair, et al., *Volume IV*, 78.

39. Walker, *Alam Halfa and Alamein*, 478.

40. Alexander's Despatch, Supplement to *The London Gazette*, 5 February 1948, CAB 106/613, TNA, 858.

41. North, *The Alexander Memoirs*, 28.

42. Playfair, et al., *Volume IV*, 78.

43. Barr, *Pendulum of War*, 404.

44. Playfair et al., *Volume IV*, 79.

45. Ibid., 79. Footnote.

46. Johnston and Stanley, *Alamein: The Australian Story*, 264.

47. Fennell, *Combat and Morale in the North African Campaign*. (Cambridge: Cambridge University Press, 2011), 252.

48. Ibid., 256.

49. Walker, *Alam Halfa and Alamein*, 481. Appendix III.

50. Barr, *Pendulum of War*, 405.

51. Quoted in Johnston and Stanley, *Alamein: The Australian Story*, 270.

52. Nigel Hamilton, *Monty: The Field-Marshal 1944–1976*. (London: Hamish Hamilton, 1986), 941.

53. Pugsley, *A Bloody Road Home*, 358.

54. Playfair et al., *Volume IV*, 77.

55. Ibid.

56. Hamilton, *The Full Monty*, 778.

57. Hamilton, *Monty: The Field-Marshal*, 925.

58. Fraser, *Knight's Cross*, 560, 562.

59. Lewin, *Rommel as Military Commander*, 318.

60. Martin Blumenson, "Rommel," in *Hitler's Generals*, ed. Correlli Barnett. (London: Phoenix Giants, 1995), 293, 315.

61. Antulio J. Echecarria II, "'The Highest Rule': Rommel as Military Genius" in *El Alamein and the Struggle for North Africa: International Perspectives from the Twenty-first Century*, ed. Jill Edwards. (Cairo: The American University in Cairo Press, 2012), 181.

62. Von Thoma, conversation with Crüwell, Most Secret Special Report to CSDIC Middle East No.612 (G), El Alamein Miscellaneous Papers, WO 106/2286, TNA.

63. Generalmajor Hans-Henning Holtzendorff, "Reasons for Rommel's Success in Afrika 1941–42," FMS D739, DO 24, AHEC, 38.

64. Guy Walters, "Was Monty's finest hour just a pointless bloodbath? Historians claim El Alamein—which began 70 years ago today—sacrificed thousands for the sake of propaganda," *Mail Online*, 23 October 2012, accessed 11 April 2016.

65. Barnett, *The Desert Generals*, 272.

66. Fraser, *And We Shall Shock Them*, 395.

67. George Marshall, interview with Dr. Matthews, Majors Lemson and Hamilton and Dr. Howard Smith, 23 July 1949, Verifax 530, Item 5008, Marshall Library, Lexington, VA. (ML).

68. Walter Gorlitz, ed., *The Memoirs of Field-Marshal Wilhelm Keitel: Chief of the German High Command, 1938–1945* (New York: Cooper Square Press, 2000), 185, 195.

69. Bungay, *Alamein*, 196.

70. Playfair et al., *Volume IV*, 76.

71. Eckhardt Christian, "The El Alamein Crisis and its After-effects in the OKW," MS D-172, AHEC, 1, 9.

72. North, *The Alexander Memoirs*, 29.

73. Churchill, *Vol, IV*, 541.

74. Bierman and Smith, *Alamein: War without Hate*, 334.

75. Fraser, *And We Shall Shock Them*, 246.

76. Ibid., 223.

77. Morshead, letter to Douglas L. Dowdell, 12 November 1942, 3 DRL 2562, File 419/28/10, Morshead Papers, AWM.

78. Hamilton, *The Full Monty*, 777.

79. Walker, *Alam Halfa and Alamein*, 477.

80. Churchill, *Vol. IV*, 494.

BIBLIOGRAPHY

ALEXANDER TURNBULL LIBRARY

MS Papers 0421   Papers of Lindsay Inglis

ARCHIVES NEW ZEALAND

WAII Series 1 Unit/Formation War Diaries and Records and Miscellaneous Papers

DA 21.1/1–51   Headquarters 2 New Zealand Division, General Staff- War Diary
January 1940 – 1944

DA 52/1/13–51   Headquarters 5 New Zealand Infantry Brigade - War Diary, January
1941 – March 1944

DA 58/1/21–27   Headquarters 6 New Zealand Infantry Brigade - War Dairy, 1 June –
31 December 1942

WAII Series 2 Unclassified Material

WAII 2/4   "Problems of Desert Warfare" L.C.F. Turner, May 1955

Series 3

WAII 3/22   Minqar Qaim Original Notes and Sketches (Kippenberger's comments)

WAII 3/16A   W.G. McClymont's Papers

WAII Series 8 The Freyberg Papers

Part 1
A Files
WAII 8/24   Minqar Qaim and Ruweisat Ridge
WAII 8/25A   General Officer Commanding's Papers "Lightfoot" and "Super-charge"

WAII 8/26	General Papers 1942
WAII 8/44	Freyberg's Diary
WAII 8/5/45	General Officer Commanding's Diary- Part III, September 1942 – September 1943

Part II

| WAII 8/AA | Miscellaneous. 1942 |
| WAII 8/V | GOC Personal Private Correspondence Part II |

WAII Series 11 War History Branch Unregistered Papers

WAII 11/2	Correspondence of Howard Kippenberger 1947–1955
WAII 11/3	R. Walker's notes; Battle for Egypt, Syria, Minqar Qaim
WAII 11/9	Miscellaneous Papers
WA II 2/16	Interviews and Speeches November 1939-December 1944
WAII 11/17	German Operations
WAII 11/19	Records of 90th Light and 164 Light Division
WAII 11/23	Afrika Korps Records

AUSTRALIAN WAR MEMORIAL

Private Records

PR 3DRL/2632, Papers of Lt General Sir Leslie Morshead
PR 82/190, Diaries of Lt T. Derrick. 2/38 Battalion AIF
PRO 0368, Papers of Lt General Sir Leslie Morshead

Official Records

AWM 52, Unit and Formation War Diaries
9 Australian Division General Staff Branch
26 Australian Infantry Brigade
2nd/13 Infantry Battalion
2nd/15 Infantry Battalion
2nd/17 Infantry Battalion
2nd/23 Infantry Battalion
2nd/24 Infantry Battalion
2nd/28 Infantry Battalion
2nd/43 Infantry Battalion
2nd/48 Infantry Battalion

AWM 54, Written Records 1939–1945
9 Australian Division Intelligence Summaries
9 Australian Division Operational Orders
9 Division Report, 527/6/9

ARMY HERITAGE EDUCATION CENTER, CARLISLE PENNSYLVANIA

D-739.F6713, Foreign Military Studies. D020-D039, Box 78

D-084, Foreign Military Studies. Supplement to "Reasons for Rommel's Successes in
Africa 1941–42"

D-172, Foreign Military Studies. "El Alamein Crisis and its After-Effects in the OKW"

D-739, Foreign Military Studies. "German Experiences in Desert Warfare during World
War II"

D-739, Foreign Military Studies. "Desert Warfare – German Experience in World
War II"

GEORGE C. MARSHALL RESEARCH LIBRARY, LEXINGTON VIRGINIA

National Archives Cards, Verifax 530, Item 5008, Interview with General Marshall 25
July 1949, Marshall Papers.

National Archives Cards, Verifax 3086, Item 2979, Marshall Papers

Box 66, Marshall Papers

IMPERIAL WAR MUSEUM (IWM), NORTH LAMBETH, LONDON

"Oppa's War Years 1939–46," Private Papers of Geoffrey Giddings, Documents 2256.

Douglas Wimberley, "A Scottish Soldier," Vols I-III, unpublished memoir, Private Papers
of Major General D.N. Wimberley, Documents 430.

LIDDLE COLLECTION, BROTHERTON LIBRARY, UNIVERSITY OF LEEDS

ARMY 009 F. Bradley
ARMY 015 Percy Boothroyd
ARMY 023 William Stuart Campbell
ARMY 031 Ian Graham Clark
ARMY 034 Geoffrey Coning
ARMY 042 John I. Kennedy-Craufurd-Stuart
ARMY 043 George Harold Hamilton Crook
ARMY 075 Ewen Frazer
ARMY 077 Geoffrey N. Giddings
ARMY 080 Acheson Harding Glendinning
ARMY 086 G. Douglas Gordon
ARMY 095 Brian Henson
ARMY 102 Fred G. Hancock
ARMY 115 Ronald Ineson
ARMY 116 Charles F. Irvine
ARMY 122 John Laing
ARMY 123 Richard A. Lake
ARMY 124 John F. Langdon
ARMY 130 H. Arthur Miller
ARMY 132 Jack W. Mitchley
ARMY 135 Joe Moon

ARMY 136 Peter J. Moore
ARMY 145 Harold Padfield
ARMY 150 Richard Peacock
ARMY 151 Geoffrey Pearson
ARMY 158 Eric William Ratcliffe
ARMY 162 Theo Redman
ARMY 163 Donald Graham Russell Reid
ARMY 170 Victor Heckman Robinson
ARMY 171 Ronald Carter Robson
ARMY 180 W. Harry Slaney
ARMY 188 Max S.A. Swan
ARMY 193 E.G. Waggett
ARMY 195 Maurice Walton
ARMY 200 Richard Whitfield
NAVY 005 Richard Campbell Begg
RAF 029 W. James Begg
RAF 059 Donald M. Jack
RAF 072 Robert G. Lomas
RAF 082 George Montgomery
RAF 099 Ian Shand
RAF 103 Roy Stevens
WOMEN IN UNIFORM OVERSEAS Margaret Edith Boyce (nee Jennings)
WOMEN IN UNIFORM OVERSEAS Mary Elizabeth Davidson

NATIONAL ARCHIVES, KEW UNITED KINGDOM

WO 32/10160, Auchinleck's Despatch
WO 106/2286, El Alamein Miscellaneous Papers
WO 169/4233, 9th Armoured Brigade War Diary
WO 201/2826, 9 Australian Division – Reports and on Operations
WO 201/535, RA Notes on the Offensive by Eighth Army from 23 Oct – 4 Nov on the El
    Alamein Position
WO 201/556, Appreciation by Commander in Chief, Middle East, 1 August 1942
WO 201/556, Appreciation by Commander 13 Corps, 1 August 1942
WO 201/2495, 9 Australian Division – Report on Operations El Alamein
AIR 8/1087, The Advance from El Alamein
PREM 3/1837, Prime Minister's Personal Minutes
WO 234/25, Deception Scheme [Repairing Department]
W 1/723, German Records [Enigma]
HW 1/723 German Records [Enigma
CAB 106/613, Alexander's El Alamein Despatch
CAB 106/703Western Desert Copy of address to officer of Headquarters 8th Army by
    General B.L. Montgomery on taking over command, 13 August 1942,
KV 2/2136, German Records: questions to Joachim Rohleder
HW 1/1015, German Records [Enigma]
HW 1/728, German Records [Enigma]
HW 1/733, German Records [Enigma]

HW 1/747, German Records [Enigma]
HW 1/717, German Records [Enigma intercepts]
CAB 44/420, Crisis in the Desert (South Africa)
WO 204/7977, Main Deception Scheme

PRIVATE PAPERS

Report on "The New Zealand Division in Egypt and Libya: Operations 'Lightfoot' and 'Supercharge,'" copy in author's possession.
GOC's diary [Lt Gen Sir Bernard Freyberg] 2 NZDiv, provided by Sir John White, copy in author's possession.

UNPUBLISHED PRIVATE PAPERS

The Private Collection of W.A. Glue. Stoke, Nelson, New Zealand.
Harper, Glyn. "'Kip' Major General Sir Howard Kippenberger, KBE, CB, DSO and Bar, ED: A Study of Command." A thesis submitted for the degree of Doctor of Philosophy of the University of New England, NSW, Australia. 1996.

INTERVIEWS

Sir Leonard Thornton, Wellington, 25 January 1993.
Angus Ross, Dunedin, 17 January 1995.

BOOKS

Anon. *The Tiger Kills*. Bombay: HMSO Government of India, 1944.
Atkinson, Rick. *The Guns at Last Light: The War in Western Europe, 1944–1945*. New York: Picador, 2014.
Ball, Simon. *The Bitter Sea: The Struggle for Mastery in the Mediterranean, 1935–1949*. London: Harper Press, 2009.
Barnett, Correlli, ed. *Hitler's Generals*. London: Phoenix Giants, 1995.
——— *The Desert Generals*. Revised Edition. London: Pan Books Ltd. Orion Books Ltd, 2007.
Barr, Niall. *Pendulum of War: The Three Battles of El Alamein*. London: Pimlico, 2005.
Behrendt, Hans-Otto. *Rommel's Intelligence in the Desert Campaign 1941–1943*. London: William Kimber & Co, 1985.
Bierman, John and Colin Smith. *Alamein: War without Hate*. London: Viking, 2002.
Bryant, Arthur. *The Turn of the Tide*. London: The Reprint Society, 1958.
Bungay, Stephen. *Alamein*. London: Aurum Press Ltd., 2002.
Carver, Michael. *El Alamein*. London: Fontana Books, 1973.
Churchill, Winston S. *The Second World War Volume III: The Grand Alliance*. London: Cassell & Co, 1950.
Churchill, Winston S. *The Second World War Volume IV: The Hinge of Fate*. London: Cassell & Co, 1951.
Cody, J.F. *Official History of New Zealand in the Second World War 1939–45: 28 (Maori) Battlion*. Wellington: Historical Publications Branch, Department of Internal Affairs, 1956.

Danchev, Alex and Todman, Daniel, eds. *War Diaries 1939–1945: Field Marshal Lord Alanbrooke*. London: Weidenfeld & Nicolson, 2001.

de Guingand, Francis. *Operation Victory*. London: Hodder & Stoughton, 1947.

Edwards, Jill, ed. *El Alamein and the Struggle for North Africa: International Perspectives from the Twenty-first Century*. Cairo: The American University in Cairo Press, 2012.

Farago, Ladislas. *Patton: Ordeal & Triumph*. London: Granada Publishing, 1969.

Fennell, Jonathan. *Combat and Morale in the North African Campaign*. Cambridge: Cambridge University Press, 2011.

Fraser, David. *And We Shall Shock Them: The British Army in the Second World War*. London: Book Club Associates, 1983.

——— *Knight's Cross: A Life of Field Marshal Erwin Rommel*. London: HarperCollins Publishers, 1994.

Gardiner, Wira. *Te Mura O Te Ahi: The Story of the Māori Battalion*. Auckland: Reed Books, 1992.

Gorlitz, Walter (ed.). *The Memoirs of Field-Marshal Wilhelm Keitel: Chief of the German High Command, 1938–1945*. New York: Cooper Square Press, 2000.

Greacen, Lavinia. *Chink: A Biography*. London: MacMillan London, 1998.

Hamilton, Nigel. *Monty: The Making of a General: 1887–1942*. London: Hamish Hamilton Ltd., 1981.

——— *Monty: Master of the Battlefield 1942–1944*. London: Hamish Hamilton, 1983.

——— *Monty: The Field-Marshal 1944–1976*. London: Hamish Hamilton, 1986.

——— *The Full Monty: Montgomery of Alamein, 1887–1942*. London: Allen Lane, 2001.

Harper, Glyn. *Kippenberger: An Inspired New Zealand Commander*. Auckland: HarperCollins Publishers (New Zealand) Ltd., 1997.

Hastings, Max. *All Hell Let Loose: The World at War 1939–45*. London: HarperPress, 2011.

Hinsley, F.H. *British Intelligence in the Second World War: Volume 2: Its influence on Strategy and Operations*. London: HMSO, 1981.

Holland, James. *Together We Stand: North Africa 1942–1943: Turning the Tide in the West*. London: HarperCollins Publishers, 2005.

Holmes, Richard. *The World at War: The Landmark Oral History from the Previously Unpublished Archives*. London: Ebury Press, 2007.

Horrocks, Brian. *A Full Life*. London: Collins, 1960.

Howard, Michael. *Strategic Deception in the Second World War*. London: Pimlico, 1992.

Irving, David. *The War Between the Generals*. London: Penguin Books, 1982.

——— *The Trail of the Fox*. New York: Avon Books, 1978.

Johnston, Mark. *That Magnificent 9th: An Illustrated History of the 9th Australian Division*. Sydney: Allen & Unwin, 2003.

Johnston, Mark & Peter Stanley. *Alamein: The Australian Story*. Melbourne: Oxford University Press, 2006.

Keegan, John. *The Second World War*. London: Arrow Books, 1990.

Keegan, John, ed. *Churchill's Generals*. London: Weidenfeld & Nicolson, 1991.

Kippenberger, Howard. *Infantry Brigadier*. London: Oxford University Press, 1949.

Levine, Alan J. *The War Against Rommel's Supply Lines, 1942–1943*. Westport, CT: Praeger Publishers, 1999.

Lewin, Ronald. *Rommel as Military Commander*. New York: Ballantine Books, 1968.

——— *The Life and Death of the Afrika Korps*. London: Corgi Books, 1979.

Liddell Hart, Basil. *History of the Second World War*. London: Phoebus Publishing Company, 1980.

———, ed. *The Rommel Papers*. London: Arrow Books Ltd, 1987.

Llewellyn, Peter. *Journey towards Christmas: Official history of the 1st Ammunition Company Second New Zealand Expeditionary Force 1939–45*. Wellington: Historical Publications Branch, Department of Internal Affairs, 1949.

Lyman, Robert. *The Longest Siege: The Battle That Saved North Africa*. Sydney: Macmillan, 2009.

McKee, Alexander. *El Alamein, Ultra and the Three Battles*. London: Souvenir Press, 1991.

Macmillan, Harold. *The Blast of War 1939–1945*. London: Macmillan & Co. Ltd., 1967.

Mathieson, Sally, ed. *Bill Gentry's War: 1939–45*. Palmerston North: The Dunmore Press, 1996.

Maughan, Barton. *Australia in the War of 1939–1945: Tobruk and El Alamein*. Canberra, William Collins in association with the Australian War Memorial, 1987.

Mawdsley, Evan. *World War II: A New History*. Cambridge: Cambridge University Press, 2009.

Montgomery, B.L. Field-Marshal. *The Memoirs of Field-Marshal The Viscount Montgomery of Alamein, K.G.* London: Collins, 1958.

——— *El Alamein to the River Sangro*. London: Arrow Books Ltd., 1960.

Mulgan, John. *Report on Experience*. Auckland: Blackwood and Janet Paul, 1967.

Murphy, W.E. *Official History of New Zealand in the Second World War 1939–34. The Relief of Tobruk*. Wellington: War History Branch Department of Internal Affairs, 1961.

——— *Official History of New Zealand in the Second World War 1939–45. 2nd New Zealand Divisional Artillery*. Wellington: War History Branch, 1966.

Neillands, Robin. *The Desert Rats: 7th Armoured Division 1940–1945*. London: Weidenfeld and Nicolson, 1991.

——— *Eighth Army: From the Western Desert to the Alps, 1939–1945*. London: John Murray (Publishers), 2004.

Neitzel, Sönke and Harald Welzer. *Soldaten: On Fighting, Killing and Dying: The Secret World War II Tapes of German POWs*. London: Simon & Schuster UK Ltd., 2013.

North, John, ed. *The Alexander Memoirs: 1940–1945*. London: Cassell & Company Ltd., 1962.

Patton, George S. Jr. *War as I knew it*. New York: Bantam Books, 1981.

Pitt, Barrie. *The Crucible of War: Year of Alamein 1942*. London: Jonathan Cape, 1982.

Playfair, I.S.O. *The Mediterranean and the Middle East, Volume III: British Fortunes Reach their Lowest Ebb (September 1941 to September 1942)*. London: HMSO, 1960.

Playfair, I.S.O. and Molony, C.J.C. with Flynn, F.C. and Gleave, T.P. *The Mediterranean and the Middle East, Volume IV. The Destruction of the Axis Forces in Africa*. London: HMSO, 1966.

Pugsley, Christopher. *A Bloody Road Home: World War Two and New Zealand's Heroic Second Division*. Auckland: Penguin Books, 2014.

Scoullar, J. L. *Official History of New Zealand in the Second World War 1939–45: Battle for Egypt: The Summer of 1942*. Wellington: War History Branch, Department of Internal Affairs, 1955.

Selwyn, Victor, ed. *Poems of the Second World War: The Oasis Selection*. London: J.M. Dent & Sons Ltd, 1985.

Shores, Christopher, and Massimello, Giovanni, with Guest, Russell; Olynyk, Frank and Bock, Winifred. *A History of the Mediterranean Air War 1940–1945 Volume Two: North African Desert February 1942-March 1943*. London: Grub Street, 2012.

Stevens, W.G. *Official History of New Zealand in the Second World War: Bardia to Enfidaville*. Wellington: Historical Publications Branch, Department of Internal Affairs, 1962.

Strachan, Hew. *The Oxford Illustrated History of the First World War: New Edition*. Oxford: Oxford University Press, 2014.

Thompson, Julian. *Forgotten Voices: Desert Victory*. London: Ebury Press, 2011.

Tuker, Francis. *Approach to Battle: A Commentary; Eighth Army, November 1941 to May 1943*. London: Cassell and Co, 1963.

Verney, G.L. *The Desert Rats: The History of the 7th Armoured Division 1938–1945*. London: Greenhill Books, 1990.

Walker, Ronald. *Official History of New Zealand in the Second World War: Alam Halfa and Alamein*. Wellington: Historical Publications Branch, Department of Internal Affairs, 1967.

Warner, Philip. *Auchinleck: The Lonely Soldier*. London: Sphere Books Ltd., 1982.

JOURNAL ARTICLES

Carrier, Richard. "Some Reflections on the Fighting Power of the Italian Army in North Africa, 1940–1943." *War in History* Vol.22, Number 4, November 2015, 503–528.

Fennell, Jonathan. "'Steel my soldiers' hearts': El Alamein Reappraised." *Journal of Military and Strategic Studies*. Vol.14, Issue 1, Fall 2011, 1–31.

——— "Air Power and Morale in the North African Campaign of the Second World War." *Air Power Review*. Vol.15, Number 2, Summer 2012, 1–16.

——— "Courage and Cowardice in the North African Campaign: The Eighth Army and Defeat in the Summer of 1942." *War in History*. Vol.20, Number 1, November 2013, 99–122.

Moody, Simon J. "Was There a 'Monty Method' after the Second World War? Field Marshal Bernard L. Montgomery and the Changing Character of Land Warfare, 1945–1958." *War in History*. Vol.23, Number 2, April 2016, 210–229.

MAGAZINE AND NEWSPAPER ARTICLES

Dorman O'Gowan, Eric. "Battle of First Alamein." *History of the Second World War*. Vol. 3. No. 7. ed. Barrie Pitt. London: Purnell & Sons and Imperial War Museum, 1967.

Dorman O'Gowan, Eric. "Alamein: The Aftermath." *History of the Second World War*. Vol. 3. No. 7. ed. Barrie Pitt. London: Purnell & Sons and Imperial War Museum, 1967.

Walters, Guy. "Was Monty's finest hour just a pointless bloodbath? Historians claim El Alamein—which began 70 years ago today—sacrificed thousands for the sake of propaganda," *Mail Online*, October 23, 2012, accessed April 11, 2016, http://www.dailymail.co.uk/news/article-2221706/Battle-El-Alamein-Was-Montys-finest-hour-just-pointless-bloodbath.html

INDEX

GLYN HARPER is Professor of War Studies at Massey University in New Zealand, and Massey Project Manager of the "New Zealand and the First World War" Centenary History Project.